Poverty and Place
Ghettos, Barrios, and the American City

Paul A. Jargowsky

Russell Sage Foundation
New York

The Russell Sage Foundation

The Russell Sage Foundation, one of the oldest of America's general purpose foundations, was established in 1907 by Mrs. Margaret Olivia Sage for "the improvement of social and living conditions in the United States." The Foundation seeks to fulfill this mandate by fostering the development and dissemination of knowledge about the country's political, social, and economic problems. While the Foundation endeavors to assure the accuracy and objectivity of each book it publishes, the conclusions and interpretations in Russell Sage Foundation publications are those of the authors and not of the Foundation, its Trustees, or its staff. Publication by Russell Sage, therefore, does not imply Foundation endorsement.

Library of Congress Cataloging-in-Publication Data

Jargowsky, Paul A.
  Poverty and place : ghettos, barrios, and the American city / Paul Jargowsky.
      p.   cm.
  Includes bibliographical references and index.
  ISBN 0-87154-405-9 (cloth)   ISBN 0-87154-406-7 (paperback)
    1. Community development, Urban—United States. 2. Inner cities—United States. 3. Urban poor—United States. 4. Pluralism (social sciences)—United States. 5. United States—Race relations.
I. Title.
HN90.C6J37 1996
307.3'366'0973—dc20   96-2109
                                                                           CIP

The paper used in this publication meets the minimum requirements of American National Standard for Information Sciences—Permanence of Paper for Printed Library Materials. ANSI Z39.48-1992.
Text design by Rozlyn Coleman.

RUSSELL SAGE FOUNDATION
112 East 64th Street, New York, New York 10021
10 9 8 7 6 5 4 3 2 1

Contents

Foreword

Since *The Truly Disadvantaged* was published in 1987, studies of neighborhood poverty have mushroomed. *Poverty and Place*, however, is the first work to provide a comprehensive analysis of changes in neighborhood poverty nationwide. This outstanding book not only critically examines existing studies and conclusions about neighborhood poverty but also offers the most definitive explanation of neighborhood poverty change and challenges a number of claims made by social scientists about the causes of increasing neighborhood poverty. It also presents the clearest discussion to date of the policy direction our nation should take to address the problem of the spreading urban blight.

Poverty and Place is a careful and methodologically sophisticated study. Based on his own field research of how best to empirically conceptualize neighborhoods of high poverty concentration, Jargowsky operationally defines high-poverty neighborhoods as those with poverty rates of at least 40 percent. The overwhelming majority (84.5 percent) of high-poverty neighborhoods are located in metropolitan areas. Jargowsky's field research reveals that the residents of high poverty areas are predominantly minority, but that an increasing number of whites reside in these neighborhoods. However, most blacks, Hispanics and whites in high-poverty areas "live where their own group is dominant" (p.16). Jargowsky therefore introduces an important conceptual distinction that will sharpen descriptions of these areas in empirical studies. Following the work of Kenneth B. Clark, who emphasized that black ghettos feature both racial and class subordination, Jargowsky uses the term "ghettos" to refer to black high-poverty areas, "barrios" to connote comparable Latino areas, and "slums" to designate similar white areas. The term "mixed slums" is used to refer to those high-poverty neighborhoods where there is no one dominant racial or ethnic group. This conceptual distinction is important because although ghettos, barrios, and slums have poverty rates of at least 40 percent in common, they obviously differ in terms of cultural patterns and group experiences associated with racial and ethnic differences in the United States.

Regardless of the ethnic or racial makeup of these neighborhoods, as Jargowsky notes, "the concentration of poverty indicates the percentage of the poor who not only have to cope with their poverty but also that of those around them" (p. 21). And between 1970 and 1990, the number of poor people in high-poverty areas very nearly doubled (from 1.9 million to 3.7 million), which exceeded even the extremely high increase in the overall population in these neighborhoods (92 percent).

It is important to note that nearly all of the increase in the number of the poor in high-poverty neighborhoods has occurred in central cities and inner-ring suburbs which feature middle-class flight and commercial abandonment. Moreover, "the number of persons residing in ghettos, barrios, and slums increased not because people moved into such neighborhoods, but because the poverty spread to more and more neighborhoods" (p. 35).

What accounts for this remarkable spread of poverty neighborhoods and the concurrent sharp increase in the number of residents residing in such neighborhoods? Jargowsky critically examines a number of popular academic hypotheses that address this question, including those on the roles of deindustrialization, industry deconcentration, and neighborhood sorting (which includes middle- and working-class flight from poor neighborhoods) presented in my book *The Truly Disadvantaged,* and the role of segregation, prominently featured in the work of Douglas Massey and his colleagues.

Jargowsky finds little support for the hypothesis that deindustrialization plays a role in the growth of ghetto poverty, except in northern metropolitan areas. Why manufacturing employment is more important for understanding increases in ghetto poverty in the north is not fully known. "It may be," states Jargowsky, "that the industrial jobs outside the north paid less well to begin with primarily because of different rates of unionization, and hence are less different from the jobs that subsequently replaced them" (p. 121). Accordingly, it could be that the focus should not be on deindustrialization per se, but on the decline of union jobs as a result of deindustrialization.

The original hypothesis on the role of industry deconcentration (that the spatial mismatch affects the earnings and employment of minorities in the central city) advanced by John F. Kain is supported by a mounting body of evidence. Jargowsky points out that "the effect seems to be growing over time, as metropolitan areas continue to move toward a more decentralized paradigm" (p. 125). Nonetheless, only one study has attempted to provide a direct test of the deconcentration hypothesis on increasing neighborhood poverty and it clearly demonstrates that deconcentration "has been a contributor to increasing neighborhood poverty" (p. 126).

The most controversial of the three hypotheses on the growth of ghetto neighborhoods advanced in *The Truly Disadvantaged* is the role of neighborhood sorting (flight of higher income African Americans from the inner city leading to increasing economic segregation). This hypothesis has been challenged by Douglas Massey and his colleagues, who maintain that it is racial segregation not economic segregation that has played a major role in the recent growth of ghetto poverty.

Jargowsky, however, raises serious questions about the validity of Massey's thesis. The results presented in a previous study of neighborhood poverty in several cities by Jargowsky and Mary Jo Bane, and Jargowsky's analysis of tract-level data for Milwaukee (see chapter 3) indicate that economic segregation played an important role in the general increase of neighborhood poverty between 1970 and 1990, "given that racial segregation declined over that period, and, on average, poverty rates in metropolitan areas changed very little" (p. 138). Jargowsky points out that it is one thing to maintain that "racial segregation is a key determinant of black poverty . . . and therefore indirectly helps to create and sustain ghetto poverty" (p. 142), but it is an entirely different argument to assert that racial segregation explains a good deal of the recent increases in ghetto poverty, especially since racial segregation has actually declined during this period. According to Jargowsky, the evidence to support Massey's central thesis that racial segregation interacts with increases in rates of African American poverty to create ghettos "comes mostly from a badly flawed econometric model" (p. 143).

The following conclusions flow from Jargowsky's review of the literature and evidence presented in the first five chapters of *Poverty and Place*. Structural changes in the economy have adversely affected those with lower levels of education and job skills leading to slow or negative growth in wages. The decline in the demand for low-skilled labor has disproportionately impacted inner-city minorities who are disadvantaged due to the poor quality of education in inner-city schools. The direct correlation between educational attainment and socioeconomic background therefore heightens their dilemma. The deconcentration of employment further reduces the probability of finding employment because it creates a spatial mismatch between inner-city residents and available jobs. Census tract-level evidence reveals that economic segregation within a minority group—that is, the flight of higher income groups from minority poverty neighborhoods—is an important factor in the increase of neighborhood poverty. Finally, although racial segregation is fundamental in understanding the presence of black high-poverty neighborhoods, the empirical evidence to support the hypothesis that racial segregation plays a direct role in the recent growth of such neighborhoods "is mixed at best" (p. 144).

Jargowsky is fully aware that many of the hypotheses and empirical conclusions concerning the growth of high-poverty areas are controversial. He states that "part of the difficulty in resolving these issues lies in the lack of a clearly specified model of how high-poverty neighborhoods are related to their metropolitan areas" (p. 145). I believe that Jargowsky's most significant contribution in this important book is the development and testing of such a model in chapter 6.

According to this empirical model, ghetto poverty and barrio poverty are largely determined by economic opportunities at the metropolitan level, that is, metropolitan-wide processes of income generation. Moreover, processes of neighborhood sorting are also important determinants of ghetto poverty since changes in the economic segregation among blacks increased ghetto poverty between 1980 and 1990. The overall level of economic segregation also helps account for levels of ghetto poverty in 1990.

Given the findings from this model, one can question the importance some observers have attributed to the cultural explanations of high neighborhood poverty. Indeed, as Jargowsky points out, "If the cultural effects of ghetto and barrio poverty persisted long after changes in economic opportunities, then levels of neighborhood poverty would respond slowly to such changes" (p. 192). Yet in many cities in the south and some in the north, large increases in average income generated substantial reductions in neighborhood poverty. As Jargowsky correctly observes, if barrios and ghettos were self-perpetuating, then his model would not have been able to explain so much of the variance in neighborhood poverty. In other words, if a self-sustaining neighborhood culture were so important, increased economic opportunity would have little effect, if any at all, on neighborhood poverty. However, the evidence presented in this book reveals that from 1970 to 1990 changes in economic opportunity at the metropolitan level are related to both rapid increases and decreases in neighborhood poverty. Economic booms in the southwest in the 1970s and in the northeast in the 1980s sharply decreased ghetto poverty. Jargowsky's multivariate analysis in chapter 6 reveals that a rise in the overall metropolitan mean income resulted in sharp declines in ghetto poverty concentration among blacks.

"Neighborhood poverty is not primarily the product of 'the people who live there' or a 'ghetto culture' that discourages upward mobility," states Jargowsky, "but the predictable result of the economic status of minority communities and the degree to which minorities are residentially segregated from whites and from each other by income" (p. 193). Accordingly, ghetto culture and pathologies should be viewed more appropriately as symptoms, and not as root causes of ghetto poverty.

Jargowsky concludes that policies designed to increase productivity, lower inequality, and reduce spatial and economic segregation will consequently reduce ghetto poverty. Without broader changes in the metropolitan economy and in rates of segregation, programs in barrios and ghettos alone, including those aimed at changing behavior, are unlikely to have much success. "If deterioration in the economy is impoverishing more and more people, and if employed and middle-class people keep fleeing from the path of poor neighborhoods," states Jargowsky, "no 'self-help' program will be able to stem the spread of the urban blight. As a consequence, such policies should be pursued with the understanding that they can have only a marginal impact" (p. 193). Other policies that target neighborhoods such as local economic development and enterprise zones will also be less effective without larger economic changes in the metropolitan community.

After reading this thoughtful book, any reasonable person would have to take these policy conclusions seriously. Jargowsky is to be congratulated for laying out a clear and compelling case for rethinking the way we talk about addressing the problems of high-poverty neighborhoods.

WILLIAM JULIUS WILSON

Acknowledgments

I first became interested in the study of poor neighborhoods when I joined the staff of Mario Cuomo's Task Force on Poverty and Welfare in 1986. The commission included many of the nation's leading economists, sociologists, and policy analysts, individuals with strong opinions on most policy issues and no shyness about expressing them. But I noticed the room would fall silent when William Julius Wilson talked about the growth of ghetto neighborhoods in Chicago and the disturbing social conditions within them. The group was genuinely perplexed about ghetto and barrio neighborhoods—not sure what the problem was, how bad it was, whether it was getting worse, and what if anything could be done about it. Though Wilson's work had documented the situation in Chicago, much more research needed to be done. Neighborhood poverty has been the primary focus of my research ever since.

This book carries on in spirit the work of the Urban Poverty Project at the John F. Kennedy School of Government, which was my intellectual home as a graduate student. My advisors then, Mary Jo Bane and David T. Ellwood, created an incredibly rich and challenging environment. I am even more amazed at what they accomplished in retrospect, as I struggle to emulate for my own students the kind of mentoring and teaching that Mary Jo and David routinely provided. They have influenced my thinking so much I would have to footnote every sentence to give them proper credit.

If you find any mistakes, it is because I have forgotten something they taught me, or at least tried to teach me.

The Russell Sage Foundation has generously supported my work on neighborhood poverty for nearly a decade. When the Foundation agreed to publish my dissertation, I was delighted. The only caveat was that I should add the soon-to-be-released 1990 census data to bring it up to date. My enthusiasm blinded me to the fact that the comparable shaping and analysis of the 1970 and 1980 data had taken years. In the end, revision by revision and chapter by chapter, I have written an entirely new book. During the long process, through many delays and changes of plans, Eric Wanner continued to be supportive and patient for which I will be eternally grateful.

Royce Hanson, formerly the Dean of the School of Social Sciences at the University of Texas at Dallas, steadfastly protected me from slow death by committee assignments, on the theory that I had work to do. George Farkas cared about me enough to say, "You're just wrong!" when I needed to hear it. He read numerous drafts, and continues to enlighten me in the ways of scholarship. George's knowledge of the history and development of sociology and economics saved me from reinventing the wheel on many occasions. John Kain provided valuable feedback and criticism, to which I have responded as well as I am able. It is difficult if not impossible to list all the people who influenced my thinking, but in addition to those already mentioned I have benefitted greatly from the work of Brian Berry, Mary Corcoran, Sheldon Danziger, Reynolds Farley, George Galster, Robert Hauser, Don Hicks, Mark Hughes, Christopher Jencks, Jack Kasarda, Sandy Korenman, Doug Massey, Ron Mincy, Myron Orfield, David Rusk, Richard Scotch, and Julie Wilson.

Janet Gamble and Rozlyn Coleman made excellent editorial suggestions on a number of chapters. Marie Chevrier, my wife and colleague, also provided excellent editorial assistance on several chapters, but this was the least of her many contributions. She consistently challenged me to think through my arguments and to express them more clearly. She let me go into seclusion when the going got tough, and showed pictures of me to my children so they would not forget who I was. Without her, the book and I would be unfinished.

Chapter 1

Studying Neighborhood Poverty

Every large city in the United States, whether economically vibrant or withering, has areas of extreme poverty, physical decay, and increasing abandonment. Most city residents will go to great lengths to avoid living, working, or even driving through these areas. Usually, these neighborhoods are seen only on nightly news broadcasts after a gang-related shooting or drug raid, or they are depicted on television shows populated with every stereotype. But millions of Americans cannot keep a safe distance from them because they live in one. In these "deadly neighborhoods" (Jencks 1988), families have to cope not only with their own poverty, but also with the social isolation and economic deprivation of the hundreds, if not thousands, of other families who live near them. This spatial concentration of poor people acts to magnify poverty and exacerbate its effects.

In different times and different places, such neighborhoods have gone by a variety of names. Depending on the race and ethnicity of the residents, they might be called slums, ghettos, barrios, or a host of other, often derogatory names. Many books have been written about specific poor neighborhoods and the social and economic relationships that evolve within them. One of the great classics is *The Social Order of the Slum* by Gerald Suttles (1968), about the Addams neighborhood in Chicago. Lee Rainwater's *Behind Ghetto Walls* (1970) concerns the now-demolished Pruitt-Igoe housing project in St. Louis. *Talley's Corner*, by Eliot Liebow (1967), focuses on the people who frequented a single street corner in Washington, D.C. In contrast, *The Truly Disadvantaged* by William Julius Wilson (1987), adopts a somewhat broader context by examining the growth of poor neighborhoods and the conditions within them in an entire metropolitan area—in his case, Chicago. Wilson's book has led to a resurgence of scholarly interest in poor neighborhoods and their residents. However, no book to date has presented a nationwide study of poverty at the neighborhood level, covering all regions and metropolitan areas. The purpose of this book is to fill that gap and provide, to the extent possible, a comprehensive portrait of neighborhood poverty in the United States.

Interest in the issue of neighborhood poverty seems to wax and wane in response, unfortunately, to outbreaks of urban violence. The riots that broke out in Los Angeles and a number of other cities after the initial Rodney King verdict in 1992 put the problem of poor neighborhoods back on the public agenda after years of relative neglect. Prior to that, the last major expression of public concern over the "ghetto problem" came after the urban riots of the 1960s. At the time, President Johnson responded to the "civil disorders" by appointing the Kerner Commission to investigate the causes of the violence. The commission's oft-cited conclusion was that "our nation is moving toward two societies, one black, one white—separate and unequal" (Kerner Commission 1968, 1). Stating that "it is time now to end the destruction and the violence, not only in the streets of the ghetto but in the lives of people" (p. 483), the commission's massive report included a detailed list of policy recommendations.

In March 1968, Tom Wicker was moved to write in the report's introduction, "Reading it is an ugly experience but one that brings, finally, something like the relief of beginning" (Kerner Commission 1968, xi). At that unique moment—shortly before the assassinations of Martin Luther King, Jr., and Robert Kennedy—it was possible to hope that dramatic changes could occur, that the United States not only recognized its urban poverty problem but that it could also harness the nation's affluence and solve the problem outright through government policies and programs. Yet, the nation has not done that. Resources were drained by the expanding war in Viet Nam. Fear of violence and crime, fueled by the civil disorders that prompted appointment of the Kerner Commission, disillusioned many white Americans about issues related to race and poverty. The commission's recommendations were not adopted in any serious way. Neighborhood poverty has thus persisted over the past two decades, and in many cities it has grown worse.

As this book will show, the physical areas of urban blight have expanded rapidly and a greater proportion of the population lives within their borders. Social conditions in high-poverty neighborhoods have deteriorated, fueling more abandonment in a cycle of decay that, with few exceptions, seems immune to policy intervention or private initiatives. Visits to blighted urban neighborhoods, such as the South Bronx, have become a staple of presidential campaigns, just as neglect of urban issues has become standard operating procedure for the years between elections. The Clinton administration professed a deeper concern than its immediate predecessors about the plight of inner-city neighborhoods. As a nation, however, we are more disillusioned than ever by past failures and more bound by fiscal constraints. Although the Kerner Commission made the correct diagnosis, we now know enough to question some of the specific treatments it recommended. Can we adopt more cost-effective, less bureaucratic means to pursue the goals the commission laid out? Can we now find the courage and the resources to tackle problems identified so clearly in a report published nearly thirty years ago? Ultimately, how we as a nation respond to these problems will determine whether we can slow down or even reverse the decay of urban neighborhoods and its pernicious effects on our children, our cities, and our sense of community.

Why Study Neighborhood Poverty?

The existence and expansion of blighted neighborhoods are matters of great concern for city planners. That city planners must contend with high-poverty neighborhoods does not, however, necessarily make the topic important for study in an academic sense. Indeed, an argument could be made that the real problem is poverty itself, which has its roots in the workings of the labor market and changing patterns of family formation. Poor people have to live somewhere. Variations in housing costs drive many to settle in public housing projects or areas of cheap private housing, often located near the projects. In addition, if a substantial portion of the poor are members of minority groups, as is often the case, housing market discrimination and historical patterns of racial segregation further constrict the poor to a subset of neighborhoods where they are overrepresented. Whether the poor live tightly concentrated in a few neighborhoods or are dispersed, the argument continues, has little relevance to the problems that generate poverty. The logical conclusion is that poverty, not the neighborhoods poor people live in, should be the focus of scholarly attention and the target of public policies.

In certain ways, this line of reasoning is correct. First, the majority of the poor—even the majority of the black poor—do not live in high-poverty neighborhoods. Second, for those in two-parent families, the primary causes of poverty can be traced to the vicissitudes of the labor market, and for those in female-headed families to the lack of financial support from absent fathers (Bane and Ellwood 1986; Ellwood 1988). An undue focus on the poorest neighborhoods, particularly those exhibiting high levels of crime, drug use, out-of-wedlock childbearing, and other behaviors that rankle middle-class Americans, can deflect attention from the broader structural aspects of poverty. The seemingly intractable poverty in ghettos and barrios might also lead the public and policymakers to despair, and so overlook the important contributions to reducing poverty that could be achieved by straightforward measures like the Earned Income Tax Credit (EITC), which are not tied to specific locations, and better enforcement of child support.

Still, there are many reasons to be concerned with high-poverty neighborhoods *in addition to* the poverty of individuals. First among them is the premise that neighborhoods matter, that the economic and social environments of high-poverty areas may actually have an ongoing influence on the life course of those who reside in them. That is, poor neighborhoods have an independent effect on social and economic outcomes of individuals even after taking account of their personal and family characteristics, including socioeconomic status (Tienda 1991). Of greatest concern are the effects that harsh neighborhood conditions have on children, whose choices in adolescence can have lifelong consequences. If teenagers drop out of school or bear children out of wedlock in part because of neighborhood influences, then the study of neighborhood poverty is important.

The relative importance and exact nature of neighborhood effects are, however, a matter of continuing debate in the economic and sociological literatures.[1] Here, it will suffice to say that there are many different channels through which such effects could operate— for example, a ghetto culture that stresses short-term goals (Anderson 1990, 1991); a lack of role models and stabilizing institutions to buffer social dislocation (Wilson 1987); or underfunded schools and reduced access to new jobs in suburban areas (Kain 1968, 1992). Through these and other channels, neighborhoods can influence the choices children make, the breaks they get, and the way they are treated by family, peers, and employers. In the extreme, if living in destitute neighborhoods leads children to adopt self-destructive values and behaviors, the result is a vicious cycle of poverty: children in such circumstances are "growing up . . . under conditions that make them better candidates for crime and civil disorder than for jobs providing an entry into American society" (Kerner 1968, 263).

Neighborhood effects are not the only reason to be concerned with high-poverty areas. Concern over the quality of schools and fear of crime are two major factors behind middle-class flight to the urban periphery. In neighborhoods with borderline poverty, often located at the periphery of high-poverty areas, the population is declining, with the nonpoor leaving faster than the poor (Gramlich, Laren, and Sealand 1992; Jargowsky and Bane 1991). This flight leads to more economic segregation and worsens fiscal tensions between central cities and suburbs. Metropolitan areas become economically "hollow," with poor central cities at odds with rich and defensive suburbs. Moreover, recent studies suggest that central-city poverty has dynamic effects on the economic development of suburbs (Adams and others 1994; Voith 1994). While the evidence on the point is hardly definitive, it seems doubtful that a suburban ring can long prosper around a dying urban core. Such concerns have led several metropolitan areas—for example, Portland, Oregon, and Minneapolis–St. Paul—to take a comprehensive view of growth and development, one that explicitly recognizes the value of a stable, livable urban core (Orfield 1996; Pearce 1993; Rusk 1993).

Perhaps the most compelling reason to study poor neighborhoods is that the quality of life for their residents is often dreadful.

The conditions described by the Kerner Commission thirty years ago largely still hold, "The culture of poverty that results from unemployment and family disorganization," stated the commission, "generates a system of ruthless, exploitative relationships within the ghetto." People must live and work in "an environmental jungle characterized by personal insecurity and tension" (Kerner Commission 1968, 262). Journalists such as *Wall Street Journal* reporter Alex Kotlowitz and Leon Dash of the *Washington Post* have documented the conditions of life in some of the nation's poorest African American ghettos (Dash 1989; Kotlowitz 1991). Anthropological and sociological research spanning many decades has given us detailed accounts of people's struggles to survive in the midst of severely impoverished neighborhoods.[2]

Although some would characterize residents of high-poverty areas as members of an "underclass" who bring their poverty upon themselves, I will show in chapter 4 that most ghetto and barrio residents do not engage in the behaviors considered typical of the underclass. Moreover, the analysis in chapter 6 shows that neighborhood poverty is largely determined by the overall economic conditions prevailing in a metropolitan area and the levels of segregation by race and income. Since these metropolitan-wide factors account for most of the variation in neighborhood poverty, the characteristics of the residents and local culture of the neighborhoods play a secondary role, at best. Moreover, it would take a cold heart indeed to think of the children *born* into high-poverty neighborhoods as "undeserving," regardless of their parents' behavior. The fact that substantial numbers of children, most of whom are minorities, grow up in such profoundly harmful environments raises fundamental questions about the American ideal of equality of opportunity.

Neighborhood Poverty: Conceptual and Operational Issues

Most people who live in metropolitan areas could tell you which neighborhoods they consider to be ghettos, barrios, or slums. Such notions, as commonly applied, are inherently subjective; what one person considers a slum, another may see as an up-and-coming neighborhood, ripe for gentrification. If one were conducting a study in a single metropolitan area, one could rely on the local consensus, if there were one, concerning the specific areas that constitute "bad" neighborhoods. To conduct a nationwide study, however, a common metric is needed, one that can be applied in a consistent fashion to thousands of neighborhoods in hundreds of metropolitan areas throughout the United States.

Moreover, there are important conceptual issues that have to be resolved. Are we talking about race and ethnicity or are we talking about class? Terms such as ghetto and barrio clearly have racial and ethnic connotations, but not all African American and Hispanic neighborhoods are poor, nor are all poor neighborhoods exclusively minority. Yet, as currently used, the terms ghetto and barrio also have class connotations. Moreover, discussions of "the underclass" presume or imply certain types of behaviors and attitudes among the residents of the affected neighborhoods. In the sections that follow, I discuss the choices I have made in analyzing the data on neighborhood poverty and the rationale for them. Since the methodology can have a large effect on the portrait of neighborhood poverty that emerges, I am explicit about the choices I make in developing an operational definition of high-poverty neighborhoods. I also compare my approach with several alternatives that are commonly employed in the urban poverty literature.

Neighborhoods in the Census

Before one can specify what a high-poverty neighborhood is, one has to clarify what is meant by the term "neighborhood" itself. Suzanne Keller (1987) described some of the term's nuances and the difficulty in reconciling them:

> The term "neighborhood," most investigators agree, is not without its ambiguities. Essentially, it refers to distinctive areas into which larger spatial units may be sub-divided, such as gold coasts and slums, central and outlying districts, residential and industrial areas, middle class and working class areas. The distinctiveness of these areas stems from different sources whose independent contributions are difficult to assess: geographical boundaries, ethnic or cultural characteristics of the inhabitants, psychological unity among people who feel that [they] belong together, or concentrated use of an area's facilities for shopping, leisure, and learning. Neighborhoods combining all four

elements are very rare in modern cities. In particular . . . the geographical and the personal boundaries do not always coincide (p. 87).

Michael White, in his census monograph on American neighborhoods, wrote that most uses of the term "have in common the meaning of physically bounded area characterized by some degree of relative homogeneity and/or social cohesion" (White 1987, 3). Despite this core concept, White noted that there is little agreement about the land area or population size that would constitute "sociologically meaningful" neighborhoods.

In a study of neighborhood poverty, it makes sense to find a definition of neighborhood that identifies the area within which concentrations of poverty might influence outcomes of individuals. Even this focus, however, provides little real guidance. To a preschooler, the potentially influential neighborhood may be the hallway of his floor in a housing project, while to his teenage brother it may be the local school district. Yet, to study neighborhood poverty, we need an areal unit that approximates what we mean by the term neighborhood and for which data is available for the nation as a whole.

Wilson's pathbreaking work made use of Chicago's "community areas," which are relatively large neighborhoods with identifiable names and clearly defined boundaries (Wilson 1987). Unfortunately, Chicago is one of the few cities to have established and maintained a system of defined neighborhoods. In most places, the exact names and boundaries of neighborhoods fluctuate over time and depend on whom you ask. For a national study, *census tracts* are the only realistic choice; they are defined by the Census Bureau as "small, relatively permanent statistical subdivisions of a county . . . census tracts usually have between 2,500 and 8,000 persons and, when first delineated, are designed to be homogeneous with respect to population characteristics, economic status, and living conditions" (U.S. Bureau of the Census 1992, appendix A).

Unlike Chicago's community areas, census tracts have been created nationwide, in cooperation with local planning officials, for all metropolitan areas and "other densely populated counties." The remaining counties are divided up into block numbering areas (BNAs) "using guidelines similar to those for the delineation of census tracts" (U.S. Bureau of the Census 1992, appendix A).[3] As of 1990, there were about 60,000 tracts and BNAs, with an average population of about 4,000 persons. "Tracts," concluded White, "offer the best compromise with respect to size, homogeneity, data availability, and comparability" (White 1987, 19).

High-Poverty Neighborhoods

When comparing census tracts, various measures are available for classifying neighborhoods by economic status. These include mean or median household income, the neighborhood poverty rate, and composite measures of socioeconomic status. Most researchers have favored a criterion based on the neighborhood poverty rate. Unlike mean or median income, the poverty rate of a neighborhood implicitly incorporates information about mean family income and the variance of the neighborhood income distribution. For statistical purposes, the Census Bureau defines a person as poor if their total family income falls below the federally defined poverty level, which varies by family size and is adjusted each year for inflation.[4] For example, the poverty threshold for a family of three was $10,419 in 1990, the last census year. The *poverty rate* for a particular neighborhood is determined by dividing the number of poor persons who live there by the total of poor and nonpoor persons.[5]

Wilson, using community areas, focused on neighborhoods with poverty rates of 30 percent or more. As researchers began to extend Wilson's work beyond Chicago, the common practice was to use census tracts with poverty rates of 40 percent.[6] Initially, this level was chosen for a decidedly nonsubstantive reason: it was the highest rate for which the Census Bureau published aggregated figures in special topic reports on high-poverty areas in central cities (U.S. Bureau of the Census 1973, 1985). However, the acquisition and analysis of data on individual census tracts, since the late 1980s, allow any poverty rate to be chosen, and so the choice of a specific threshold level must be discussed and justified.

Figure 1.1 shows the distribution of the U.S. population in 1990 by a neighborhood's poverty rate. Two conclusions are immediately apparent. First, the distribution of neighborhoods by poverty rate is continuous, not bimodal (with one group of "nice" neighborhoods and a separate group of "bad" neighborhoods). Nor is there any

Figure 1.1   U.S. Population by Neighborhood Poverty Rate; Metropolitan and Non-Metropolitan Areas, 1990

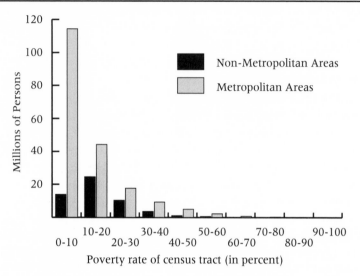

Poverty rate of census tract (in percent)

Source: Census tract data for 1970–90 (see appendix A), tabulations by the author.

obvious place in the distribution to divide high-poverty areas from all other neighborhoods.

Second, almost no neighborhoods are entirely poor. Out of nearly 60,000 census tracts, only sixty-seven had poverty rates of 90 percent or greater. Such tracts contained only two-hundredths of 1 percent of the U.S. population. Combining all neighborhoods with a 60 to 100 percent poverty rate yields 1.4 million persons, still less than 1 percent of the U.S. population. In contrast, if a 20 percent poverty threshold is used to define high-poverty areas, then such neighborhoods would contain more than one-fifth of the nation's citizens.

These examples show that neighborhood poverty can be made to look bigger or smaller depending on how it is measured. The poverty threshold is properly chosen when it achieves the greatest predictive validity—that is, it should come closest to identifying those census tracts that are considered ghettos, barrios, or slums by experienced observers of individual neighborhoods, such as city planners and public officials, local Census Bureau officials, and workers in social service agencies. To address this question, Mary Jo Bane and I made site visits to a number of metropolitan areas across the country (see Jargowsky and Bane 1991).[7] According to that research, neighborhoods selected using a 40 percent poverty rate came closest to matching those that were subjectively identified by knowledgeable local individuals.

In our fieldwork, we found that such neighborhoods were predominantly minority. They tended to have a threatening appearance, marked by dilapidated housing, vacant units with broken or boarded-up windows, abandoned and burned-out cars, and men "hanging out" on street corners. In Philadelphia and Chicago, the housing stock consisted of high-rise public housing projects or multistory tenement buildings built right to the sidewalks. In Detroit, the high-poverty areas consisted of single-family homes built decades ago for auto workers earning the unheard of wage of $5 a day; now old and undermaintained, some had simply fallen down and only rubble remained. In Jackson, Mississippi, such neighborhoods had tin-roofed shacks. In Pine Bluff, Arkansas, trailers sat rusting alongside tiny Depression-era houses.

In contrast, neighborhoods with poverty rates in the 20 to 40 percent range generally had a quite different look and feel. Fewer units were vacant or in disrepair. There was less litter and broken glass. Fewer people were "hanging out." Such neighborhoods, although still showing signs of distress, appeared to be working-class or lower-middle-class communities. City planners and other local individuals usually did not call our attention to these neighborhoods, although they often bordered the main high-poverty areas.

The few census tracts we visited with poverty rates above 60 percent were dominated by public housing projects, where income was used as a screening device to select residents. Such artificially created neighborhoods lacked the economic heterogeneity of most other neighborhoods, even high-poverty areas. For these reasons, I use a 40 percent poverty rate to identify the high-poverty neighborhoods. In 1990, 3,417 census tracts or BNAs out of 59,678 (5.7 percent) had poverty rates at least that high.[8] The majority of these (2,886, or 84.5 percent) were located in metropolitan areas; the remainder (551) were in smaller towns and rural areas.[9]

At the margin, any threshold is arbitrary; there is little difference between a neighborhood with a 39.9 percent poverty rate and one with a 40.1 percent poverty rate. Moreover, the poverty rate in a census tract is an estimate based on a sample.[10] Thus, classification errors will occur in both directions. With the large number of tracts nationally and in the larger metropolitan areas, such errors will tend to cancel out; in smaller metropolitan areas, however, the misclassification of a few tracts seriously distorts the extent of neighborhood poverty. For this reason, I do not report the figures for the smallest metropolitan areas separately; they are included in aggregate regional and national figures.

Race Versus Class

In prior research, a number of scholars including myself defined the term *ghetto* to refer all to high-poverty neighborhoods, regardless of the racial and ethnic makeup of the neighborhood's residents. A number of researchers have criticized this practice on the grounds that *ghetto* refers to neighborhoods formed by the residential segregation of racial and ethnic minorities, particularly African Americans (Kain 1992, 10).[11] In view of these concerns, it is worthwhile to review the conceptual meaning of the term ghetto and to clarify the terminology I will employ in this book to refer to high-poverty neighborhoods with differing racial and ethnic compositions.

Historically, *ghetto* referred to urban enclaves that were composed primarily of one racial or ethnic group, particularly the Jewish area of a city. Louis Wirth, in his 1928 book *The Ghetto*, stated without qualification that "the word 'ghetto' applies to the Jewish quarter of a city" (Wirth 1928, 1).[12] The *Oxford English Dictionary* suggests that the word derives from the Italian *getto*, meaning foundry, because the original Jewish quarter in Venice was on the site of a foundry (*OED* 1989, 491–92). In the United States, most large cities at the turn of the century had several neighborhoods in which persons of one nationality or race were highly concentrated, among them Irish, Italian, Polish, and black ghettos. To a certain extent, these concentrations were voluntary assemblages; new immigrants found many advantages to living in areas where they shared a language and culture with others (Forman 1971, 5). Of course, these ghettos were also maintained by active and often legally sanctioned housing discrimination, especially in the case of African Americans.

European-ethnic ghettos served as launching pads for later economic and residential assimilation. In most cases, these neighborhoods have disappeared or continue to survive mainly as tourist
attractions. The vast majority of their former residents and especially their children have dispersed. In contrast, black ghettos
emerged as an enduring feature of the metropolitan landscape
(White 1987). In Northern cities at least, European immigrants
were never as highly segregated as blacks became following the
great northward migration during World War I. Racial segregation
was enforced by zoning, restrictive covenants, and overt violence
directed against anyone who dared cross the color line (Massey and
Denton 1993, 32–42).

Because European immigrants and later black migrants from the
rural South were usually quite poor, ghettos came to be associated
with poverty. Writing in 1971, Forman described the difference
between the ghettos and slums as follows:

> Whereas residence in a ghetto is the result of racial or cultural char-
> acteristics, residence in a slum is determined primarily by economic
> factors. The typical slum resident lives in poor housing because he
> cannot afford to live in anything better. While *slum* implies poverty,
> this is not necessarily true of the ghetto. (Forman 1971, 3).

Forman proposed the awkward term "slum-ghetto" to refer to
minority neighborhoods that are also poor and argued that the
word ghetto should be applied to any minority neighborhood,
regardless of economic level.

In the past, the issue was almost a distinction without a difference, because most minority neighborhoods were also poor. As a
result, ghetto became a loose synonym for slum. In *Dark Ghetto*, for
example, Ken Clark wrote that "the pathologies of the ghetto community perpetuate themselves through cumulative ugliness, deterioration, and isolation and strengthen the Negro's sense of worth-
lessness, giving testimony to his impotence" (Clark 1965, 12).
Without question, Clark conceives of the ghetto as a racial construct, but he also implicitly assumes a high degree of economic
deprivation. In many other books and articles as well as in every-
day speech, the trend for some time has been to use the term ghetto
to refer to neighborhoods both segregated and poor. For the average

American, white or black, it has been true for some time that a song lyric about "life in the ghetto" or a statement like "he grew up in the ghetto" has both racial *and* economic connotations.

Further developments have served to highlight the economic sense of the term ghetto in common usage. First, since 1965 a substantial black middle class and nascent black affluent class have emerged. Second, the central cities of several large metropolitan areas have become majority black. As a result, many black professionals now live in highly segregated, but quite wealthy suburban communities (Dent 1992). These neighborhoods are not "ghettos" in the current sense of the term. Indeed, residents of such neighborhoods could argue that they moved out of the ghetto and are quite happy about it. Clark would not use phrases like "pathologies of ghetto communities" and "cumulative ugliness, deterioration, and isolation" in reference to such prosperous neighborhoods as Hamilton Heights in New York City, Baldwin Hills in Los Angeles, MacGregor Park in Houston, Cascade Heights in Atlanta, and Chatham in Chicago—even though these neighborhoods are predominantly black (*Ebony* 1987).

Based on this usage, I will use *ghetto* to refer to a neighborhood that is both predominantly black and also meets the 40 percent poverty threshold. Such neighborhoods are a subset of all high-poverty neighborhoods. Similarly, the term *barrio* will be used to refer to high-poverty neighborhoods that are predominantly Hispanic. For lack of a better term, I refer to predominantly white and non-Hispanic high-poverty neighborhoods as *white slums*. The remainder, neighborhoods where no one racial or ethnic group predominates, I call *mixed slums*.

The next step is to find out how many neighborhoods of each type exist and their relative populations. Very few high-poverty neighborhoods are composed exclusively of one racial or ethnic group—only 125 of the 2,866 census tracts.[13] Thus, in a sense, the vast majority of high-poverty neighborhoods are mixed to some degree. Figure 1.2 shows that the distribution of high-poverty census tracts by percent non-Hispanic black is bimodal. The largest categories are less than 10 percent black and more than 90 percent black. Yet about an equal number of high-poverty neighborhoods fall in a continuous distribution between the two peaks. Only about

Figure 1.2   High-Poverty Neighborhoods by Percent Non-Hispanic Black, 1990

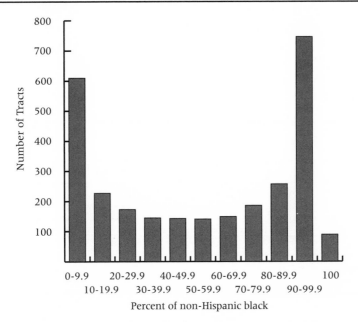

Source: Census tract data for 1970–90 (see appendix A), tabulations by the author.

half of all blacks in high-poverty neighborhoods live in monolithic black ghettos (greater than 90 percent black). About 600,000 of all blacks living in high-poverty areas (14.4 percent) live in neighborhoods that are less than 50 percent black.

Table 1.1 shows the distribution of high-poverty neighborhoods in metropolitan areas by the existence of a dominant racial or ethnic group in 1990. While the exact cutoff for what constitutes a "dominant" group is arbitrary, I have used two-thirds for the purpose of illustration. In all, there are nearly three thousand high-poverty neighborhoods in the United States with about 8.5 million residents. Black ghettos are the most common neighborhood type and account for about half of all high-poverty neighborhoods and 42 percent of their residents. The next most common neighborhood

Table 1.1   Population of High-Poverty Neighborhoods

| | Number of High-Poverty Tracts | Persons in High-Poverty Tracts (thousands or percent) | | | |
| | | Total | Non-Hispanic | | Hispanic |
			White	Black	
Total	2,866	8,446	1,900	4,198	2,052
Neighborhood type					
White slum	387	13.7%	50.4%	2.1%	2.3%
Ghetto	1,329	42.4	11.1	76.9	5.5
Barrio	334	17.1	5.0	2.3	60.0
Mixed slum	816	26.9	33.6	18.7	32.2

Source: 1990 census, Summary Tape File 3A (CD-ROM), tabulations by the author.
Note: Total persons include other races not shown separately. Percentages may not add to 100 due to rounding. Neighborhood types include only metropolitan census tracts in which the poverty rates are 40 percent or higher. *White slums* are census tracts in which the population is at least two-thirds white; *ghettos* are at least two-thirds black; *barrios* are at least two-thirds Hispanic. All other tracts are *mixed slums.*

type has no dominant group, in the sense that no group accounts for more than two-thirds of the neighborhood's residents. Finally, there are about equal numbers of barrios and white slums.

An interesting implication of table 1.1 is that it makes a difference whether you focus on blacks living in high-poverty neighborhoods or the residents of black ghettos. Most whites, blacks, and Hispanics residing in high-poverty neighborhoods live where their own group is dominant—white slums, ghettos, or barrios, respectively. But nontrivial proportions of those in poor neighborhoods are "off the diagonal," living in neighborhoods where a different group is dominant or in mixed areas. Of the 4.2 million blacks living in some type of high-poverty area, nearly one-fourth live in barrios, white slums, or mixed slums. Half the non-Hispanic whites in high-poverty neighborhoods live outside white slums. Forty percent of Hispanics in high-poverty neighborhoods do not live in barrios.[14]

Since black ghettos are the most common type of high-poverty neighborhood, I sometimes use the term ghetto as a shorthand term for all high-poverty neighborhoods, particularly when referring to regions or metropolitan areas where most of the residents of such areas are African American. However, unless otherwise noted, all high-poverty neighborhoods, including ghettos, barrios, and both types of slums, are covered in the analysis.

Neighborhood Poverty Versus the "Underclass"

The concept of neighborhood poverty developed above is related to, but distinct from, the concept of the "underclass." That term has become a popular way to refer to the urban poor, particularly those who reside in the high-poverty neighborhoods. Thus, I want to digress for a moment to discuss the relationship between neighborhood poverty and the underclass and to emphasize that this book addresses the former rather than the latter.

In a metropolitan area at any given point in time, there is a fixed number of persons living in families or households with incomes below the federal poverty line, corresponding to an overall metropolitan poverty rate. Whatever the overall level of poverty in a metropolitan area, the poor can be more or less residentially segregated from the nonpoor. At one extreme, every neighborhood can have the same poverty rate as the metropolitan area. In this case, there would be no ghettos, barrios, or slums, unless the overall poverty rate was at least 40 percent, in which case the whole city would be considered a high-poverty area. At the other extreme, poor and nonpoor persons could live in completely separate neighborhoods, in which case some neighborhoods would have poverty rates of 100 percent and the rest 0 percent.

In reality, of course, cities fall somewhere in between, with a wide distribution of neighborhood poverty rates, and most cities have some neighborhoods that classify as ghettos or barrios. Within such neighborhoods, one may observe a greater or lesser degree of behaviors associated with the underclass, such as dropping out of school, having children out of wedlock, drug and alcohol abuse, welfare receipt, and low attachment to the labor force.

Thus, there are three conceptually distinct subjects that a researcher interested in urban poverty could choose to study. The first are the economic, institutional, and social processes that lead to some level of poverty within the metropolitan area and that determine differences in poverty levels among metropolitan areas

(Eggers and Massey 1991, 1992). The second is the extent to which poverty is concentrated in certain neighborhoods, the trends over time in this tendency, and the forces that drive them, which are the subjects of this book. The third potential subject is the way in which geographic concentrations of poverty cause certain behavioral responses. This is the study of the underclass.

Among journalists and the general public, the term underclass is used loosely to describe inner-city poor persons who exhibit any deviant or self-destructive behavior. However, when the term is used in academic research, it has a much more specific meaning. Mincy and Wiener (1993), for example, define underclass as "a group of people who have trouble entering and remaining in the labor force, who derive a large share of their income from sources other than legal employment, and who exist in a social context that prevents labor force attachment."[15]

In *The Truly Disadvantaged: The Inner-City, the Underclass and Public Policy*, William Julius Wilson (1987) argues that when the poor are residentially isolated from the nonpoor, they are spatially and socially cut off from mainstream resources, opportunities, and role models. The result is "a disproportionate concentration of the most disadvantaged segments of the urban black population," which creates a "social milieu" that fosters low labor force attachment, out-of-wedlock childbearing, drug and alcohol use, and other social pathologies (Wilson 1987, 58).

Years earlier, Oscar Lewis (1965) advanced the notion that, in such situations, a "culture of poverty" becomes self-sustaining, impervious to real changes in the structure of opportunities, and is passed from generation to generation. Wilson distanced himself from this extreme position, arguing that social isolation and community decline "magnified the effects of living in highly concentrated urban poverty—effects that are manifested in ghetto-specific cultures and behaviors." But, Wilson continued, "as economic and social conditions change, cultural traits, created by previous situations, likewise *eventually* change even though it is possible that some will linger on and influence behavior for a period of time" (emphasis in the original; Wilson 1987, 138). In other words, in Wilson's view, the underclass culture is primarily an effect of economic transformation and social isolation, rather than a major sustaining force of neighborhood poverty.

Ghettos and barrios are fundamental to the underclass debate in that they provide the social and economic context for the development of class-specific behaviors (Van Haitsma 1989). One can, however, study neighborhood poverty without taking a position on whether the residents of high-poverty areas, or some subset of them, form a distinct class in the social science sense of the word. As Hughes notes in his study of ghetto poverty, "what will be discussed [here] . . . as the dependent variable . . . could be used as the independent variable . . . in a study of individual behavior" (Hughes 1989, 191). In fact, as chapter 4 shows, high-poverty areas contain a great diversity of lifestyles and socioeconomic outcomes. Thus, if an underclass subculture does exist in the sociological sense, not all residents of poverty areas become ensnared by it.

High-Poverty Tracts Outside Metropolitan Areas

I have limited my attention to high-poverty neighborhoods within metropolitan areas. Yet many pockets of extreme poverty exist outside metropolitan areas, especially among blacks in the South. As of 1990, the entire country has been divided into tracts or BNAs. Before then, only metropolitan areas were so "tracted." Mincy and Wiener (1993) argue that these new areas, the BNAs, ought to be included to give a full national picture of neighborhood poverty.

I believe that urban and rural poverty areas pose separate problems and that the two have different histories, causal structures, and characteristics. Many issues, such as the suburbanization of jobs or the fiscal strains between city and suburbs, are of concern only in urban areas. Small-town and rural "pockets of poverty" differ from urban ghettos in other important ways. With regard to measurement issues, tracts and BNAs may not be comparable as proxies for neighborhoods. BNAs tend to be much larger, with nearly *thirteen times* the land area of the average metropolitan tract. At the same time, their average population is 15 percent lower. Hence, their population density is far lower, and the analogy to local neighborhoods can become quite strained. At the very least, BNAs capture a different meaning of neighborhood than do urban census tracts. Moreover, since comparable figures for such areas are not available for 1970 and 1980, it is impossible to chart trends over time for these areas, as I do for metropolitan neighborhood poverty in the next chapter.

Metropolitan Summary Measures

Identifying high-poverty neighborhoods is only the first step in evaluating neighborhood poverty. To facilitate comparisons among metropolitan areas, summary measures are needed to gauge the size and seriousness of a city's ghettos, barrios, and slums. Simply counting the number of high-poverty tracts or persons in them is inadequate because such measures would largely reflect a metropolitan area's total population. Measures are needed that give the relative size of the neighborhood poverty problem. The two key measures I use are the neighborhood poverty rate and the concentration of poverty.

The *neighborhood poverty rate* (also called the level of neighborhood poverty) is the percentage of a metropolitan area's total population that resides in ghettos, barrios, or other high-poverty census tracts. Just as the overall poverty rate is the proportion of persons in a given area who live in poor families or households, the neighborhood poverty rate is the proportion of persons living in high-poverty neighborhoods. This measure indicates the fraction of the population that is "at risk," in terms of the negative effects associated with high-poverty neighborhoods: crime, bad schools, lack of role models, and so on. It will often be useful to examine this statistic separately by race. The black neighborhood poverty rate is the proportion of the African American population in a metropolitan area that lives in high-poverty neighborhoods; since most blacks in high-poverty neighborhoods live in highly segregated ghettos, I also refer to this statistic as the level of ghetto poverty. Similarly, the neighborhood poverty rate among Hispanics can be referred to as the barrio poverty rate.

The *concentration of the poor* is the percentage of a metropolitan area's poor population that resides in high-poverty neighborhoods, which also can be computed separately by race. The difference between the level of neighborhood poverty and the concentration of poverty can be illustrated with the following example. Suppose a hypothetical metropolitan area has a poverty rate of only 1 percent, but all of the poor persons live in one high-poverty census tract that has an equal number of nonpoor residents. The neighborhood poverty rate would be 2 percent, because both the poor

(1 percent of the population) and the nonpoor persons in the high-poverty tract (another 1 percent of the population) are included in the numerator and the total population is in the denominator. But the concentration of poverty would be 100 percent, since all the poor reside in a high-poverty neighborhood.

Both measures are useful, but they answer different questions. The former measure gives a sense of the relative size of a metropolitan area's ghetto, barrio, or slum problem, while the latter is useful when thinking about the constraints and opportunities faced by poor persons. In particular, the concentration of poverty indicates the percentage of the poor who not only have to cope with their own poverty, but also that of those around them.

The term *concentration* in this context does not refer to density. Ghetto neighborhoods are often less dense in terms of persons per areal unit because of high vacancy rates and abandoned buildings. Indeed, in 1990, high-poverty census tracts averaged 2,947 persons, compared with 4,432 persons per nonghetto census tract. Rather, concentration of the poor refers to the tendency of the poor to live in neighborhoods where many of their neighbors are also poor, rather than diffused broadly among the population.

Drawbacks to the Methodology

The poverty rate–census tract methodology is subject to several criticisms. First, because the cost of living varies by region and metropolitan area, the poverty line, in effect, varies. A family in New York City with a poverty-level income is likely to be much worse off than a family with the same income living in Tulsa.[16] By extension, a neighborhood with 40 percent of its households below the poverty line is worse off in New York than in Tulsa. (It may or may not be a "worse" neighborhood in a social sense.) The same issue applies to a comparison of poor neighborhoods between 1970 and 1980 because of the known defect in the consumer price index, which results in an overestimation of inflation during that period. An upward bias in inflation may cause poverty levels to be overstated, and neighborhoods that are objectively less impoverished may end up classified as high-poverty areas.

A second criticism is that the poverty rate, which is based on cash income, ignores differences between regions and cities in the availability of in-kind benefits, such as food stamps, Medicaid, and certain forms of housing and energy assistance. Fortunately, these benefits tend to be higher in the same areas that have a higher cost of living, so the two errors may be partly offset.

Third, the census undercounts income and people. The undercount of people is particularly worrisome since "the largest undercounts of the 1980 census occurred in central cities with large minority populations"; moreover, the undercount seems to be closely related to a city's crime rate, so the undercount is likely to be greatest in ghetto neighborhoods (Erickson, Kadane, and Tukey 1987, 111). On the other hand, the census's undercount of income tends to inflate the number of poor. Again, these two errors may offset each other, but the net effect is impossible to determine.

An ideal methodology would develop price deflators for all metropolitan areas; develop estimates for in-kind benefits; adjust the base population of census tracts to correct for the undercount; estimate the "real" distribution of income within each neighborhood; divide household incomes by an equivalence scale to get the rate of income to needs for each household;[17] compute the distribution of needs-adjusted household income within tracts; and select neighborhoods based on a characteristic of this distribution. Such a methodology is, however, computationally complex and impractical; it might also introduce more errors than it would fix. Each step would involve making assumptions, some of which would, of necessity, be arbitrary. For these reasons, the Bane and Jargowsky approach of using a 40 percent poverty rate has been adopted here.

Alternative Approaches to Measuring Ghetto Poverty

Other researchers measure ghetto poverty and the concentration of poverty in different ways. Some of the major variants are Massey and Eggers's exposure measure, Ricketts and Sawhill's underclass measure, and Mark Hughes's concept of impacted ghettos.

The Exposure Measure

Massey and Eggers (1990) criticize the measures used by Jargowsky and Bane and by Wilson because they do not "make full use of data on the spatial distribution of income" (p. 1155).[18] They argue that "asking whether the concentration of poverty has grown simply asks whether minorities' probabilities of interclass contact have risen" (Massey and Eggers 1990, 1159–60). "Interclass contact" refers to the likelihood that members of one income group share a neighborhood with members of another income group. Probabilities of "residential contact" are typically measured by the exposure index (P*). Massey uses the exposure of the poor in a given racial or ethnic group to poverty as his measure of the concentration of poverty. For example, the concentration of the black poor would be the average tract poverty rate experienced by members of that group.

Use of the exposure measure does avoid having to classify poverty areas, as Massey and Eggers claim, and does use information from the entire geographic distribution of poor persons. But this is a weakness rather than a strength. One of the chief concerns about ghettos and barrios is whether there are threshold effects, so that moving from a neighborhood with a 30 percent poverty rate to one with a 40 percent poverty rate is much worse than moving from a neighborhood with a 10 percent poverty rate to one with a 20 percent poverty rate. In other words, the experience of the poor in relatively low-poverty areas is of much less concern than those in "bad" neighborhoods. Moreover, the exposure measure does not identify specific neighborhoods, which can then be mapped and studied in detail. In short, the concentration of poverty is *not* simply about "minorities' probabilities of interclass contact," but rather about the degree to which minorities inhabit areas of extreme deprivation, with the attendant possibility that the social milieu is qualitatively different from that of the rest of society.[19]

"Underclass" Measures

Ricketts and Sawhill (1988), on the other hand, explicitly set out to measure the underclass from a behavioral perspective. They propose to identify "a subgroup . . . that engages in behaviors at variance with those of the mainstream" (p. 318). Yet their method is also geographic in that they seek to delineate "underclass neighborhoods" (again, census tracts) where large numbers of persons act in deviant ways. Specifically, they select all census tracts that are simultaneously one standard deviation above the national mean on four characteristics: the percentage of families with children headed by females; the percentage of adult males who worked fewer than twenty-six weeks or were not in the labor force in the previous year; the percentage of households receiving public assistance; and the percentage of older teenagers not in school and not high school graduates (dropouts).[20] They use the overall tract score on these indicators, not race-specific measures.

Their definition has several problems. First, the second condition groups those who were not in the labor force with those who had long spells of unemployment, thus confusing behavior with economic outcomes (Wilson 1988). Even labor force participation is partly determined by economic conditions; "discouraged workers" do not participate in the labor market because they do not expect to find work. This criterion is not strictly a measure of behavior unless it is obvious that jobs are plentiful, such as when the economy is near full employment.

Second, their methodology is highly sensitive to the multiple correlations among the four characteristics. Anything that affects the correlation of one of these variables with any of the others can have a large effect on which tracts are designated as underclass. For example, since welfare benefit levels are lower in the South, families must have lower income levels to be eligible for the program. Thus, the correlation of public assistance and the other three variables is lower in the South and fewer tracts there qualify as underclass by the Ricketts and Sawhill method.

The empirical results of Ricketts and Sawhill's approach differ somewhat from the census tract–poverty rate approach. Out of more than 40,000 census tracts, 880 met their definition of underclass areas in 1980. About 5 percent of the U.S. poor lived in underclass areas, whereas about 13 percent of the poor lived in census tracts with poverty rates of at least 40 percent (Ricketts and Sawhill 1988, table 2). "Virtually all" of the underclass tracts are located in the Northeast's urban areas (p. 322).

In 1980, more than 60 percent of Ricketts and Sawhill's underclass tracts were also high-poverty tracts. But most high-poverty tracts (72 percent) were not underclass tracts, even though the characteristics of the two are quite similar, except for the proportion of high school dropouts (see table 1.2). In a related study,

Table 1.2   Characteristics of Underclass and High-Poverty
                Census Tracts, 1980

Average Tract Characteristic	Type of Tract	
	Underclass	Ghetto
Families with female head	60%	59%
Households with public assistance	34	33
Adult males, less than 26 weeks worked	56	57
16–19-year-old high school dropouts	36	19

Source: Ricketts and Sawhill (1988), table 2.

Tobin (1993) shows that this factor explains most of the divergence
between ghetto poverty and underclass figures. Dropping out is less
correlated with the other three characteristics than they are with
each other. For this reason, Kasarda (1993) defines a new measure
called "distressed neighborhoods," which follows the same basic
approach but omits the dropout rate (see chapter 3).

Further work by Ricketts and Mincy (1989) indicates extremely
rapid growth of the underclass between 1970 and 1980. Underclass
tracts quadrupled between 1970 and 1980; the underclass population increased 230 percent. In contrast, Mincy and Wiener (1993)
show little change in the underclass between 1980 and 1990. In both
cases, the trend is very different from the results obtained with the
neighborhood poverty approach used here. Part of the explanation
lies in the way underclass standards are applied. The means and
standard deviations that constitute the thresholds are derived for the
nation as a whole in 1980 and then applied to the other years. In
other words, a 1970 census tract had to be one standard deviation
above the 1980 means on all four characteristics. Yet, given the general increase in female-headed households in all segments of society
and a general decrease in men's labor force participation, few census tracts in 1970 were very far above the 1980 means.

This approach seems to bias the analysis in favor of finding a
large growth in the underclass. Between 1980 and 1990, however,
the dropout rate generally declined, having the opposite effect. In
fact, Tobin's sensitivity analysis shows that the supposed growth of
the underclass is entirely the result of using 1980 thresholds for the
other years (Tobin 1993, 13). Both underclass and neighborhood

poverty measures can tell us interesting things about poor inner-city neighborhoods. But the underclass measures devised so far seem to suffer from an instability inherent in their construction and the limitations of census data.

Impacted Ghettos

Mark Hughes proposes a somewhat different concept—that of *impacted ghettos*, neighborhoods "so distressed that they define a new level of neighborhood deprivation" (Hughes 1989, 192). He defines census tracts as impacted ghettos if they are sufficiently worse off than metropolitan norms, specifically if they are above twice the metropolitan median on the same four characteristics used by Ricketts and Sawhill. Hughes (1989) distinguishes his work from that of Ricketts, Sawhill, and Mincy as follows:

> [By] measuring deprivation relative to metropolitan norms rather than national norms, it allows us to focus on the concentration of deprivation within certain neighborhoods as distinct from . . . relative norms of the metropolitan area and the nation. Second, by measuring deprivation relative to current norms rather than benchmark [1980] norms, the definition allows us to focus, again, on the concentration of deprivation within certain neighborhoods as distinct form changes in the "normal" levels of the characteristics between time periods. (192)

Hughes also criticizes the Ricketts and Sawhill approach on the grounds that almost any distribution, no matter how compact, will have some observations more than one standard deviation above the mean (p. 193). Census tracts more than one standard deviation above the mean may or may not have extreme values on that characteristic in a socially meaningful sense; it depends on the mean and standard deviation of that characteristic.

In contrast, it is quite possible that no census tract in a metropolitan area would have a value on a characteristic that was twice the metropolitan *median*, the standard Hughes employs. But the "twice the median" rule has its own problems. For example, if the median value for a variable expressed as a percentage, such as percent on public assistance, were greater than 50 percent, no census tract could possibly have twice the median value.

Hughes employs twice the median as a measure of "statistical distance" or "extremeness" (p. 193). Yet, the median is not a measure of dispersion, nor is twice the median or any other multiple of it. In contrast, a tract that is one or more standard deviations above the mean—as in the Ricketts and Sawhill measure—is statistically extreme at least in comparison to other census tracts. A better way to address Hughes's concern (that outliers so identified may not be extreme enough) would be to set the cutoff points based on subjective notions of what values of the characteristics are extreme enough to qualify as "underclass."

At the metropolitan level, Hughes (1989) defines the extent of "impacted ghetto formation" as the increase in the number of impacted ghetto tracts (p. 194). He finds that the highest levels of "impacted ghetto" poverty are in the Northeast and North Central regions, as are the largest increases. He also finds decreases in some cities, most of which are in the South and West (Hughes 1989, table 1). Comparison of census-tract maps (Hughes 1989, figures 1–6) show that Hughes's criteria tend to select a subset of the census tracts identified as ghettos by Jargowsky and Bane (1991 and unpublished maps).

How to Approach Neighborhood Poverty

This discussion of alternative measures of neighborhood poverty and underclass highlights a key decision for researchers: Should the focus be on the geographic concentration of the poor or on concentrations of underclass behaviors? Some measures, such as Massey and Eggers's exposure of the black poor to poverty or those I proposed above, focus on the spatial organization of the poor. Others, such as Ricketts and Sawhill's measure and its variants, add a social and behavioral element.

Each approach has its advantages and disadvantages. Whereas underclass researchers try to focus on neighborhoods exhibiting social pathologies, the census does not measure and report on alienation, crime, and drug use—the key components of most underclass characterizations. Even if underclass measures were able to overcome these problems, the approach is conceptually unsound because it assumes a causal process. Underclass theory suggests that concentrations of extreme poverty give rise to social pathologies that exacerbate poverty. That is an empirical question; to answer it, we must look at *all* concentrations of extreme poverty to learn the extent to which such pathologies are due to neighborhood effects. This book provides a systematic and comprehensive overview of neighborhood poverty in metropolitan America and analyzes the causal forces behind it in the hope that a more effective set of policies can be devised to slow down or reverse the spread of urban blight through our nation's cities.

Chapter 2

Neighborhood Poverty Between 1970 and 1990

Between 1970 and 1990, neighborhood poverty in U.S. metropolitan areas, considered collectively, grew along virtually every dimension. Ghettos, barrios, and other slum neighborhoods expanded in physical size, number of residents, number of poor residents, and the proportion of the metropolitan population living within them. The proportion of African Americans living in ghetto neighborhoods increased, despite a slight decrease in that group's poverty rate. Poor persons, whether white, black, or Hispanic, became increasingly concentrated in high-poverty areas and more isolated from the rest of society. The fastest growing measure of neighborhood poverty, however, was the number of census tracts classified as high-poverty areas. In other words, the physical space occupied by blighted urban neighborhoods expanded faster than the number of residents of such neighborhoods. Larger, but less densely inhabited, ghettos and barrios now occupy the center of many metropolitan areas, both a symptom and a cause of middle-class flight and the hollowing of American cities.

In the previous chapter, I described my general approach to measuring neighborhood poverty and distinguished it from several alternative approaches. I use census tracts as proxies for neighborhoods and identify any census tract with a poverty rate of 40 percent or more as a high-poverty area. As we have seen, few neighborhoods so identified are exclusively composed of members of a single racial or ethnic group, but high-poverty areas do include

African American ghettos, Hispanic barrios, and other slums inhabited by non-Hispanic whites or a melànge of persons from several racial and ethnic groups. Two measures summarize the relative size of neighborhood poverty within a metropolitan area. The first is the neighborhood poverty rate, or the percentage of a metropolitan area's population living in high-poverty census tracts. The second is the concentration of poverty, or the proportion of a metropolitan area's poor population that lives in high-poverty areas.

Applying this methodology to all metropolitan areas that could be tracked from 1970 to 1990 yields the following conclusions:

The number of high-poverty areas more than doubled;

The total number of persons living in such areas increased from 4.1 million to 8.0 million;

Members of minority groups are far more likely to live in high-poverty neighborhoods than non-Hispanic whites;

The number of African Americans living in high-poverty areas, mostly highly segregated ghettos, climbed from 2.4 million to 4.2 million, reflecting both population growth and an increase in neighborhood poverty among blacks from 14 to 17 percent;

The number of Hispanics living in barrios and other high-poverty neighborhoods increased dramatically, from 729,000 to 2.0 million, but this increase was driven largely by population growth, so there was little change in the neighborhood poverty rate among Hispanics;

The majority of the poor still do not reside in high-poverty areas, but the concentration of poverty rose from 12 percent to 18 percent overall, from 3 to 6 percent among the white poor, and from 26 to 34 percent among the black poor;

The timing and extent of the growth of neighborhood poverty varied substantially by region and metropolitan area, with cities in the Rust Belt states of the Midwest most affected.

The rapid expansion of ghettos and barrios documented in this chapter is not only a human tragedy but also an intensification of the divide between the "haves" and the "have-nots" within metropolitan areas. Almost all of the growth of high-poverty neighbor-hoods takes place within the confines of political jurisdictions of central cities or, in some cases, inner-ring suburbs, caused in part by middle-class flight and commercial abandonment. In contrast, wealthier suburbs and other outlying areas are growing rapidly and trying to shield themselves from the problems associated with the inner city. Whether intentional or not, the process represents a retreat from the concept of community and has very serious long-run implications for American society.

Comparability of Data Between the 1970 and 1990 Censuses

To ensure the validity of inferences about trends in neighborhood poverty, the comparability of census data over time needs to be examined. Changes in the classifications for race and ethnicity, met-ropolitan area boundaries, and the measurement of inflation all affect the analysis.

Race and Ethnicity

The manner in which the Census Bureau coded persons of Hispanic origin changed between 1970 and 1980. In the 1970 census, "Span-ish Americans" were identified by an algorithm based on surnames assumed to be Spanish, use of the Spanish language, and other fac-tors (Bean and Tienda 1987, 36–55). The algorithm also varied by region. By 1980, however, the census used a Spanish-origin ques-tion that allowed individuals to identify their ethnicity, and the same procedure was employed in 1990.

People of Spanish origin may be of any race. Most Hispanics, when answering the race question, either have identified them-selves as white or left the question blank. It is often possible to cre-ate mutually exclusive categories by combining information on race and ethnicity to obtain numbers for non-Hispanic whites, non-Hispanic blacks, Hispanics, and all others. But the exact number of non-Hispanic whites in census tracts cannot be calculated from the publicly released 1970 data. Simply reporting the data for whites in general, including some Hispanics, could be misleading, because the Hispanic population has increased rapidly. Thus, white figures for later decades would include a greater percentage of Hispanics.

To estimate the number of non-Hispanic whites in a consistent manner for 1970–90, I subtracted the number of blacks and Hispanics from the total population. Since few Hispanics are black, the resulting sum is a reasonably good estimate of non-Hispanic whites and non-Hispanic members of other races. As a check on the procedure's validity, one can compare actual 1990 figures with the estimates. Estimates derived by approximation for 1990 are very close to the actual values, which are presented in chapter 3. In tracking neighborhood poverty trends, I therefore report the values for non-Hispanic whites as estimated by the method above to facilitate comparison with the 1970 and 1980 figures.

I am also not able to separate Hispanics by subgroup (Mexican, Puerto Rican, Cuban, and so forth) in the 1970 and 1980 tract-level data. This is a drawback, since Hispanic subgroups have very different regional patterns and neighborhood poverty levels, as chapter 3 will show. The figures for Hispanics are therefore aggregates of very dissimilar subgroups.

New Metropolitan Areas

Between 1970 and 1990 the number of U.S. metropolitan areas grew from 243 to 337. These metropolitan areas did not, of course, suddenly rise from empty cornfields; rather, an existing city and its surrounding area had sufficient population growth and economic development to meet the Census Bureau's criteria for the designation of a metropolitan area.[1] Before 1990, most areas outside officially designated metropolitan areas were not divided into census tracts or other comparable units.[2] These areas may well have had poor neighborhoods in 1970 and 1980, but the data needed to count them are not available. Thus, a simple count of all the high-poverty neighborhood census tracts for each census year would overstate the increase in neighborhood poverty. The new metropolitan areas are also systematically different from the older areas in that they are smaller and more likely to be in the South or the West.

Rather than make comparisons across a shifting base, I have limited my analysis in this chapter to metropolitan areas in existence since 1970. To take account of changes in metropolitan area boundaries made by the Census Bureau between censuses, the affected census tracts have been recoded to their 1980 metropolitan areas for the entire period under analysis. Several metropolitan areas that were separate in the 1970 data, such as Dallas and Ft. Worth, were combined to reflect their status in the 1980 census, resulting in a consistent set of 239 metropolitan areas for the analysis.[3] These changes eliminate nearly one hundred more recently defined metropolitan areas. These areas are relatively small, however, and excluding them has little impact on the aggregate national figures. In 1990, more than 91 percent of metropolitan residents lived in the subset included in my analysis. Moreover, 94 percent of residents of poor neighborhoods lived in the 239 older metropolitan areas.[4] This analysis is therefore more comprehensive than most prior analyses, which have focused on a subset of metropolitan areas, typically the fifty or one hundred largest, or only on central cities of metropolitan areas. An exception is Mincy and Weiner (1993), who examined all metropolitan areas but did not exclude newly defined metropolitan areas when calculating changes over time.

Inflation

Because the poverty line and, ultimately, the definition of ghettos are based on dollar income, comparisons of ghetto poverty over time must account for inflation. The federal government adjusts the poverty line annually for inflation using the consumer price index (CPI). Until 1982, the methodology for calculating the CPI overstated the rate of inflation. A revised methodology that corrects for the problem has been in use since 1982 (U.S. Bureau of the Census 1991, 9–10). Unfortunately, tract-level data for 1970 and 1980 were not reissued with revised poverty calculations. Nor can revised tract-level poverty rates be calculated from older data with the improved CPI, because tract-level data cannot be disaggregated to the family level. The increases in neighborhood poverty presented below may therefore be somewhat overstated. The problem is probably trivial for the 1980s but could be significant for the 1970s, when the divergence between the CPI and real inflation was greatest.

National Trends in Neighborhood Poverty

In 1970, 4.1 million people lived in high-poverty neighborhoods in metropolitan areas (see table 2.1). By 1980, ghettos, barrios, and

Table 2.1   Population by Income, All Metropolitan Neighborhoods and High-Poverty
Areas, 1970–90

	1970	1980	1990	Percent Change		
				1970–80	1980–90	1970–90
All persons (000s)						
All areas	139,328	157,405	177,913	13.0%	13.0%	27.7%
High-poverty	4,149	5,174	7,973	24.7	54.1	92.2
Poor persons (000s)						
All areas	15,240	17,453	20,915	14.5	19.8	37.2
High-poverty	1,891	2,381	3,745	25.9	57.3	98.0
Census tracts						
All areas	32,287	37,207	42,098	15.2	13.1	30.4
High-poverty	1,177	1,767	2,726	50.1	54.3	131.6
Persons per tract						
All areas	4,315	4,231	4,226	−1.9	−0.1	−2.1
High-poverty	3,525	2,928	2,925	−16.9	−0.1	−17.0
Poor persons per tract						
All areas	472	469	497	−0.6	6.0	5.3
High-poverty	1,607	1,347	1,374	−16.2	2.0	−14.5

Source: Census tract data for 1970–90 (see appendix A), tabulations by the author.
Note: Table is limited to metropolitan areas in continuous existence since 1970, with geographic
adjustments to improve comparability over time (see text).

slums in those same metropolitan areas had 5.2 million residents—
a 25 percent increase in ten years. During the 1980s, the population of these neighborhoods rose even faster, to 8.0 million
people—an increase of 54 percent.[5] Despite increased spending on
social programs and a large increase in the gross national product,
the population of high-poverty neighborhoods in the United States
nearly doubled between 1970 and 1990. The number of poor
people in poor neighborhoods rose at a slightly faster pace, from 1.9
million to 3.7 million over the same period.

The change in the population of poverty areas reflects a complex
interaction among population growth, poverty, and the spatial distribution of the poor, as table 2.1 shows. The total population of the
239 metropolitan areas included in the analysis grew by about 13
percent in each decade; hence, a small but significant part of the
increase in ghetto and barrio populations can be attributed to over-

all population growth. The rate of population growth in high-poverty areas exceeds overall population growth (92 percent compared with 28 percent), and the rate of growth of *poor* residents of such neighborhoods surpasses the increase in poor people for metropolitan areas as a whole (98 percent to 37 percent). Thus, the increases in neighborhood poverty are not only a reflection of population growth or higher poverty rates. Changes in the spatial organization of the poor must also have played an important role in creating new ghettos and barrios.

The Spread of Urban Blight

As table 2.1 shows, the number of high-poverty census tracts more than doubled, from 1,177 in 1970 to 2,726 in 1990.[6] Table 2.1 also reveals that the *total* number of metropolitan tracts increased, even though the number of metropolitan areas included in the analysis was held constant. The increase in total tracts came from old tracts being divided when their population exceeded the normal range, and from completely new neighborhoods being created as peripheral and other formerly vacant areas were developed.[7] Poor census tracts, however, tend to be in areas with stable or even declining populations, so the number of high-poverty tracts created through the splitting of existing tracts is almost certainly small. Therefore, almost all the increase represents geographical areas that became poorer. Although the land area of tracts varies widely, the observed increase of more than 130 percent in high-poverty tracts probably represents at least a doubling of these neighborhoods' land area.

The number of persons *per tract* was nearly constant between 1970 and 1990, a little over 4,200 each census year. This was no accident—it is a deliberate consequence of the Census Bureau's policy of dividing tracts and creating new ones to keep up with population growth. In contrast, in 1970 the population density of high-poverty tracts was lower than the national average and by 1980 declined by one-sixth to a level of slightly less than 3,000 persons per tract. Thus, the number of persons residing in ghettos, barrios, and slums increased not because people moved into such neighborhoods, but because the poverty spread to more and more neighborhoods. Even the number of poor persons per high-poverty tract declined between 1970 and 1990, though there was a slight rise in the 1980s. Hence, the term *concentration of poverty* is potentially mis-leading, since the number of poor persons per high-poverty tract actually declined by one-sixth. The early-twentieth-century image of the "teeming slum" bears little resemblance to modern ghetto and barrio neighborhoods.

The low and declining population density of high-poverty neigh-borhoods and the great expansion in their number suggest that the recent increases in neighborhood poverty have been driven at least partly by migration out of inner-city areas, particularly of persons with incomes above the poverty line.[8] In this regard, U.S. high-poverty areas differ from those in many Third World cities, which are crowded and develop on the urban periphery as poor persons migrate in from surrounding rural areas.

Levels of Neighborhood Poverty

The increase in the population living in high-poverty areas between 1970 and 1990 was not uniform across racial and ethnic groups, as figure 2.1 shows. Blacks had substantial increases in both decades; the number of non-Hispanic whites living in high-poverty areas did not grow much in the 1970s and then increased sharply in the 1980s; and Hispanics had the most rapid rate of increase in both the 1970s and 1980s.

Table 2.2 shows how population growth and changes in resi-dential patterns interacted to produce these increases in the popu-lations of high-poverty tracts. First, the overall U.S. population grew by one-fourth between 1970 and 1990, and the population of met-ropolitan areas grew by about the same rate. In addition, there was a rise in the overall neighborhood poverty rate from 3.0 to 4.5 per-cent—in other words, residents of metropolitan areas were much more likely to reside in a ghetto, barrio, or slum.

For blacks, however, the pattern was different. The U.S. black population increased faster (32 percent) than the national average. In addition, blacks were more likely to live in metropolitan areas by the end of the period, so that blacks in metropolitan areas increased by over 40 percent. The black neighborhood poverty rate increased from 14 percent in 1970 to 17 percent in 1990. Thus, population growth, a shift toward metropolitan areas, and an increasing neigh-

Figure 2.1   Residents of High-Poverty Neighborhoods, by Race/Ethnicity,
1970–90

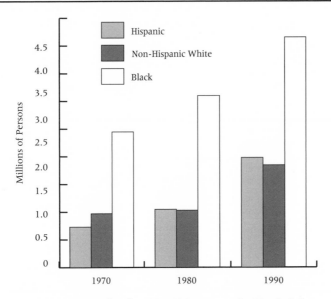

Source: Census tract data for 1970–90 (see appendix A), tabulations
by the author.
Note: See text for estimation of non-Hispanic white.

borhood poverty rate all contributed to the 70 percent growth in
blacks living in high-poverty areas.

Non-Hispanic whites experienced slower than average population growth and, unlike blacks, had no change in their propensity
to live in metropolitan areas. With virtually no change in their
neighborhood poverty rate in the 1970s, there was only a 6 percent
increase in the number of whites in high-poverty areas. But the
neighborhood poverty rate for whites nearly doubled in the 1980s,
accounting for most of the 79 percent increase in the white population living in high-poverty tracts. For Hispanics in metropolitan
areas, the likelihood of living in a barrio or other poor neighborhood
actually decreased in the 1970s.[9] The 1970s increase in the number
of barrio residents is entirely a function of population growth.

Table 2.2   Neighborhood Poverty Rates and Underlying Population Dynamics, 1970–90

	Population (000s)			Percent Change		
	1970	1980	1990	1970–80	1980–90	1970–90
U.S. total						
All persons	197,957	220,846	248,730	11.6%	12.6%	25.6%
White	167,090	180,884	197,799	8.3	9.4	18.4
Black	21,931	25,623	29,031	16.8	13.3	32.4
Hispanic	8,936	14,339	21,900	60.5	52.7	145.1
Metropolitan areas						
All persons	139,328	157,405	177,913	13.0%	13.0%	27.7%
White	114,712	124,848	135,098	8.8	8.2	17.8
Black	17,000	20,351	23,927	19.7	17.6	40.7
Hispanic	7,616	12,206	18,888	60.3	54.7	148.0
Percent of U.S. total in metro areas						
All persons	70.4%	71.3%	71.5%			
White	68.7	69.0	68.3			
Black	77.5	79.4	82.4			
Hispanic	85.2	85.1	86.2			
Living in high-poverty neighborhoods						
All persons	4,149	5,174	7,973	24.7%	54.1%	92.2%
White	972	1,030	1,843	6.0	78.9	89.6
Black	2,447	3,097	4,152	26.6	34.1	69.7
Hispanic	729	1,048	1,978	43.8	88.7	171.3
Neighborhood poverty rates						
All persons	3.0%	3.3%	4.5%			
White	0.8	0.8	1.4			
Black	14.4	15.2	17.4			
Hispanic	9.6	8.6	10.5			

Source: Census tract data for 1970–90 (see appendix A), tabulations by the author.
Note: Table is limited to metropolitan areas in continuous existence since 1970, with geographic adjustments to improve comparability over time (see text). Figures for whites are estimates.

Between 1980 and 1990, however, more Hispanics were living in metropolitan areas *and* more of them lived in poor neighborhoods, resulting in an 89 percent increase in Hispanic barrio residents.

Racial and Ethnic Composition of High-Poverty Areas

As neighborhood poverty rates have changed, so too has the racial composition of these neighborhoods. Figure 2.2 shows the percentages of residents of high-poverty areas in 1970, 1980, and 1990 that are white, black, or Hispanic. Whites, although far less likely to live in poor neighborhoods, are more numerous in the general population and thus constitute a not inconsiderable segment of these neighborhoods' populations. As noted previously, Hispanics are a rapidly growing segment of the population in high-poverty neighborhoods. As a result, the *proportion* of this population that is black is actually declining, despite large increases in the absolute number of blacks living in high-poverty areas. Despite the decreasing share, about half of the population of high-poverty areas was black in 1990.

Charles Murray and Ron Mincy, two researchers from very different ends of the ideological spectrum, have suggested that a white "underclass" may be emerging and that we should stop thinking

Figure 2.2   Racial Composition of High-Poverty Areas, 1970–90

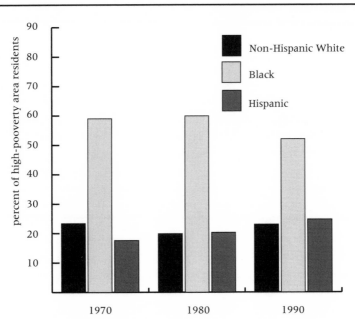

Source: Census tract data for 1970–90 (see appendix A), tabulations by the author.
Note: See text for estimation of non-Hispanic white.

about urban poverty in purely racial terms (Mincy 1991; Murray 1993). The data support their argument in that the likelihood of whites living in poor neighborhoods increased between 1980 and 1990. Whether the number of white residents in poor neighborhoods will continue to grow at more than twice the rate of blacks—as it did in the 1980s—is hard to predict. The percentage of white children in female-headed families, although starting from a lower base, has risen at least as fast as in minority groups, and the growing wage gap for people with less education appears to be color blind. If these factors explain the growth of white neighborhood poverty in the 1980s, then the trend will almost certainly continue.

The Concentration of Poverty

Although neighborhood poverty rates and the concentration of poverty are highly correlated, they measure distinct aspects of the neighborhood poverty problem. A metropolitan area with a very low overall poverty rate will have few ghettos and barrios and a low rate of neighborhood poverty, but the few people who are poor could be highly clustered in a few high-poverty neighborhoods. Moreover, two metropolitan areas with similar poverty rates could have very different concentrations of poverty, and this is a separate issue from the size of poor neighborhoods relative to the overall population, which is measured by the neighborhood poverty rate.

Table 2.3 illustrates the national trends in the concentration of poverty; although similar to table 2.2, it includes only persons who are poor by the federal poverty guidelines. The main conclusion is that the concentration of poverty grew rapidly for non-Hispanic whites and African Americans between 1970 and 1990. In 1970, only about one-fourth of the metropolitan black poor lived in ghettos or other poor neighborhoods; by 1990, one out of every three lived in a high-poverty neighborhood. Among whites, the concentration of the poor more than doubled, though it started from a much lower level (3 percent). Among Hispanics, the concentration of poverty did not grow in the sense that Hispanic poor persons in metropolitan areas were about equally likely to live in barrios in 1970 as in 1990. As a result of these trends among the subgroups, the overall concentration of poverty rose from 12 to 18 percent.

Table 2.3   Concentration of Poverty and Underlying Population Dynamics, 1970–90

	Population (000s)			Percent Change		
	1970	1980	1990	1970–80	1980–90	1970–90
U.S. poor persons						
All persons	26,931	27,393	31,743	1.7%	15.9%	17.9%
White	17,157	16,353	17,898	−4.7	9.4	4.3
Black	7,596	7,649	8,441	0.7	10.4	11.1
Hispanic	2,178	3,391	5,403	55.7	59.3	148.1
Metropolitan areas						
All persons	15,240	17,453	20,915	14.5%	19.8%	37.2%
White	8,826	9,207	10,084	4.3	9.5	14.3
Black	4,785	5,485	6,320	14.6	15.2	32.1
Hispanic	1,628	2,761	4,511	69.6	63.4	177.1
Percent of poor persons in metro areas						
All persons	56.6%	63.7%	65.9%			
White	51.4	56.3	56.3			
Black	63.0	71.7	74.9			
Hispanic	74.7	81.4	83.5			
Poor persons living in high-poverty areas						
All persons	1,891	2,381	3,745	25.9%	57.3%	98.0%
White	258	302	631	17.1	108.9	144.6
Black	1,247	1,548	2,120	24.1	37.0	70.0
Hispanic	385	531	995	37.9	87.4	158.4
Concentration of poverty						
All persons	12.4%	13.6%	17.9%			
White	2.9	3.3	6.3			
Black	26.1	28.2	33.5			
Hispanic	23.6	19.2	22.1			

Source: Census tract data for 1970–90 (see appendix A), tabulations by the author.
Note: Table is limited to metropolitan areas in continuous existence since 1970, with geographic adjustments to improve comparability over time (see text). Figures for whites are estimates.

The *number* of poor persons residing in high-poverty neighborhoods just about doubled, from 1.9 million to 3.7 million, between 1970 and 1990. Thus, the poor population increased even faster than the overall population of high-poverty areas, 98 percent compared with 92 percent, implying increasing isolation of the poor. As with the overall population of high-poverty areas, changes in the poor population of such areas reflect underlying population growth and changes in residential patterns. In addition, changes in poverty rates must also be taken into account. Table 2.4 shows the poverty rates for the nation, metropolitan areas, and high-poverty areas. In essence, it is table 2.3 divided by table 2.2. Information from all three tables contributes to an understanding of the growing poor population in ghettos, barrios, and other poor neighborhoods.

First, let us look at how population growth and changes in poverty rates affect the number of poor persons in metropolitan areas—the denominator of the concentration of poverty calculation. The U.S. population grew by about 25.6 percent between 1970 and 1990, but over that period the *national* poverty rate declined from 13.6 percent to 12.8 percent. As a result, the total number of poor in the United States grew at a slower pace—18 percent. In the 239 metropolitan areas included in this analysis, the poverty rate rose

Table 2.4   Poverty Rates Among Various Populations, 1970–90

	Income Below Poverty		
	1970	1980	1990
U.S. total	13.6%	12.4%	12.8%
White	10.3	9.0	9.0
Black	34.6	29.9	29.1
Hispanic	24.4	23.6	24.7
Metropolitan areas	10.9	11.1	11.8
White	7.7	7.4	7.5
Black	28.1	27.0	26.4
Hispanic	21.4	22.6	23.9
High-poverty areas	45.6	46.0	47.0
White	26.5	29.3	34.2
Black	51.0	50.0	51.1
Hispanic	52.8	50.7	50.3

Source: Census tract data for 1970–90 (see appendix A), tabulations by the author.
Note: Table is limited to metropolitan areas in continuous existence since 1970, with geographic adjustments to improve comparability over time (see text). Figures for whites are estimates.

from 11 percent to 12 percent. Thus, the number of poor persons in metropolitan areas grew by 37 percent, from 15.2 million to 20.9 million. And of those, a greater proportion lived in high-poverty areas, as we have seen. Thus, the doubling of poor persons in high-poverty neighborhoods reflects three factors: the underlying population growth rate, the differential growth of poverty inside metropolitan areas, and a greater concentration of the poor within metropolitan areas.

The story is markedly different among racial groups. Poverty among non-Hispanic whites in metropolitan areas changed little between 1970 and 1990. The number of poor non-Hispanic whites living in metropolitan areas therefore grew very slowly. Yet this group was more than twice as likely to live in poor neighborhoods in 1990 than in 1970, leading to a 145 percent increase in the number of white poor living in them.

The total number of black poor living in ghettos rose 70 percent, from 1.2 million to 2.1 million. Since the national and metropolitan poverty rates for blacks were both *down*, the main factors driving the increase were population growth and increased concentration of poverty—in other words, a greater tendency for poor blacks in metropolitan areas to reside in ghetto neighborhoods.

Only poor Hispanics did not experience a substantial increase in the concentration of poverty between 1970 and 1990. Despite that, the *number* of poor Hispanics living in ghettos did rise substantially, with their 158 percent increase being the highest of any group. This increase, however, was driven almost entirely by population growth (see table 2.2) along with a higher poverty rate for Hispanics in metropolitan areas (see table 2.4).

In summary, the number of poor persons living in poor neighborhoods grew substantially between 1970 and 1990, both overall and across racial and ethnic groups. The reasons for the increase differed for each group, however. Among the white poor, the increase was largely because of their much greater concentration of poverty. Among the black poor, population growth and the concentration of poverty were the key factors. Among the Hispanic poor, population growth was the main factor, combined with higher poverty rates for Hispanics in metropolitan areas.

Regional Variations in Neighborhood Poverty

The increase in neighborhood poverty described above was not distributed equally across the national landscape. There were large differences in the timing and size of changes in ghetto poverty, and these deviations seem to correspond, for the most part, to regional economic trends.

Expansion of Poor Areas

The number of census tracts with a poverty rate of 40 percent or more grew in all major sections of the country, based on the Census Bureau's nine geographic divisions.[10] The East North Central division had the largest increase. The Rust Belt states that make up this division—Illinois, Indiana, Michigan, Ohio, and Wisconsin—added 585 ghetto tracts in 1970–90. The next largest gain was in the Mid-Atlantic states (368 new ghetto tracts), followed by the Southwest (227 new ghetto tracts).

As table 2.5 illustrates, the physical expansion of the ghetto occurred at different times in different parts of the country. During the 1970s, the Mid-Atlantic and East North Central regions had a tremendous increase in high-poverty tracts—more than doubling in each case. Areas of the country that benefited economically from the high oil prices of the 1970s—the South and particularly the Southwest—saw the number of high-poverty census tracts decline. In the 1980s, however, *all* divisions had increases despite economic growth in most of the country. As in the 1970s, the Rust Belt added the most new high-poverty tracts. What was different from the 1970s were the large increases in the oil states of the Southwest, hard hit economically after the collapse of oil prices and the widespread failure of savings and loan companies in the 1980s.

Metropolitan Areas with the Most Ghetto Expansion

The great majority of metropolitan areas (182 out of 239) had more high-poverty tracts by 1990. Thirty-three areas had no change; only twenty-four had declines. Even areas with *declining levels of neighborhood poverty* often had *increases in the number of high-poverty tracts*. For example, out of eighty-seven metropolitan areas where neighborhood poverty among blacks declined between

Table 2.5   High-Poverty Census Tracts by Census Division, 1970–90

	1970	1980	1990	Change		
				1970–80	1980–90	1970–90
U.S. total	1,177	1,767	2,726	590	959	1,549
Northeast						
New England	23	50	69	27	19	46
Mid-Atlantic	141	505	509	364	4	368
Midwest						
East North Central	166	393	751	227	358	585
West North Central	49	67	142	18	75	93
South						
South Atlantic	254	272	352	18	80	98
East South Central	148	136	172	−12	36	24
West South Central	270	217	497	−53	280	227
West						
Mountain	42	37	75	−5	38	33
Pacific	84	90	159	6	69	75

Source: Census tract data for 1970–90 (see appendix B), tabulations by the author.
Note: Table is limited to metropolitan areas in continuous existence since 1970, with geographic adjustments to improve comparability over time (see text).

1970 and 1990, fifty-seven had increases in poor tracts over the same period. Of the metropolitan areas that actually lost such tracts between 1970 and 1990, the greatest decline was a mere six tracts. These examples show that the physical size of ghettos and barrios rarely shrinks much, even if their population declines substantially.

Figure 2.3 shows the metropolitan areas with the largest increases in high-poverty census tracts. Two patterns emerge: New York, Chicago, and Philadelphia saw a rapid expansion in the 1970s; whereas the other cities experienced faster growth during the 1980s. The New York metropolitan area actually showed a decline in high-poverty tracts for the latter decade. The Milwaukee metropolitan area had a particularly large increase in the 1980s. (Appendix B reports the total number of tracts and the number of poor tracts for many metropolitan areas.)

Figure 2.3   Metropolitan Areas with the Largest Increases in High-Poverty Areas, 1970–90

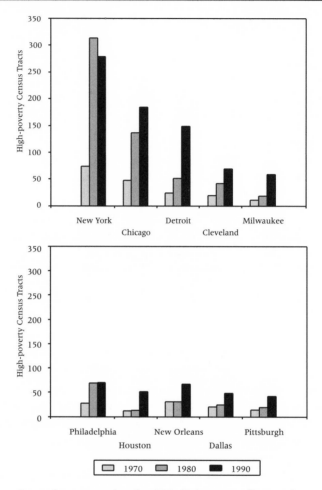

Source: Census tract data for 1970–90 (see appendix A), tabulations by the author.

Regional Patterns in Neighborhood Poverty Rates

Even more striking is how regions differ over time in their neighborhood poverty rates. Table 2.6 shows the weighted metropolitan averages for neighborhood poverty among blacks (ghetto poverty) and Hispanics (barrio poverty) within each census division. In the

Table 2.6   Black and Hispanic Neighborhood Poverty Rates by Census Division, 1970–90

	Number of MSAs	Neighborhood Poverty Rate					
		Black			Hispanic		
		1970	1980	1990	1970	1980	1990
U.S. total	239	14.4%	15.2%	17.4%	9.6%	8.6%	10.5%
Northeast							
New England	26	7.2	9.3	7.7	5.2	16.6	13.3
Mid-Atlantic	25	7.3	21.3	17.9	12.5	23.2	19.1
Midwest							
East North Central	48	9.0	16.2	26.2	1.2	3.8	8.1
West North Central	19	14.5	14.4	19.1	0.8	2.8	5.7
South							
South Atlantic	36	18.7	13.4	11.6	2.2	2.3	3.4
East South Central	14	34.9	22.0	25.3	5.8	9.6	4.4
West South Central	35	25.9	13.1	21.6	28.6	13.7	22.3
West							
Mountain	13	13.9	4.9	8.8	9.1	4.9	7.5
Pacific	23	7.0	5.1	6.7	1.6	1.2	3.6

Source: Census tract data for 1970–90 (see appendix A), tabulations by the author.
Notes: Table is limited to metropolitan areas in continuous existence since 1970, with geographic adjustments to improve comparability over time (see text). *MSAs* denote metropolitan statistical areas. Averages of metropolitan areas in each division weighted by total blacks and Hispanics, respectively.

Mid-Atlantic region (New York, New Jersey, and Pennsylvania), ghetto poverty nearly tripled and barrio poverty nearly doubled during the 1970s. After the long economic recovery of the 1980s, which was particularly strong in the Northeast, cities such as New York and Philadelphia actually showed small declines in ghetto and barrio poverty between 1980 and 1990. (Although ghetto poverty dropped from 21 to 16 percent in Philadelphia during the 1980s, the city gained one more ghetto census tract.)

Pittsburgh and Buffalo both went against the regional trend with large increases in ghetto poverty in the 1980s. In Buffalo, the share of blacks living in high-poverty areas rose from 21 to 40 percent. These two cities mirrored the pattern of the eastern portion of the Midwest, where ghetto poverty increased substantially over both decades. Larger cities suffered big increases in neighborhood poverty in the 1970s, while smaller cities in the region, such as Akron and Toledo, had their most substantial increases in the 1980s. In a sense, in the 1980s these smaller cities caught up with the major cities of their region.

Chicago is another example of a metropolitan area where the trend in high-poverty census tracts diverges from the trend in neighborhood poverty rates. The level of ghetto poverty, for example, increased a great deal over the 1970s (from 12 percent to 23 percent). During the 1980s, in contrast, there was no increase by this measure. A count of high-poverty *tracts* shows increases in *both* decades, however—from 48 to 136, and from 136 to 148 in the 1970s and 1980s, respectively.

The Southwest has been out of step with most of the country in terms of economic growth: it boomed in the 1970s and slumped in the 1980s. Similarly, the region's pattern of changes in neighborhood poverty was opposite that of the Northeast. Ghetto poverty in the average metropolitan area in the Southwest fell substantially— from 26 percent to 13 percent between 1970 and 1980—then increased to 22 percent by 1990 (table 2.6). All the region's major cities (except Austin) followed this *U*-shaped pattern. The East South Central region followed a similar, though less dramatic pattern. The southern states of the Atlantic seaboard are distinguished by being the only census division to have, on average, declines in both decades. New England and the two western census divisions had low levels of neighborhood poverty to begin with and relatively small changes in those levels by 1990.

Neighborhood poverty, then, rises and falls in response to local labor market conditions. This suggests that the formation of and experience within ghettos and barrios are inextricably linked to the broader economic conditions of their metropolitan areas. Although such a conclusion seems obvious, it challenges the popular view that ghettos and barrios are the product of the personal failings of the people who live in them. Some even claim that ghetto neighborhoods, and the deterioration of social conditions within them, can be traced to low intelligence levels of ghetto residents (Murray and Herrnstein 1994, 522). Moreover, the most politically popular approach to urban blight—the creation of enterprise zones—is largely based on the premise that the problem is caused by the lack of jobs in specific neighborhoods.

I will have more to say about enterprise zones and other policy measures in due course, but the point I wish to flag here is that the relationship between the health of regional economies and trends in ghetto poverty ought to make us wary of analyses or policies that fail to address the workings of a region as a whole. Locally focused policies may well have a role, but their impact is likely to be small relative to the effects of fluctuations in metropolitan and regional economies.

The Expansion of Milwaukee's Ghetto

Few metropolitan areas had as large an increase in neighborhood poverty between 1970 and 1990 as Milwaukee. In 1970, Milwaukee had a small ghetto area composed of fewer than a dozen high-poverty census tracts, in which lived 1.2 percent of its total population, 8.4 percent of its black population, and 16 percent of its black poor. These tracts, as well as the tracts that became part of the ghetto in the following two decades, are shown in figure 2.4. (The heavy shading represents tracts that were ghettos in 1970.) The early ghetto tracts are located in the central city, near downtown, as is common. They are also where future ghetto expansion occurs after 1970.

A handful of additional tracts—all of which were adjacent to or near the original 1970 ghetto—had become ghettos by 1980, bringing the total number to nineteen. After this expansion, 2 percent of Milwaukee's population, 15 percent of its black population, and 24 percent of its black poor lived in a ghetto neighborhood.

The ghetto formation process in Milwaukee accelerated in the 1980s, when forty new ghetto tracts were formed. The tracts form a nearly perfect circle around the original (1970) ghetto area.[11] After this enormous expansion, nearly one in ten residents of the metropolitan area were living in a ghetto. By 1990, *almost half of all of Milwaukee's blacks and nearly two-thirds of its poor blacks lived in ghetto neighborhoods.*

The potential for a continuation of ghetto expansion is indicated by the area of "borderline" neighborhoods (those with poverty

Figure 2.4   Milwaukee Metropolitan Area Ghetto Expansion, 1970–90

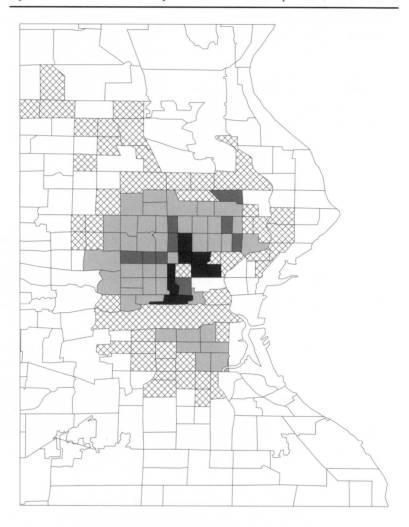

Year Census Tracts First Exceeded 40 Percent Poverty

- Never
- 1990
- 1980
- 1970
- Borderline in 1990

Source: Census tract data for 1970–90 (see appendix A), tabulations by the author.

rates of 20–40 percent). These neighborhoods form another concentric circle around what are now ghetto neighborhoods. This pattern of spreading ghetto blight is common to many metropolitan areas.

Neighborhood Transitions

Milwaukee's ghetto area grew larger as additional census tracts had their poverty rates increase past the 40 percent threshold. A "borderline" census tract's poverty rate can increase in three ways: residents of the tract can become poorer over time; poor people from other areas can move into the tract; or nonpoor people in the tract can move out, leaving their poorer neighbors behind.[12] In practice, all three processes could take place at once. Each process, however, predicts a distinct pattern of tract population changes, and these patterns can be used to identify the explanation for the increase in a tract's poverty rate. For example, if a tract's poverty rate increases through migration of poor people into the tract, we should observe roughly equal increases in the tract's poor population and total population. In contrast, if the tract became poorer because individuals already living there got poorer, the number of poor will increase but the total population will not change much.

Of course, a full understanding of the causal process driving the expansion of the poverty areas would require an understanding of why people moved where they did or why they experienced changes in their poverty status. But understanding the mechanics of the process is prerequisite to developing a more substantive explanation. The ideal data set for exploring this issue would be truly longitudinal: the data would allow one to track the geographic moves and changes in poverty status of specific individuals over time.[13] The census data on trends that are employed here are more limited, consisting of three cross-sectional views of Milwaukee's residents. For example, if the number of poor persons grew by one hundred in a census tract with a constant total population, the data do not indicate whether one hundred residents became poor or whether one hundred nonpoor persons left only to be replaced by an equal number of poor persons from elsewhere. Nevertheless, the net movements of people that can be observed from census data help explain how Milwaukee's ghetto expanded so rapidly.

Figure 2.5 illustrates the relationship between neighborhood poverty status and population change. It shows that nearly all ghetto neighborhoods had population losses. What is most striking, however, is how Milwaukee's metropolitan area neatly divides into two zones. The central zone, including but much larger than the ghetto, is losing population, whereas the outer zone, far removed from any ghetto tracts, gained population in nearly every neighborhood. One could argue about whether population dispersion caused the ghetto to grow or whether the ghetto, by scaring off middle-class people of all races, caused the dispersion. Quite likely, the process is a sort of "vicious circle."

Figure 2.6 gives an enlarged view of the ghetto region. At the very edge of the ghetto area, there are some tracts with population gains. Some are ghetto tracts and some have poverty rates of 20 to 40 percent. These tracts—situated on the border between the ghetto and the rest of the city—may well be receiving most of the population outflow from ghetto neighborhoods.

Simple comparisons of high-poverty census tracts at one point in time to such tracts at another point in time can be misleading, because the census tracts themselves can change. Table 2.7 avoids this problem and provides further insight into Milwaukee's ghetto expansion by identifying geographically constant census tracts and presenting changes in their populations, poverty levels, and racial compositions between 1970 and 1990. All high-poverty neighborhoods in 1990 are divided into those that were already high-poverty areas in 1970, those which became ghettos in the 1970s, and those which became ghettos in the 1980s. For comparison, census tracts that had borderline poverty levels and low poverty levels in 1990 are also shown.[14]

The 1970 ghetto tracts—the "old ghetto"—had a much lower population density in 1970 than all other tracts and continued to lose population in the following twenty years. At the same time, the average number of poor persons in these neighborhoods rose, suggesting more of the remaining residents became poor. It is also possible that poor people moved in from elsewhere in the area. Interestingly, although the black population in these tracts declined in the 1970s and held constant in the 1980s, the percentage of blacks increased as nonblacks left.

Figure 2.5   Milwaukee Metropolitan Area: Poverty and Population Change

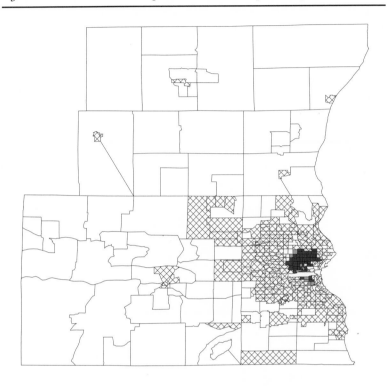

Poverty Status, 1990: Population Change 1970–90

Ghetto: Decline   Ghetto: Increase

Not Ghetto: Decline   Not Ghetto: Increase

Source: Census tract data for 1970–90 (see appendix A), tabulations by the author.

To understand the ghetto formation process, we must look at the tracts that *became* ghettos between 1970 and 1990. Tracts that became ghettos during the 1970s showed an increase in poor persons per tract over the decade, despite a net decrease of more than six hundred persons per tract. It appears that people living in these tracts became poor, although it is possible that some of the new poor were persons who moved into these tracts from elsewhere. In any case, there must have been a substantial outmigration of non-

Figure 2.6   Milwaukee Metropolitan Area: Close-up View of Poverty and
            Population Change

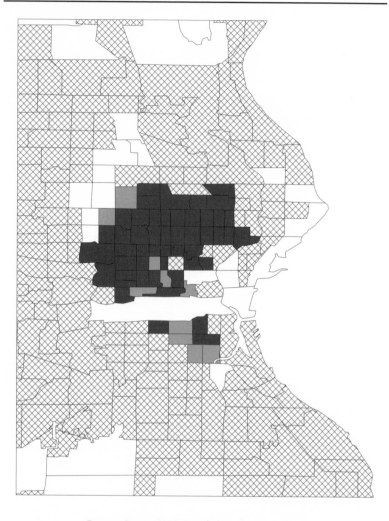

Poverty Status, 1990: Population Change 1970–90

■ Ghetto: Decline		▨ Ghetto: Increase
⊠ Not Ghetto: Decline		☐ Not Ghetto: Increase

Source: Census tract data for 1970–90 (see appendix A), tabulations by the
author.

Table 2.7 Ghetto Expansion in the Milwaukee Metropolitan Area, 1970–90

	Year First Became Ghetto			Poverty Status in 1990		All Census Tracts
	1970	1980	1990	20–40% Poor	0–20% Poor	
Number of tracts	8	9	42	49	266	374
Total persons (000s)						
1970	13.4	27.3	132.8	150.6	1,079.1	1,403.3
1980	10.0	21.5	110.2	130.8	1,124.2	1,396.7
1990	9.7	20.2	111.0	133.9	1,157.2	1,431.9
Persons per tract						
1970	1,675	3,030	3,163	3,074	4,057	3,752
1980	1,250	2,393	2,624	2,669	4,226	3,735
1990	1,209	2,244	2,642	2,733	4,350	3,829
Poor persons per tract						
1970	767	824	667	381	183	291
1980	524	984	749	421	172	296
1990	764	1,189	1,273	745	208	434
Poverty rate						
1970	45.8%	27.2%	21.1%	12.4%	4.5%	7.8%
1980	41.9	41.1	28.5	15.8	4.1	7.9
1990	63.2	53.0	48.2	27.3	4.8	11.3
Black persons per tract						
1970	1,057	1,696	1,237	450	28	281
1980	846	1,715	1,443	754	109	398
1990	850	1,640	1,680	1,049	202	527
Percentage black						
1970	63.1%	56.0%	39.1%	14.6%	0.7%	7.5%
1980	67.6	71.7	55.0	28.2	2.6	10.7
1990	70.4	73.1	63.6	38.4	4.6	13.8

Source: Census tract data for 1970–90 (see appendix A), tabulations by the author.
Note: Some tracts were joined to create constant boundaries over time. Tracts created after 1970 are excluded from the analysis.

poor residents. The net effect of these changes drove the poverty rate up for these nine tracts from 27.2 percent in 1970 to 41.1 percent in 1980. Again, the black population was relatively constant, whereas the total population declined. Since the number of Hispanics was nearly constant (figures not shown), most who moved out were non-Hispanic whites, and most of them were not poor.

Tracts that became ghettos during the 1980s show a somewhat different pattern. Like the older ghetto tracts, which the newer tracts virtually encircle, these new ghettos lost population in the 1970s but held constant over the 1980s. In the 1980s, however, the number of poor persons in these tracts increased rapidly, though roughly in proportion to the increase in poverty in the metropolitan area as a whole. The poverty rate of the tracts that became ghettos between 1980 and 1990 rose from 28.5 to 48.2 percent, compared to an increase from 7.9 to 11.3 percent for the metropolitan area. This suggests that the residents of these neighborhoods were impoverished by a general economic downturn that affected the labor market as a whole, not by such factors as the neighborhood's culture or a local lack of jobs.

These newest ghetto tracts also differed from their predecessors in terms of race. The older ghetto tracts (from both 1970 and 1980) had an increase in the proportion of black residents, owing largely to middle-class, mostly white outmigration. In the new ghetto tracts, the actual number of blacks (and Hispanics) increased across both decades. Moreover, in the new ghettos white residents per tract dropped from 1,767 in 1970 to 613 by 1990. In other words, there was a racial succession—a displacement of whites by minorities in these neighborhoods. In part, this reflects Milwaukee MSA's rapid increase in black population. Between 1970 and 1990, the black population grew by 86 percent; among major metropolitan areas with substantial black populations, only Atlanta and Miami had larger increases.

Continued Ghetto Expansion?

What lies ahead for borderline tracts? Table 2.7 offers some clues. Their future does not appear promising. Like the other tracts subsumed by the ghetto, the population in these borderline neighborhoods declined in the 1970s and then leveled off. Also like the ghettos formed in the 1980s, these tracts now have more poor people. The poverty rate rose to 27.3 percent in 1990—similar to the 1980 poverty rate for the tracts that became ghettos by 1990. The number of black residents also increased sharply, pushing the percentage of blacks from 14.6 percent in 1970 up to 38.4 percent in 1990.

These tracts would be extremely vulnerable to any further increase in the metropolitan area's poverty rate and are already enduring the racial succession and population decline that contributed to the previous ghetto expansions.

The tracts listed in the fifth column of table 2.7 (those with poverty rates lower than 20 percent in 1990) stand in sharp contrast to the others. Of all the groups, only this one had higher than average population densities and a steady pattern of population increases. The number of poor people was essentially unchanged, and the poverty rate was less than 5 percent. The one similarity to ghetto tracts is that black persons per tract increased, and the percentage of blacks rose, albeit from less than 1 percent to about 5 percent.

Milwaukee's experience in the 1980s was extreme, but it serves to illustrate the processes at work in the expansion of ghettos across the nation. One conclusion is that selective outmigration plays an important role in ghetto formation and, in the 1970s, was the key factor in Milwaukee's ghetto expansion. In the 1980s, it was selective outmigration together with racial succession and a decline in the region's economy. A second conclusion is that regional economic downturns can have a devastating impact on areas already under stress.

Emerging Lessons from Recent Trends in Neighborhood Poverty

Neighborhood poverty expanded in the majority of U.S. metropolitan areas between 1970 and 1990. Some regions and cities had their greatest increases in the 1970s; others suffered more in the 1980s. The Rust Belt fared the worst, with marked ghetto and barrio expansion in both the 1970s and 1980s.

Levels of neighborhood poverty and concentration of the poor increased for non-Hispanic whites and African Americans, especially in the 1980s. The Hispanic barrio population had the greatest increase in sheer numbers, but this was largely a reflection of the underlying growth of that group. The fastest *rate* of increase in the likelihood of living in a poor neighborhood was actually among non-Hispanic whites, although the absolute levels are, for now at least, quite low. Despite the growth in Hispanic and white neighborhood poverty, African Americans are still the majority of ghetto residents. The black share of the total residents of ghetto neighborhoods has declined substantially, however.

We have seen that the ups and downs of regional and metropolitan economies have a very strong effect on the level of neighborhood poverty. Yet even in cities with little or no increase in neighborhood poverty, the physical boundaries of the high-poverty area have widened. Evidence from Milwaukee and other cities suggests that changes in the spatial patterning of metropolitan populations—by race and income—have played an important role in the expansion of ghettos. In chapters 5 and 6, I empirically test those and other hypotheses about the causes of ghetto and barrio expansion. Before turning to that analysis, however, I present more detailed empirical findings on neighborhood poverty in 1990 in chapters 3 and 4.

Chapter 3

Neighborhood Poverty in 1990

The rapid expansion of ghetto and barrio neighborhoods and the growth of populations living within them have not gone unnoticed. Newspapers run detailed portraits of "life on the edge of nowhere" (Eig 1992). Romanticized depictions of alienated young men who disdain authority, mistreat women, and battle each other for control of the streets are presented in popular music and films. For most Americans, however, the most powerful and memorable images of the inner city are probably those of the Los Angeles riots, particularly the beating of Reginald Denny and fires blazing out of control.

Such jarring images often capture our attention, but they rarely lead to wise policies. My goal in this chapter is provide a more factual basis for the policy debate surrounding urban poverty by looking closely at the size and scope of neighborhood poverty in 1990. One important finding is that the vast majority of America's poor are *not* living in high-poverty urban neighborhoods, nor are those who live in such neighborhoods all poor. The reality is more complex. This chapter also compares the results of this study with findings from other studies that have used somewhat different methodologies for studying neighborhood poverty. Chapter 4 delves even deeper, providing a statistical portrait of high-poverty areas that reveals a surprising amount of social and economic diversity.

Advantages of 1990 Census Data

Between 1970 and 1990 neighborhood poverty expanded rapidly in many metropolitan areas both in the size of blighted areas and in the percentage of the population living in ghettos, barrios, and other poor neighborhoods. This increase in neighborhood poverty has taken place despite little change in poverty measured at the individual level. As a result, there is now a greater tendency to associate poverty with particular neighborhoods, and public discussions often equate "the poverty problem" with "the inner-city problem." It is incorrect to lump these issues together, however. Even after two decades of an increasing concentration of poverty, only about one-sixth of the poor and one-third of the African American poor live in high-poverty neighborhoods. Yet, these ghettos, barrios, and slums provide the most visible and disturbing evidence of poverty in the United States.

In looking at the changes in neighborhood poverty over the past twenty years, my analyses in the previous chapter were constrained by the level of detail available in the earlier census years, particularly 1970. For example, the number of non-Hispanic whites living in high-poverty neighborhoods could not be calculated directly. The 1990 data are far more detailed and provide an opportunity for a more thorough examination of neighborhood poverty. The analysis in this chapter therefore differs from that in the previous chapter in the following ways:

The Hispanic category is disaggregated into Mexican, Puerto Rican, Cuban, and other Hispanic;

Figures for blacks refer to non-Hispanic blacks, eliminating the double-counting of black Hispanics;

Figures for whites refer to non-Hispanic whites instead of a composite group arrived at by subtraction (see chapter 2).

As a result of these changes in methodology, the 1990 figures in this chapter differ slightly from those reported in chapter 2. For obtaining an accurate snapshot of neighborhood poverty at one point in time, the figures in this chapter are preferable.

One further difference is that, for completeness, *all* metropolitan areas defined by the Census Bureau in the 1990 census are now included in the analysis, rather than the constant group of 239 areas that were analyzed to study the changes in neighborhood poverty between 1970 and 1990. This adds nearly one hundred newly designated metropolitan areas, although most are small and contain few high-poverty neighborhoods. These additions raise the count of high-poverty census tracts from 2,726 to 2,866 and the total population of high-poverty areas from 8.0 million to 8.4 million. All analyses in this chapter and the next are based on the more comprehensive geographic coverage.

As in previous chapters, high-poverty neighborhoods are defined as census tracts with poverty rates of 40 percent or more. Again, the neighborhood poverty rate refers to the percent of a metropolitan area's population residing in high-poverty areas. The level of *ghetto* poverty is the neighborhood poverty rate for blacks: the percentage of a metropolitan area's black population residing in high-poverty neighborhoods—usually, but not always, highly segregated ghettos. Similarly, the level of *barrio* poverty is the neighborhood poverty rate among Hispanics. Finally, the concentration of poverty is the percentage of a metropolitan area's *poor* persons who reside in poor neighborhoods.

Racial and Ethnic Composition of High-Poverty Areas

One common impression of poor neighborhoods is correct: they are predominantly inhabited by members of minority groups. In 1990, nearly four out of five residents of high-poverty neighborhoods were members of minority groups, as shown in figure 3.1. Non-Hispanic blacks accounted for nearly half of the 8.4 million residents of these neighborhoods. Hispanics, primarily Mexicans and Puerto Ricans, accounted for nearly one-fourth, and a nontrivial number—nearly one-fourth of the total—were non-Hispanic whites.

Table 3.1 compares the racial and ethnic composition of high-poverty areas to that of metropolitan areas in general and the nation as a whole. Non-Hispanic whites, who in 1990 made up 76 percent of the U.S. population, were only 23 percent (1.9 million) of the population of poor neighborhoods. African Americans, in

Figure 3.1   Racial and Ethnic Composition of High-Poverty Neighborhoods

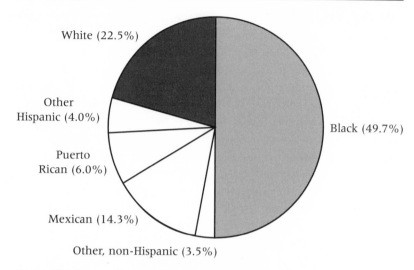

White (22.5%)

Other
Hispanic (4.0%)

Puerto
Rican (6.0%)

Mexican (14.3%)

Other, non-Hispanic (3.5%)

Black (49.7%)

Source: 1990 Census, Summary Tape File 3A (CD-ROM), tabulations by the author.
Notes: The base is the 8,446,000 persons living in high-poverty neighborhoods in
1990. "Other Hispanic" includes Cubans. The categories for "white" and "black" are
for non-Hispanics.

contrast, were overrepresented: although only one-eighth of the
population of metropolitan areas, they were one-half of the population of ghetto neighborhoods. Hispanics, as a group, were overrepresented as well, but to different degrees depending on ethnic
origin. Mexicans were 14 percent of the residents of high-poverty
areas, compared with 5 percent of the population, and for Puerto
Ricans, the figures were 6 and 1 percent respectively. But the
Cuban population in high-poverty areas was roughly proportional
to their representation in the general U.S. population, less than 1
percent in both cases.

Unfortunately, the census data do not provide unduplicated
counts of white, black, and Hispanic *poor* persons in high-poverty
neighborhoods.[1] Of the 3.9 million poor residents of high-poverty
areas, 27 percent were classified as white, 56 as black, and 26 percent as Hispanic. These figures add to more than one hundred
because Hispanics frequently specified a race category as well as an
ethnic one when answering the census.[2] As discussed in chapter 2, a

Table 3.1   Population Distribution by Race/Ethnicity and by Poverty Status for the United States, Metropolitan Areas, and High-Poverty Areas, 1990

	United States		Metropolitan Areas		High-Poverty Areas	
	In Thousands	In Percent	In Thousands	In Percent	In Thousands	In Percent
All incomes	248,710	100.0	194,273	100.0	8,446	100.0
Non-Hispanic	226,810	91.2	174,431	89.8	6,394	75.7
White	188,425	75.8	142,170	73.2	1,900	22.5
Black	29,285	11.8	24,525	12.6	4,198	49.7
Other	9,100	3.7	7,736	4.0	296	3.5
Hispanic	21,900	8.8	19,842	10.2	2,052	24.3
Mexican	13,393	5.4	11,818	6.1	1,209	14.3
Puerto Rican	2,652	1.1	2,565	1.3	506	6.0
Cuban	1,053	0.4	1,029	0.5	34	0.4
Other	4,802	1.9	4,431	2.3	302	3.6
Below poverty	31,743	100.0	22,833	100.0	3,938	100.0
White	19,025	59.9	12,612	55.2	1,066	27.1
Black	8,441	26.6	6,660	29.2	2,196	55.8
Hispanic	5,403	17.0	4,756	20.8	1,030	26.2
Non-Hispanic white and other (est.)	17,898	56.4	11,417	50.0	712	18.1

Source: 1990 census, Summary Tape File 3A (CD-ROM), tabulations by the author.
Notes: Incorporates certain adjustments to metropolitan area boundaries to improve comparability over time; see chapter 2 for details. For discussion of the non-Hispanic white and other estimate for poor persons, see text. Percentages and numbers may not add to totals because of rounding.

rough estimate of non-Hispanic whites can be obtained by subtracting totals for blacks and Hispanics from area totals. Using this method, non-Hispanic whites are only 18 percent of the concentrated poor, even though they account for more than half of the poor population nationally.[3] Again, blacks were disproportionately represented: although only one-fourth of poor persons nationally, they were more than one-half the poor residents of high-poverty areas.

The racial composition of high-poverty areas differs along several dimensions. Table 3.2 highlights the differences by region. Southern metropolitan areas accounted for nearly 40 percent of neighborhood poverty whereas western metropolitan areas accounted for only 12 percent. In part, this difference reflects the distribution of the nation's population as a whole.

The highest percentage of blacks among poor neighborhood residents was in the Midwest, where six in ten were non-Hispanic blacks. The highest percentage of non-Hispanic whites was also found in the Midwest, where nearly one-third of the residents of poor neighborhoods were white. Only 5 percent of the Midwest's ghetto residents were Hispanics whereas in other regions they make up between 26.6 and 41.6 percent of poor neighborhood residents. The composition of those Hispanics by ethnic subgroup differed sharply by region. Three-fourths of Hispanic residents of poor neighborhoods in the Northeast were Puerto Rican; in contrast, five out of six in the West and seven out of eight in the South were of Mexican descent.

Table 3.2   Residents of High-Poverty Neighborhoods by Region and Race/Ethnicity, 1990

	All Metro-politan Areas	Region			
		Northeast	Midwest	South	West
Thousands of persons	8,446	1,795	2,287	3,369	994
Distribution by region	100.0%	21.3%	27.1%	39.9%	11.8%
Distribution by race/ethnicity	100.0%	100.0%	100.0%	100.0%	100.0%
Non-Hispanic	75.7	65.0	95.0	73.4	58.4
White	22.5	16.9	32.2	17.3	27.7
Black	49.7	45.5	59.4	54.6	18.4
Other	3.5	2.6	3.4	1.5	12.3
Hispanic	24.3	35.0	5.0	26.6	41.6
Mexican	14.3	0.8	2.5	23.6	34.5
Puerto Rican	6.0	24.9	1.8	0.4	0.4
Cuban	0.4	0.4	0.1	0.7	0.1
Other Hispanic	3.6	8.8	0.6	1.9	6.7

Source: 1990 census, Summary Tape File 3A (CD-ROM), tabulations by the author.
Notes: Figures and percentages may not add to totals because of rounding. Overlapping metropolitan areas assigned to region with greatest population.

Racial Composition by City Size

Much of the early work on neighborhood poverty focused on the fifty, sixty, or one hundred largest cities. Ronald Mincy has argued that the focus on large metropolitan areas "darkened our picture of the underclass" (Mincy 1991, 1).[4] The result, he argues, is "a true chilling effect on social policy," since the problem is dismissed by the larger community as a minority problem (pp. 19–20).

Table 3.3 shows that Mincy's point is well taken. The proportion of white residents of poor neighborhoods decreases steadily as the metropolitan population rises. In the smallest metropolitan areas (those with fewer than 250,000 residents), 46 percent of the residents in high-poverty tracts were white.[5] The figure falls off rapidly in the next group (250,000–500,000 residents) to 27 percent and continues to decline steadily to 10 percent for the largest metropolitan areas (more than four million). In the smallest metropolitan areas, blacks are only one-third of poor neighborhoods' residents. The figure rises to nearly 60 percent for metropolitan areas with between two and four million people.

Interestingly, the pattern for Hispanics appears bimodal, which reflects the different distributions of the two main Hispanic subgroups. In large metropolitan areas, Mexicans are a much smaller

Table 3.3   Racial and Ethnic Composition of High-Poverty Areas, by Size of Metropolitan Area, 1990

	U.S. Total (000s)	Non-Hispanic			Hispanic
		White	Black	Other	
All metropolitan areas	8,446	22.5%	49.7%	3.5%	24.3%
Metropolitan area size					
Less than 250,000	1,142	46.3	34.0	3.8	15.8
250,000 to 499,999	1,347	27.2	36.7	2.8	33.3
500,000 to 999,999	1,427	25.7	51.1	4.9	18.3
1 to 2 million	1,160	19.9	56.3	3.2	20.5
2 to 4 million	1,084	17.2	59.5	5.0	18.3
More than 4 million	2,285	9.6	56.4	2.4	31.7

Source: 1990 census, Summary Tape File 3A (CD-ROM), tabulations by the author.
Note: Numbers and percentages may not add to totals because of rounding.

proportion of residents in high-poverty tracts than in smaller areas; Puerto Ricans, on the other hand, are concentrated in the largest metropolitan areas, where they constitute 17 percent of such residents. In addition, the category "other Hispanic," which mainly includes people of Central or South American origin, is a negligible proportion of barrio residents except in the very largest cities, where they constitute 8 percent of poor neighborhoods' population. Cubans are not a significant part of the barrio population in any urban population category.

White Neighborhood Poverty?

Although there is diversity in the racial and ethnic composition of poor neighborhoods, is Mincy correct to suggest that white slums and white "underclass" neighborhoods are a significant and neglected problem? After all, whites do account for more than one in five residents of poor neighborhoods nationally and more in smaller metropolitan areas. "Jargowsky and Bane," he states, "omit whites from discussions of ghetto poverty. . . . The concentration of poverty among whites is [treated as] some kind of anomaly, unworthy of policy attention" (Mincy 1991, 11).

To some degree, the data on neighborhood poverty among whites are corrupted by one of the faults of the poverty line. My first attempt to locate white neighborhood poverty was in Boston. Mary Jo Bane and I used census data and maps to identify the two leading candidates suggested by the statistics: one was the notorious "Southie" housing project, which has resisted integration for decades and shows all the signs of decay that other poor neighborhoods do; the other turned out to be the neighborhood surrounding Boston University. Many college students are counted as poor because of their low current income. Some students engage in behaviors associated with the underclass, such as heavy drug and alcohol use and promiscuous sex. Still, we felt safe assuming, and most analysts would agree, that most college students progress to the middle and upper classes, and therefore a large concentration of college students should not be considered a slum.

Table 3.4 shows the metropolitan areas with the most whites living in poor neighborhoods. The list includes several areas with very large public universities, such as Gainesville, Florida, Ann Arbor,

Michigan, and Bryan, Texas. In these cities, a high proportion of the adults living in high-poverty census tracts had completed at least one year of college.[6] A significant fraction of the residents of poor neighborhoods in these cities were living in college dormitories. Those in dorms, however, are not counted in either the numerator or the denominator of the neighborhood poverty rate.[7] But the presence of dorms means that other students are likely to be living nearby in private housing, and they *are* counted in the neighborhood's poverty rate. And some college dorms, in fact, are located in high-poverty neighborhoods; Temple University, for example, is located in the heart of North Philadelphia, one of the most devastated ghettos in the country.

Other cities on the list, however, are not college towns, nor were very many of the residents of their high-poverty areas attending college. These include New York, Detroit, and Philadelphia. Clearly, many of the whites residing in high-poverty areas in these metropolitan areas are not college students and should be included in an analysis of neighborhood poverty.

Table 3.4   Non-Hispanic Whites in High-Poverty Areas, Selected Metropolitan Areas, 1990

	Living in High-Poverty Areas		
Metropolitan Area	Non-Hispanic Whites	Percent of Adults with Some College	Number Living in College Dormitories
Detroit, MI	69,838	25.0%	60
New York, NY	69,044	19.8	3,511
Columbus, OH	45,192	32.3	11,171
Minneapolis, MN	37,562	41.1	4,808
Akron, OH	33,438	38.0	9,258
Philadelphia, PA	32,827	18.2	7,037
Toledo, OH	32,506	29.6	9,203
Gainesville, FL	30,289	65.1	6,694
Ann Arbor, MI	28,984	87.4	15,289
Bryan, TX	28,718	74.6	11,066

Source: 1990 census, Summary Tape File 3A (CD-ROM), tabulations by the author.

Because data on individuals are not reported at the tract level (because of confidentiality issues), it is not possible to exclude college students from each tract.[8] It is possible, however, to drop census tracts that are disproportionately composed of students. As a sensitivity test, I recalculated the high-poverty-area population after excluding tracts that had 10 percent or more of their population living in college dorms. This correction probably goes too far in that some of the remaining 90 percent are persons who should be included in the analysis. The count of non-Hispanic white residents of high-poverty neighborhoods drops nearly 30 percent, but the figures for blacks and Hispanics are little changed.[9]

My conclusion is that the growing levels of white neighborhood poverty noted in chapter 2 should be treated with suspicion, but that the white slum problem is real—70 percent of white poverty-area residents were not eliminated by throwing out those with 10 percent or more dorm residents. Even after excluding the "college" tracts, 17.5 percent of the residents of high poverty areas were non-Hispanic whites. Fortunately, the problem does not seem to compromise the analysis of ghetto poverty among blacks or barrio poverty among Hispanics, which is the primary focus of this book.

Variations in Neighborhood Poverty by Race and Ethnicity

How likely are members of a given demographic group to live in a high-poverty neighborhood? Table 3.5 shows the percentage of various demographic groups who lived in ghettos, barrios, and other poor neighborhoods in 1990. Overall, the 8.4 million residents of such neighborhoods made up less than 4 percent of the total U.S. population in 1990. Given that the majority were members of minority groups, it follows that the probability of living in a high-poverty neighborhood differs dramatically by race and ethnicity, as shown in the leftmost column of table 3.5. Only 1 percent of all U.S. non-Hispanic whites lived in a high-poverty area in 1990. In contrast, 14 percent of all U.S. non-Hispanic blacks—*nearly one in seven*—lived in ghettos or other high-poverty neighborhoods. Although this figure shows that blacks are far more likely to live in poor neighborhoods than whites, a much smaller percentage of blacks reside in them than is commonly imagined. While most res-

Table 3.5   Neighborhood Poverty Rates and the Concentration of Poverty, by Race/Ethnicity and Region, 1990

	United States[a]	All Metropolitan Areas	Metro. Areas by Region			
			Northeast	Midwest	South	West
Neighborhood Poverty Rates[b]						
All incomes	3.4%	4.3%	4.0%	5.3%	5.5%	2.2%
Non-Hispanic	2.8	3.7	2.8	5.2	4.5	1.6
White	1.0	1.3	0.9	2.1	1.4	1.0
Black	14.3	17.1	15.8	25.1	16.3	7.0
Other	3.3	3.8	3.3	9.0	3.7	3.0
Hispanic	9.4	10.3	17.6	7.7	15.5	4.6
Mexican	9.0	10.2	9.6	5.9	22.1	4.8
Puerto Rican	19.1	19.7	25.3	16.9	3.6	2.0
Cuban	3.3	3.3	3.8	6.5	3.3	1.4
Other Hisp.	6.3	6.8	10.8	6.1	5.9	4.0
Concentration of Poverty[c]						
Below poverty	12.4%	17.2%	18.3%	22.1%	19.6%	8.2%
White	5.6	8.4	7.1	9.5	10.7	5.3
Black	26.0	33.0	32.6	43.0	30.9	15.0
Hispanic	19.1	21.7	33.5	17.5	30.0	9.8
Non-Hispanic white and other (est.)	4.0	6.2	3.4	10.2	5.4	5.7

Source: 1990 census, Summary Tape File 3A (CD-ROM), tabulations by the author.
[a] Column represents residents of high-poverty census tracts in metropolitan areas as a percent of total U.S. populations.
[b] Neighborhood poverty rate is the proportion of a metropolitan area's residents living in high-poverty areas, defined as census tracts with poverty rates of 40 percent or more.
[c] Concentration of poverty is the proportion of a metropolitan area's poor persons living in high-poverty areas, as defined above.

idents are minorities, most minority individuals do not live in ghettos and barrios. Indeed, the vast majority do not.

Once again, treating Hispanics as a single group would obscure several important points. The term "Hispanic" is used mostly in the Anglo community to refer collectively to several groups of people with different countries of origin, histories of immigration and assimilation, and traditions and cultures (Bean and Tienda 1987). The overall probability of a Hispanic living in a barrio neighborhood was 9.4 percent in 1990—far greater than whites but substantially lower than blacks. Disaggregating by ethnic origin, however, one finds that Puerto Ricans were far more likely to live in barrios in 1990 than other Hispanics. In fact, Puerto Ricans—at 19 percent— were more likely to live in high-poverty areas than African Americans. Only 9 percent of Mexicans, the next highest Hispanic subgroup, lived in barrios, whereas only 3 percent of Cubans lived in high-poverty neighborhoods.

Regional Differences in Neighborhood Poverty Rates

The second column of table 3.5 shows the average neighborhood poverty rates for all metropolitan areas in the United States. The remaining columns show the average rates in the major regions of the United States.[10] In 1990, 4.3 percent of metropolitan residents lived in ghettos, barrios, or other poor neighborhoods. Whites were not likely to live in such neighborhoods in any region of the country, but the level is highest in the Midwest (2 percent). Blacks are also most likely to live in high-poverty tracts in the Midwest, but the level is much higher (25 percent) than that for whites. Ghetto poverty is much lower in the West. For example, only 7 percent of blacks in western states lived in ghettos.

Among Hispanics, neighborhood poverty rates differ sharply by ethnic subgroup and region. Mexicans in the Northeast and South have relatively high levels of neighborhood poverty but low levels elsewhere. One-fourth of all Puerto Ricans in the Northeast live in poor neighborhoods, mostly barrios, and nearly 17 percent in the Midwest, but the levels are sharply lower in the South and West. Cubans are unlikely to live in barrios in any region. The figures for "other Hispanics," principally from countries in Central and South America, are relatively low. One caution is in order, however. Since these figures include only those who were counted by the census, illegal immigrants and recent legal immigrants with limited English proficiency were among those most likely to be undercounted.

Poverty Versus the Concentration of Poverty

When thinking about public policies to address poverty, politicians and the public tend to have a certain image of the poor in mind.

The stereotype, more often than not, is a black single mother on welfare living in a ghetto neighborhood. Ghetto and barrio residence is not typical, however, of the poor (see the bottom panel of table 3.5). Only 12 percent of all poor persons in the United States in 1990 lived in a high-poverty neighborhood.

In other words, about seven in eight poor persons did not live in ghettos and barrios, contradicting the often implicit assumption that poverty is synonymous with the inner city. The vast majority of the white poor do not live in high-poverty tracts. They are more widely dispersed than Hispanics and blacks. Moreover, even among minority groups, most of the poor in 1990 did not live in urban ghettos or barrios. Nationally, three-quarters of the black poor and four-fifths of the Hispanic poor lived outside high-poverty areas. In the average metropolitan area, about one in six Hispanic poor and one in three black poor were residents of ghettos, barrios, or other high-poverty neighborhoods.

Again, there was substantial variation by region. The concentration of poverty in the Midwest, where the stereotype comes closest to being fulfilled, was 43 percent for African Americans.[11] In northeastern and southern metropolitan areas, close to one-third of the black poor lived in ghettos; only in the West does the figure drop off. Poor Hispanics are most heavily concentrated in the Northeast and South. Unfortunately, Hispanic *poor* are not disaggregated by ethnic subgroup in census tract data.

Geographic Distribution of the Poor

If most of the poor do not live in ghettos, barrios, and slums, where do they live? Table 3.6 shows the distribution of the poor in 1990 by residence inside and outside metropolitan areas and by neighborhood poverty rate.[12] Some nonmetropolitan neighborhoods have poverty rates of 40 percent or more.[13] In fact, 2.7 percent of the U.S. poor lived in these high-poverty areas. In some ways, people living in them may be even more isolated than urban ghetto and barrio dwellers, given the low density of these areas. The majority of the U.S. poor lived in metropolitan neighborhoods not poor enough to be considered ghettos, barrios, or slums: 37 percent in areas with low poverty levels (0–20 percent poor) and 23 percent in areas with intermediate poverty levels (20–40 percent poor). Another one-fourth lived in nonmetropolitan areas with poverty rates less than 40 percent.

Table 3.6   Distribution of the Poor by Type of Neighborhood, by Race/Ethnicity and Region, 1990

	Poor Persons (000s)	Neighborhood Poverty Level Outside Metropolitan Areas			Neighborhood Poverty Level Inside Metropolitan Areas		
		0–19.9%	20–39.9%	40–100%	0–19.9%	20–39.9%	40–100%
Total	31,743	13.9%	11.4%	2.7%	36.6%	22.9%	12.4%
Northeast	5,214	10.0	2.0	0.2	45.4	26.3	16.0
Midwest	6,971	21.8	7.8	1.3	33.7	20.1	15.3
South	13,065	12.9	19.6	4.6	30.0	20.6	12.3
West	6,492	10.6	6.3	2.5	46.0	27.9	6.6
Total black	8,441	4.9	11.9	4.4	20.5	32.4	26.0
Northeast	1,305	0.6	0.4	0.1	24.6	42.0	32.3
Midwest	1,763	1.5	1.9	0.5	17.0	37.8	41.3
South	4,800	7.8	19.9	7.4	18.5	26.4	20.1
West	574	1.1	1.2	0.5	38.4	44.2	14.6
Total Hispanic	5,403	3.8	6.1	2.1	30.3	38.6	19.1
Northeast	1,019	0.8	0.3	0.0	25.7	40.0	33.1
Midwest	343	9.8	2.9	0.4	34.6	37.1	15.2
South	1,831	3.6	9.6	5.0	24.0	33.3	24.5
West	2,211	4.3	6.4	0.9	37.1	42.6	8.6
Total white	17,898	21.3	12.8	2.1	46.1	13.7	4.0
Northeast	2,891	17.5	3.4	0.3	61.7	14.4	2.7
Midwest	4,865	30.0	10.2	1.6	39.7	12.5	5.9
South	6,434	19.5	22.2	2.4	40.2	12.7	3.0
West	3,708	15.9	7.1	3.7	52.5	16.6	4.2

Source: 1990 census, Summary Tape File 3A (CD-ROM), tabulations by the author.
Note: Numbers and percentages may not sum totals because of rounding. Non-Hispanic white estimated by subtracting black and Hispanic figures from total.

The geographic distribution of the poor, and hence the qualitative experience of poverty, differs dramatically by race and ethnicity. The white poor are more likely to live outside metropolitan areas (36 percent) than either blacks (21 percent) or Hispanics (12 percent). More than two-thirds of the white poor actually lived in low-poverty areas. In contrast, about one-fourth of the black poor and one-third of the Hispanic poor lived in low-poverty neighborhoods. Thus, in addition to suffering much higher poverty rates than whites, minorities who are poor are much less able to draw on the resources of a financially healthy community.

Table 3.6 also shows the regional pattern of residence by race and ethnicity. Virtually no poor blacks or Hispanics live outside metropolitan areas in the Northeast, regardless of neighborhood poverty level. In fact, poor blacks are hardly ever found outside metropolitan areas, except in the South. More than one-third of poor blacks in the South reside outside metropolitan areas, including 7 percent living in neighborhoods with poverty rates of 40 percent or more. More than four in ten of the white poor live outside metropolitan areas in both the Midwest and the South.

Although this book's focus is poor neighborhoods in metropolitan areas, it is important to remember that they are only a part of the nation's poverty problem. Many of the poor are white, and many poor people live in the suburbs and other intermediate locations. Large segments of both the white and black poor live outside metropolitan areas, especially in the Midwest and South. All these subgroups likely share some problems, but important differences distinguish them, especially concerning the factors that cause or contribute to their poverty. To some extent, the poor subgroups may even be in conflict. For example, Citibank's decision in 1980 to relocate much of its credit-card processing operation to South Dakota (Meislin 1980) was part of a more general trend of job relocation that reduced jobs for poor inner-city minorities while increasing opportunities for poor rural whites. Thus, anti-poverty policies based on a particular image of the poor and where they live would almost certainly fail to serve many in need.

Neighborhood Poverty and Children

Policymakers have a particular interest in the welfare of children, especially poor children. Children may be more vulnerable to the influence of their neighborhood than adults and have fewer connections to the world beyond it. Not surprisingly, the percentages of children living in poor neighborhoods by race, ethnicity, and poverty status are similar to those of the groups as a whole. For several reasons, however, children are more likely to live in ghettos and barrios than adults. For one, each child born into a family increases the poverty threshold for the family. For another, many poor families are headed by a single parent. With one less adult, such families are disproportionately composed of children.

Table 3.7 shows the distribution of children by neighborhood poverty level in 1990. Of all sixty-two million U.S. children, 4 percent lived in ghettos, barrios, and slums. Another 1 percent lived in high-poverty areas outside metropolitan areas. Younger children (0–4 years of age) were more likely to live in poor neighborhoods than older children. Minority children were much more likely to live in high-poverty areas than non-Hispanic white children. Although black and Hispanic children were more likely to live in poor neighborhoods than adults, non-Hispanic white chil-

Table 3.7   Distribution of Children by Type of Neighborhood, by Poverty Status, Age, and Race/Ethnicity, 1990

	Thousands of Children (000s)	Neighborhood Poverty Level Outside Metropolitan Areas			Neighborhood Poverty Level Inside Metropolitan Areas		
		0–19.9%	20–39.9%	40–100%	0–19.9%	20–39.9%	40–100%
All children	62,279	15.9%	6.0%	0.9%	61.2%	11.9%	4.1%
0 to 4 years	17,978	14.6	5.5	0.9	61.9	12.7	4.4
5 to 17 years	44,301	16.4	6.3	0.9	60.9	11.6	4.0
Black	9,336	5.5	8.8	2.6	38.1	29.1	16.0
Hispanic	7,473	4.8	4.4	1.1	48.6	30.8	10.3
Non-Hispanic white	45,470	19.8	5.7	0.5	68.0	5.3	0.6
Poor children	11,162	13.0	11.7	3.0	32.4	25.5	14.5
0 to 4	3,617	12.7	10.8	2.7	32.9	26.2	14.7
5 to 17	7,545	13.1	12.1	3.1	32.1	25.1	14.4
Black	3,717	4.6	11.8	4.5	19.5	32.6	27.0
Hispanic	2,407	4.1	6.3	2.1	28.2	39.4	19.8
Non-Hispanic white	5,037	23.5	14.1	2.3	43.8	13.5	2.7

Source: 1990 census, Summary Tape File 3A (CD-ROM), tabulations by the author.
Note: Numbers and percentages may not add to totals because of rounding. Non-Hispanic white estimated by subtracting black and Hispanic figures from total.

dren were slightly less likely to live in them than adults. This suggests that, compared with minorities, whites living in slums are more likely to be single males, college students, and elderly couples, and are less likely to be poor families with children.

Poor children were more likely to live in ghetto neighborhoods than poor adults. Nationally, about one in seven poor children lived in high-poverty neighborhoods in a metropolitan area; another 3 percent lived in high-poverty areas outside metropolitan areas. Yet, nearly half of all poor children lived in neighborhoods with low poverty rates (less than 20 percent). This latter group, however, is very disproportionately composed of non-Hispanic whites. Although more than two-thirds of poor white children lived in low-poverty neighborhoods, less than one-fourth of poor black children and less than one-third of poor Hispanic children did so.

These findings are important for programs that deliver services to poor children. Targeting geographical concentrations of poor children by establishing, for example, "one-stop shopping" service centers in poor communities may be a good way to reach a large number of poor children in a cost-effective manner. Still, most children living in poor families do not live in ghetto or barrio neighborhoods, even among minority groups. Policies and programs that require direct service delivery will have a difficult time reaching all poor children because many of them, especially poor white children, live widely dispersed in nonpoor communities.

An argument can be made that children in poor families living in poor neighborhoods are doubly disadvantaged and are more in need of certain kinds of services. Counterarguments also could be made in support of poor children isolated in an otherwise nonpoor community. The issue cannot be addressed in the abstract, because different types of disadvantage interact with neighborhood poverty in different ways. Gang involvement is a more serious problem when poverty is concentrated for obvious reasons. In contrast, a poor family may have fewer options for obtaining free or subsidized food if they live in a nonpoor neighborhood. What table 3.7 does suggest is that programs that do not rely on geographical service provision are better if the goal is to reach all poor children. A recent example is the expansion of the tax code's Earned Income Tax Credit, which increases the take-home pay of working poor families with children regardless of where they live.

A Big City Problem?

Neighborhood poverty rates and the concentration of the poor also depend on city size, but the effect of city size varies by region (see table 3.8). Ghetto poverty—the neighborhood poverty rate for blacks—appears to differ little by city size, unless the figures are further disaggregated by region. In the Northeast, much higher levels of ghetto poverty are found in the larger cities; the same is true for the concentration of the black poor. In both cases, the figures more than double when going from the smallest to the largest metropol-

Table 3.8   Neighborhood Poverty Rates and Concentration of the Poor, by Region and Size of Metropolitan Area, for Blacks and Hispanics, 1990

	Number of Metro. Areas	Neighborhood Poverty Rates		Concentration of the Poor	
		Black	Hispanic	Black	Hispanic
All metropolitan areas	337	17.1%	10.3%	33.0%	21.7%
Less than 500,000	249	18.3	18.4	30.5	32.3
500,000 to 1 million	47	16.8	10.5	31.2	21.6
More than 1 million	41	16.8	8.3	34.4	18.3
Northeast					
Less than 500,000	50	7.3	6.4	16.2	14.1
500,000 to 1 million	11	12.3	10.1	25.9	23.7
More than 1 million	8	17.3	21.1	35.3	38.5
Midwest					
Less than 500,000	70	21.7	7.8	33.1	13.9
500,000 to 1 million	7	24.6	7.1	38.5	17.7
More than 1 million	10	25.8	7.8	45.5	18.3
South					
Less than 500,000	93	20.3	34.0	32.4	51.0
500,000 to 1 million	21	16.5	15.4	30.8	28.8
More than 1 million	11	13.3	7.8	29.5	16.5
West					
Less than 500,000	36	4.7	6.7	9.2	12.1
500,000 to 1 million	8	12.3	7.3	22.3	14.7
More than 1 million	12	6.6	3.8	14.7	8.4

Source: 1990 census, Summary Tape File 3A (CD-ROM), tabulations by the author.

itan areas. Midwestern cities have higher ghetto poverty regardless of size, but the larger metropolitan areas have slightly higher levels. Large Midwestern cities have the worst ghetto problem: more than one-quarter of all blacks and nearly half of all poor blacks lived in high-poverty neighborhoods.

In the South, however, the relationship is turned on its head: the smallest metropolitan areas have the highest levels of ghetto poverty and concentration of the poor. What idiosyncratic regional factors could create this puzzling pattern? Part of the answer may lie in the fact that blacks only recently migrated to large northern cities with thriving industrial economies, whereas the black population in smaller southern cities stems in part from blacks' historical settlement patterns driven largely by agriculture. Such a pattern suggests that a causal model of ghetto poverty must take into account regional and historical differences among cities, and not merely current demographic and economic factors.

The reversal in the relationship between metropolitan size and neighborhood poverty is even more dramatic for Hispanics (see table 3.8). In the Northeast, Hispanics are more than three times as likely to live in high-poverty areas in the largest metropolitan areas compared to the smallest. In the South, Hispanics are more than four times as likely to live in barrios in the smaller metropolitan areas. In this case, however, the differences can be readily attributed to the heterogeneity of Hispanic subgroups.

Ghettos and Barrios in Specific Cities

Thus far, the analysis has taken a national and regional view of neighborhood poverty. Here the experiences of selected metropolitan areas are examined. Table 3.9 shows the ten metropolitan areas with the largest ghetto and barrio populations. New York tops the list: in 1990, nearly one million people—one in every ten residents of the New York metropolitan area—lived in one of the city's 279 high-poverty census tracts. New York's neighborhood poverty problem is overwhelmingly a minority problem, about evenly split between blacks and Hispanics: one in five black New Yorkers and one in four Hispanic New Yorkers lived in a high-poverty area. Detroit—not Chicago or Los Angeles—comes in a distant second with less than half a million residents of high-poverty areas, of

Table 3.9   Metropolitan Areas with the Largest Ghettos, Barrios, and
           Slums, by Race/Ethnicity, 1990

	Number of High-Poverty Tracts	Living in High-Poverty Neighborhoods		
		Total[a]	Non-Hispanic		Hispanic
			White	Black	
High-poverty areas					
1 New York	279	960,292	69,044	411,155	459,525
2 Detroit	149	418,947	69,838	332,118	12,202
3 Chicago	184	396,200	20,768	325,446	43,732
4 Los Angeles	56	267,666	26,321	75,976	149,110
5 Philadelphia	70	241,863	32,827	143,185	59,706
6 McAllen, TX	37	234,467	17,526	186	216,231
7 New Orleans	67	165,751	12,791	144,581	2,926
8 Houston	51	162,487	10,915	92,608	56,847
9 San Antonio	31	152,936	9,071	13,364	129,356
10 Miami	33	148,083	12,824	88,097	46,284
Percent of metropolitan totals					
1 New York	10.3%	10.2%	1.4%	20.0%	24.3%
2 Detroit	12.8	9.9	2.2	35.4	15.8
3 Chicago	10.6	5.5	0.4	23.1	5.4
4 Los Angeles	3.4	3.0	0.7	8.0	4.5
5 Philadelphia	5.6	5.0	0.9	15.6	36.3
6 McAllen, TX	58.7	61.1	32.3	27.3	66.1
7 New Orleans	17.8	13.4	1.7	33.8	5.7
8 Houston	6.8	4.7	0.5	15.0	7.8
9 San Antonio	12.4	11.7	1.6	15.5	21.0
10 Miami	12.4	7.6	2.2	23.7	4.9

Source: 1990 census, Summary Tape File 3A (CD-ROM), tabulations by the author.
[a]Total includes other races, not shown separately.

whom the vast majority are non-Hispanic blacks. In 1990, one in
three blacks in the Detroit metropolitan area lived in a ghetto
neighborhood. Chicago follows a similar pattern.

Los Angeles presents something of a paradox. It ranked fourth in
ghetto and barrio residents in 1990 but did not show particularly
high neighborhood poverty rates among either blacks or Hispanics.
Los Angeles has populous ghettos and barrios, mainly because of its
enormous size, not because its residents are more likely to live in

high-poverty areas. Philadelphia's high-poverty-area population was mainly black in 1990, but on a percentage basis the city's Hispanics were more than twice as likely to live in a poor census tract. Virtually all the residents of New Orleans's poor neighborhoods are black, representing one-third of the city's black population.

The figures for McAllen, Texas, are in a class by themselves. Nearly two-thirds of the city's residents live in high-poverty neighborhoods, and nearly 60 percent of the city's census tracts are so classified. McAllen is on the border with Mexico in southern Texas. Geographically, culturally, and demographically the city has more in common with Tijuana, Mexico, than Houston or Dallas. Part of the explanation for such a large proportion of the city's census tracts having poverty rates of 40 percent or more is that the poverty line is not adjusted for local differences in the cost of living. On the other hand, part of the reason the cost of living is so low is that the entire Rio Grande Valley is economically depressed. There is no simple way to disentangle these issues.

Ethnic Composition of Barrios

The ethnic makeup of Hispanic barrios varies greatly from city to city. Table 3.10 shows the ethnic composition of the barrio population for those metropolitan areas with the largest number of Hispanics living in high-poverty areas in 1990. Predictably, most of the cities with the largest Hispanic barrio populations are in the South and West, New York and Philadelphia being the two exceptions. In 1990, New York's high-poverty-area residents were nearly one-half Hispanic, of which about two-thirds were Puerto Rican. In general, Puerto Ricans who come to the mainland are highly concentrated in New York City; in 1990, one-third of the Puerto Ricans in New York lived in high-poverty neighborhoods. As a result, more than 60 percent of all Puerto Rican barrio residents in the entire country live in New York City. Virtually all of the Hispanics in Philadelphia's poor neighborhoods were Puerto Rican.

The cities with large Puerto Rican populations tend to have small Mexican populations, and the opposite was true as well. Mexican barrios are strongly concentrated in the South and West, although they are not nearly as concentrated in any one city. Like Puerto Ricans, most Cubans (56 percent) in high-poverty areas are con-

Table 3.10   Metropolitan Areas with Largest Hispanic Barrios, Totals and Subgroups, 1990

	Total in High-Poverty Tracts[a]	Hispanics Living in High-Poverty Neighborhoods				
		Total	Mexican	Puerto Rican	Cuban	Other Hispanic
High-poverty areas						
1 New York	960,292	459,525	12,084	305,069	5,576	136,796
2 McAllen, TX	234,467	216,231	209,726	374	22	6,109
3 Los Angeles	267,666	149,110	105,676	800	469	42,165
4 San Antonio	152,936	129,356	123,391	419	97	5,449
5 Brownsville, TX	136,312	125,353	119,844	176	84	5,249
6 El Paso	110,735	101,951	99,531	394	51	1,975
7 Laredo, TX	66,005	64,000	62,096	102	87	1,715
8 Philadelphia	241,863	59,706	665	53,708	324	5,009
9 Houston	162,487	56,847	49,979	329	113	6,426
10 Miami	148,083	46,284	2,866	6,052	19,262	18,104
Percent of metropolitan totals						
1 New York	10.2%	24.3%	18.3%	33.5%	7.9%	16.2%
2 McAllen, TX	61.1	66.1	66.5	54.3	8.5	58.5
3 Los Angeles	3.0	4.5	4.2	1.9	1.0	6.0
4 San Antonio	11.7	21.0	21.6	5.6	7.5	15.1
5 Brownsville, TX	52.4	59.0	59.3	32.8	41.4	53.8
6 El Paso	18.7	24.8	25.2	8.8	12.1	16.4
7 Laredo, TX	49.5	51.2	51.3	40.2	44.4	47.1
8 Philadelphia	5.0	36.3	6.0	46.6	5.8	15.4
9 Houston	4.7	7.8	8.4	3.2	1.3	5.6
10 Miami	7.6	4.9	12.4	8.8	3.4	6.1

Source: 1990 census, Summary Tape File 3A (CD-ROM), tabulations by the author.

[a] Total includes non-Hispanic white and black and other races, not shown separately.

centrated in just one city—Miami. Two-thirds of the "other Hispanics" in the United States who in 1990 lived in poor neighborhoods could be found in just three cities. They share barrio neighborhoods with Puerto Ricans in New York City, with Mexicans in Los Angeles, and with Cubans in Miami.

These disparate regional patterns suggest that one should not speak of the "Hispanic barrio problem" in the abstract. Rather, there are at least three separate problems that need to be understood on their own terms. Puerto Rican barrios need to be understood in the context of the economic disparities between the island and the mainland and the unique legal status of Puerto Rico itself. Mexican barrios need to be understood in the context of the economic disparities between the United States and Mexico, the problem of a largely unenforceable border, and border regions' historical dependence on Mexican agricultural labor. Cuban barrios add international geopolitical maneuvering by both Cuba and the United States to the mix.

One caveat must be inserted into this discussion: because of the undercount of Mexicans and other Hispanics who are illegal immigrants, my calculations may substantially underestimate the number of Mexicans and other Central and South Americans in barrio neighborhoods. Although Puerto Ricans are U.S. citizens and have no reason to fear the census taker, they may still be undercounted because of language barriers and census takers' reluctance to enter neighborhoods they perceive to be dangerous, but probably to a lesser degree than for the other Hispanic subgroups.

Cities with the Highest Neighborhood Poverty Rates
The previous discussion of numbers of ghetto and barrio residents could lead to the impression that neighborhood poverty is confined to the largest cities, except for those border towns, such as McAllen, that serve as ports of entry for Mexicans. But as a percent of total population, many smaller metropolitan areas have severe problems as well.

Table 3.11 shows the ten metropolitan areas with the highest neighborhood poverty rates among blacks and Hispanics.[14] New York, so prominent in the previous tables, does not even make the list. In Milwaukee, nearly half of all blacks and about two-thirds of poor blacks lived in high-poverty neighborhoods in 1990. This extraordinary degree of ghettoization was not always the case in Milwaukee. Its levels were low to modest in 1970 and 1980 but grew rapidly in the 1980s, as discussed in chapter 2.

Several other large cities—Buffalo, Detroit, and New Orleans—were among the cities with the highest levels of ghetto poverty in 1990. But six of the ten are small, with a population of half a million or less, and are located in the deep South or Midwest. It is a new phenomenon for Midwestern cities to be on this list; a similar list for 1970 or 1980 would be composed almost entirely of south-

Table 3.11   Population and Poor Population of High-Poverty Areas, Metropolitan Areas with Highest Black and Hispanic Neighborhood Poverty Rates, 1990

	Metropolitan Areas Population	Total	Neighborhood Poverty Rate	Total Poor	Concen-tration of Poverty
Non-Hispanic blacks					
1 Milwaukee	1,432,149	195,991	46.7%	79,254	64.6%
2 Albany, GA	112,561	51,217	42.4	20,314	57.9
3 Mobile	476,923	129,924	41.9	54,980	54.7
4 Buffalo	1,189,288	120,355	40.4	43,912	54.0
5 Flint, MI	500,229	83,703	40.4	30,524	56.1
6 Shreveport, LA	376,330	129,756	39.8	58,256	47.0
7 Youngstown, OH	492,619	54,279	38.5	21,658	52.5
8 Lafayette, LA	208,740	51,185	35.6	22,661	40.4
9 Detroit	4,248,699	936,866	35.4	305,202	53.9
10 New Orleans	1,238,816	427,723	33.8	171,700	49.0
Hispanics					
1 McAllen, TX	383,545	326,923	66.1%	152,679	75.8%
2 Brownsville, TX	260,120	212,592	59.0	95,829	68.7
3 Laredo, TX	133,239	125,084	51.2	48,857	65.2
4 Philadelphia	4,856,881	164,601	36.3	55,806	62.3
5 Hartford, CT	789,923	56,646	27.6	20,907	47.4
6 Las Cruces, NM	135,510	76,319	25.0	26,515	32.6
7 El Paso	591,610	411,248	24.8	138,399	38.6
8 New York	9,372,226	1,891,039	24.3	588,698	40.6
9 San Antonio	1,302,099	616,878	21.0	177,961	35.8
10 Corpus Christi	349,894	180,586	18.7	54,369	31.6

Source: 1990 census, Summary Tape File 3A (CD-ROM), tabulations by the author.
Note: Restricted to metropolitan areas with at least 50,000 residents of indicated group.

ern cities, which started from extremely high levels in 1970 and in most cases have experienced declines. Midwestern cities, by comparison, had little or no ghetto poverty in 1970 and saw increases over the last two decades.

Other Analyses of Neighborhood Poverty

Any set of research findings is dependent upon the definitions and methodology employed by its authors. The findings are of limited value, however, if they are radically dependent on the chosen methodology. For this reason, I contrast my findings with previous research that has employed somewhat different analytical approaches.

Underclass Research

Mincy and Wiener (1993) have continued the research begun by Ricketts and Sawhill (1988). The latter's underclass measure attempts to determine "the geographic concentration of multiple social characteristics that act as barriers to labor force attachment" (Mincy and Wiener 1993, 5).[15] A neighborhood was defined as underclass if it was one standard deviation above the mean on all four of the following characteristics: men not attached to the labor force; teenagers who are high school dropouts; families headed by a women with children; households dependent on welfare (p. 6).[16]

Mincy and Wiener also calculate "concentrated poverty" according to Bane and Jargowsky's criterion. The latter term, as they use it, is identical to what I have called neighborhood poverty. But their computations include all U.S. census tracts and BNAs, rather than just metropolitan census tracts, as in my analysis. Thus, the scope of their study is broader, but at the cost of combining two phenomena—metropolitan ghettos and rural poverty areas—that likely have very different characteristics and causal structures.

Kasarda's Analysis of "Concentrated Urban Poverty"

John Kasarda has examined four distinct approaches to measuring concentrated urban poverty. I will focus on two of them: "extreme poverty neighborhoods," equivalent to high-poverty areas as defined here, and "distressed neighborhoods" (Kasarda 1993, 253–57). The latter concept includes three of Ricketts and Sawhill's four components; the omitted factor is teenage school dropouts.[17] To these, Kasarda adds poverty and defines "distressed neighborhoods" as census tracts that are simultaneously one standard deviation above the mean tract on all four dimensions.[18]

Kasarda's study has a more limited geographic focus than either Mincy and Wiener or this volume. First, Kasarda includes central cities rather than entire metropolitan areas in his analysis, arguing that "the 100 largest central cities not only capture most of the nation's ghetto poor but, given the size of their ghettos, represent the greatest challenges to urban policy" (Kasarda 1993, 255). This statement is true but misses the point that a key dimension of neighborhood poverty is the percentage of an area's population (and of various racial and ethnic subgroups) that lives in ghettos, barrios, and slums. Using only central cities excludes a decidedly nonrandom part of the subgroups from the analysis. In other words, Kasarda is right about the numerator but not about the denominator of neighborhood poverty calculations.

To complicate matters, the proportion of a metropolitan area located within the boundary of the central city differs widely from city to city, depending on such factors as state laws, historical idiosyncrasies, and the timing of the area's growth and development. Boston and San Francisco are two examples of central cities that constitute relatively small parts of their metropolitan areas, whereas San Antonio and Memphis have managed to annex most of their surrounding suburbs. Because the base is inconsistent, both among cities and within a metropolitan area as it expands across fixed political boundaries, both cross-sectional and longitudinal statistics based on central-city data are potentially misleading.

A second geographic limitation to Kasarda's analysis is that it includes only the one hundred largest central cities, out of more than three hundred metropolitan areas. Clearly, large cities contain many of the nation's most impoverished neighborhoods. But the preceding analysis documented how the racial and ethnic composition of ghettos, barrios, and slums varies dramatically by city size; thus, Kasarda's analysis will tend to miss relatively more of the whites and Mexicans living in poor neighborhoods and relatively more blacks in the South.

Race-Specific Poverty Rates

In previous research, I identified high-poverty areas using the poverty rate for a particular race group rather than the overall neighborhood poverty rate. In other words, a census tract was considered a ghetto for *black* residents if the *black poverty rate* was 40 percent or more, and likewise for whites and Hispanics. The basic assumption of this method is that members of different racial and ethnic groups residing in the same census tract interact little, and so the poverty rate of one's own group is more germane to the level of neighborhood deprivation experienced by residents (Jargowsky 1994).

Geographic Coverage

Table 3.12 compares the results of these studies. Columns A, C, and E report results based on the use of an overall tract poverty rate of 40 percent or more to identify poor neighborhoods and differ only in their geographic coverage. About two-thirds of the ghetto, barrio, and slum neighborhoods in metropolitan areas are located in the one hundred largest central cities studied by Kasarda. About 5.7 million persons live in these neighborhoods, compared with 8.4 million when all metropolitan areas are included and more than ten million when the entire nation is included.

Consistent with Mincy's concern about the focus on large cities coloring our perception of neighborhood poverty, the distribution of poverty-area residents by race and ethnicity changes as we move across the columns in table 3.12. A focus on large central cities leads to a more racially polarized picture. In the nation as a whole, one out of four residents of high-poverty areas in 1990 was a non-Hispanic white, compared with only one out of ten in the one hundred largest central cities. The proportion of poverty-area residents that is Hispanic varies little across the studies, in part because they are not disaggregated by ethnic subgroup by Mincy and Wiener or by Kasarda. Kasarda shows much higher probabilities of living in a high-poverty area for all racial and ethnic groups. This is a consequence of limiting the analysis to neighborhoods in central cities, since the remaining census tracts are on average more suburban and less likely to have high poverty rates.

Alternative Criteria for Neighborhood Selection

It is perhaps more interesting to compare the results from different types of measures, keeping geography constant. Using race-specific neighborhood poverty rates to define high-poverty areas, instead of overall poverty rates, increases the number of ghetto and barrio residents from 8.4 million to 11.2 million (compare columns C and D; see Jargowsky 1994). Since the white poverty rate in a census tract is often lower than the black and Hispanic poverty rates, the total

Table 3.12 Alternative Concepts/Measures for Studying Neighborhood Poverty, 1990

	Mincy and Wiener, Metro and Nonmetro Areas		Jargowsky, All Metro Areas		Kasarda, 100 Largest Central Cities	
	Pov > 40%	Underclass	Pov > 40%	Pov > 40% by Race	Pov > 40%	Distressed
	(A)	(B)	(C)	(D)	(E)	(F)
Census tracts	3,417	928	2,866	varies	1,954	1,850
Residents (thousands)						
All incomes	10,394	2,682	8,446	11,157	5,496	5,704
Below poverty	4,802	1,188	3,938	5,476	2,650	2,640
Racial composition (%)						
White, non-Hispanic	26.0%	26.5%	22.5%	11.8%	15.5%	10.4%
Black, non-Hispanic	46.7	56.7	49.7	52.5	57.3	67.7
Hispanic	21.8	20.1	24.3	29.7	23.8	19.6
Percent of covered population in areas						
White, non-Hispanic	1.4	0.3	1.3	0.9	3.2	2.2
Black, non-Hispanic	16.6	5.2	17.1	23.9	24.2	29.7
Hispanic	10.4	2.5	10.2	16.7	15.4	13.2
Percent of covered poor in areas						
White	7.1	1.3	—	—	—	—
Black	30.4	8.8	33.0	—	41.6	47.3
White, non-Hispanic	—	—	6.2	4.7	—	—
Black, non-Hispanic	—	—	—	45.7	—	—
Hispanic	21.2	4.7	21.7	34.6	27.2	22.9

Sources: Columns A and B—Mincy and Wiener (1993), tables 1, 3, 4, 6, and 7; column C—this volume; column D—Jargowsky (1994) and unpublished tabulations; columns E and F—Kasarda (1993), tables 1, 3, 4, and 5. See also Tobin (1993).
Note: See text for discussion of differing concepts and coverages.

poverty rate in the tract tends to be lower as well. Thus, using race-specific poverty rates increases the count of blacks and Hispanics and reduces the count of whites living in high-poverty areas. Based on this procedure, more than half were non-Hispanic blacks, 30 percent were Hispanic, and only 12 percent were non-Hispanic whites. The number of non-Hispanic whites living in ghettos is 1.9 million using the overall poverty rate, as compared with 1.3 million using race-specific poverty rates.

Most blacks *outside* metropolitan areas live in the South, in BNAs that have very different white and black poverty rates. It could be argued (although I have not done the fieldwork necessary to confirm it) that the larger land area of BNAs means that the case for using race-specific poverty rates to represent true social neighborhoods is even stronger outside metropolitan areas. Nearly half of blacks outside metropolitan areas are in BNAs with black poverty rates of 40 percent or more.[19] Given the overwhelming urban focus of the neighborhood literature to date, very little is known about the conditions of life in BNAs with high poverty rates or about the way social and environmental conditions shape the life experiences of the residents in these areas.

The underclass measure (column B) includes a much smaller number of census tracts and people than use of the poverty rate. Nearly all the difference, however, comes from only one of the four measures—the percentage of teens in high school (Tobin 1993). For that reason, Kasarda defines "distressed neighborhoods" by omitting the dropout component and adding a poverty component, making it a hybrid measure (column F). This criterion yields about the same total number of neighborhoods and people as the 40 percent criterion (compare columns E and F). But distressed neighborhoods include more blacks and fewer whites and Hispanics, probably because of the measure's female-headed-families component.

Although there are differences across the columns of table 3.12, they are mostly small and in expected directions. The main exception is Ricketts and Sawhill's measure (column B), which yields sharply lower counts of the "underclass" compared with my concept of "neighborhood poverty." The driving force behind the difference is the decrease in the dropout rate during the 1980s, making it less likely that a census tract would be one standard deviation above the 1980 mean. The conceptual issues discussed in chapter 1 and the empirical evidence suggest that the underclass measure is sensitive to small changes in its construction. In contrast, the neighborhood poverty numbers are more robust.

The Future American City

More than eight million Americans live in ghettos, barrios, and slums, nearly one-third of them children. If the trends of the 1970 to 1990 period continue, these numbers will increase as the middle class abandons ever-larger areas of central cities. Such neighborhoods are more than an eyesore or an inconvenience; they are at the very core of our metropolitan system that is the backbone of the national economy. It does not make sense to ignore the fact that so many of our citizens are born and grow up in neighborhoods that may well limit their ability to become productive citizens. This burden is borne very disproportionately by members of minority groups.

Several points are worth emphasizing. Despite the large and growing population of ghettos and barrios, most blacks and Hispanics and most poor of any race do not live in high-poverty areas. White employers should not assume that every black job applicant grew up in the 'hood, nor every Hispanic applicant in a gang-infested barrio. Second, not all residents of poor neighborhoods are themselves poor. In fact, more than half of the residents of high-poverty areas had family incomes above the poverty line. As the next chapter shows, most residents of ghettos and barrios do not conform to the stereotype of hardened antisocial members of the underclass, even if such persons are disproportionately found in these neighborhoods.

Another important point, and one that will be useful in the analysis of why neighborhood poverty has been increasing, is that neighborhood poverty rates vary greatly across demographic groups, regions of the country, and metropolitan areas. This variation provides an opportunity to employ multivariate techniques to learn what causes some metropolitan areas to have higher neighborhood poverty rates than others and what is behind its rapid growth since 1970. Understanding the causal mechanisms ' underlying neighborhood poverty is an important first step in the design of effective and politically viable policies to stabilize inner-city neighborhoods and improve economic opportunities for ghetto and barrio residents.

Chapter 4

Characteristics of
High-Poverty Neighborhoods

The harsh realities of life in poor inner-city neighborhoods have been vividly described by journalists (Auletta 1982; Dash 1989; Kotlowitz 1991; Kozol 1996). Such accounts tend to evoke a combination of rage and sympathy in those who read them. On the one hand, most readers feel compassion for the plight of those depicted in these accounts, especially the children. On the other hand, many readers find the behavior and attitudes of at least some of the adults and teenagers to be self-defeating and, in some cases, utterly contrary to their own values. Newspaper articles and books about ghettos and barrios, even the best of them, usually have the effect on readers of confirming what they already believe about urban poverty. Those who see the roots of poverty in individual failings can draw plenty of evidence from the life stories of the people described, while those who fault limited opportunities can find many examples of structural impediments to escaping poverty.

Sociologists and anthropologists who do ethnographic work in poor neighborhoods realize that merely depicting life in ghettos and barrios is not enough. By studying the lives of a few individuals in depth, as well as the social processes that take place within a neighborhood, these researchers attempt to learn how conditions in poor neighborhoods limit the opportunities of individuals and how individuals adapt to these conditions. To understand these interactions better, researchers often seek out those in whom the process seems to be most advanced. Much recent ethnographic research has therefore focused on individuals in high-poverty neighborhoods who reject mainstream values and become part of an oppositional culture marked by the absence of marriage, welfare dependency, inconsistent attachment to the labor force, frequent drug use, and criminal behavior (Anderson 1990, 1991, 1994; MacLeod 1995, 149; Ogbu 1986, 49; Sullivan 1989, 241–50). Social theorists trace the origin of these "underclass" characteristics to cultural adaptations taking place in the context of economic deprivation and social isolation (Mincy, Sawhill, and Wolf 1990; Ricketts and Sawhill 1988; Van Haitsma 1991; Wilson 1987). Such research is invaluable for understanding social stratification and the dynamics of poverty and dependency.

The logic of the research process can lead scholars to focus on the very worst neighborhoods, or the most pathological people within such neighborhoods (Liebow 1967, 20). Yet, many persons who live in high-poverty areas go to work each day, avoid the street for fear of crime, and do not hang out on street corners, unlike the subjects of Liebow's classic study, *Talley's Corner*.[1] In the tradition of an earlier generation of studies of urban slums (see Hannerz 1969, Liebow 1967, Suttles 1968), today's researchers are careful to point out that not all residents participate in underclass lifestyles. Unfortunately, this caveat is often ignored outside the research community, perhaps overshadowed by the dramatic portraits of the most alienated and socially dysfunctional residents of poor neighborhoods. As a result, current research may have unintentionally contributed to a "truncated and overly negative" image of ghetto or barrio residents (Snow, Anderson, and Koegel 1994, 472).[2] For suburban Americans, the image is continually reinforced by politicians arguing that social programs have destroyed the moral values of the poor, by sensational movies and television programs set in violent drug-infested neighborhoods, and by music videos that feature and glamorize urban gangs and rejection of authority.

While in no way denying the social problems associated with urban poverty nor the importance of research focusing on them, this chapter provides a useful balance to such accounts by filling in the rest of the picture. I use the 1990 census to construct a sociodemographic profile of all residents of high-poverty areas, and find that there is more heterogeneity within such neighborhoods than is commonly believed. Most important, residents of high-poverty neighborhoods are not nearly so cut off from the mainstream economy and mainstream values as popular stereotypes suggest. These findings have important implications for understanding the processes by which urban poverty coalesces, for assessing the nature and magnitude of neighborhood effects on individual outcomes, and for designing policies and programs to address urban blight.

Unfortunately, census data are somewhat "shallow" and can never provide as intimate a portrait of individuals or a community as actual research in the field. That is clearly a limitation; but what this method lacks in depth it makes up in breadth. *All* high-poverty neighborhoods in metropolitan areas are included and all persons who live in these neighborhoods are represented as long as they were not missed by the census. Because a nontrivial number of persons were missed, the findings here may be biased in the direction of "mainstream" sociodemographic patterns—that is, to the extent that the omissions are related to deviance from mainstream norms (Erickson, Kadane, and Tukey 1987). Thus, the findings presented below should be understood as a supplement to ethnographic studies, not an attempt to contradict or refute them.

As in the previous chapter, I use the 1990 data on nearly 45,000 metropolitan census tracts, which serve as proxies for neighborhoods. In table 4.1, neighborhoods are assigned to one of three categories, depending on their poverty rate: 0 to 19.9 percent; 20 to 39.9 percent; and 40 percent or more (high-poverty areas). The

Table 4.1 Census Tracts and Population by Income Level, by Neighborhood Poverty Level, 1990

	All Metropolitan Neighborhoods	Neighborhood Poverty Level		
		0–19.9%	20–39.9%	40–100%
Census tracts	44,748	77.9%	15.7%	6.4%
Persons				
All income levels	194,056,425	81.7	13.9	4.4
Below poverty level	22,832,835	50.9	31.9	17.2

Source: 1990 census, Summary Tape File 3A (CD-ROM), tabulations by the author.
Note: Percentages may not add to 100 because of rounding.

great majority of metropolitan neighborhoods—nearly eight in ten—fall into the lowest poverty category. Given that the U.S. poverty rate was about 13 percent at the time of the census, the neighborhoods in this category should be considered broadly typical of the residential experience in metropolitan America, and not some group of highly affluent neighborhoods selected to serve as a convenient "straw man." In fact, slightly more than half the metropolitan *poor* lived in the low-poverty neighborhoods in 1990, compared with only 17 percent in ghettos and barrios.

It is very important to distinguish between the issues of spatial concentrations of poor people and poverty among individuals. That many of the poor do not live in poor neighborhoods suggests that useful comparisons can be made between poor people who live in typical American neighborhoods and those who live in ghettos and barrios. Such comparisons could shed light on how poor neighborhoods affect people's behavior over and above the effects of poverty itself. Unfortunately, the structure of the publicly released tract data does not allow full use of this "comparison group." The data are provided by the Census Bureau as a series of neighborhood-level summaries rather than as data on individuals. Thus, only a few tables in the tract-level data can be cross-tabulated with poverty status.[3]

Physical Characteristics

The most visible sign of neighborhood poverty and abandonment is dilapidated housing. Sometimes the housing was shabby to begin with. In Jackson, Mississippi, ghetto housing often consists of shacks with tin roofs; the units were substandard the day they were built. In Memphis, some of the ghetto neighborhoods have shotgun shacks, especially north of Chelsea Avenue. In Little Rock, some housing in poor neighborhoods consists of one-room houses and deteriorating trailers. In other areas, the ghetto housing stock was originally middle-income housing that fell into disrepair through aging, disinvestment, and vandalism.

Vacant Units

Upon visiting ghetto neighborhoods, one notices almost immediately the high proportion of vacant housing units. This impression is consistent with the general exodus and decline in population density noted in chapter 2. For example, in Chicago's notorious Cabrini Green housing project, the top two floors were entirely vacant when I visited, as were many units on lower floors. Vacant units are far more than a sign of neighborhood abandonment. They become havens for drug use and other criminal activity, and the violence such activities bring with them threatens all the residents of a neighborhood. Table 4.2 shows the distribution of housing units within each neighborhood type by occupancy status (owner-occupied, rented, or vacant). Vacancy rates in high-poverty areas are nearly twice that in low-poverty ones.

State of Repair

Housing units in poor neighborhoods are also physically older. There is no direct measure in the census for the housing stock's state of repair, but the median year built of all housing units in each census tract is reported. (On average, one could expect older structures to be in worse condition than newer ones.) For high-poverty tracts, the median year built was 1954, eleven years older than the median for low-poverty neighborhoods (1965).[4] The median-year-built figures are truncated at 1939, which probably affects high-poverty tracts more, so the actual difference in ages may be greater than eleven years.

Table 4.2 Occupancy Status of Metropolitan Housing Units, by Neighborhood Poverty Level, 1990

	All Metropolitan Neighborhoods	Neighborhood Poverty Level		
		0–19.9%	20–39.9%	40–100%
Thousands of housing units	78,314	64,409	10,728	3,178
Occupancy status				
Owner-occupied	56.8%	61.6%	37.5%	24.1%
Rental unit	34.9	30.8	51.5	62.3
Vacant	8.3	7.6	11.0	13.6

Source: 1990 census, Summary Tape File 3A (CD-ROM), tabulations by the author.
Note: Percentages may not add to 100 because of rounding.

The median value of owner-occupied units in ghettos and barrios was $38,188 compared with $123,043 in low-poverty neighborhoods; median rents were $305 and $535, respectively.[5] These discrepancies in market values and rents are indicative of the general condition of the housing stock in poor neighborhoods. Other factors surely enter in, however, such as the local crime rate and, as is said in the real estate business, "location, location, location." But since high-poverty tracts are typically *closer* to downtown, one would expect property values to be *higher* there, other things being equal. Moreover, the economic incentive to invest in maintenance is lower for units with lower market values, assuming similar costs for standard maintenance.

Tenure

I had mentioned earlier an elderly couple who could not sell their house in Detroit's ghetto; even though it was very well maintained, its market value was less than $5,000. Many owners of rental properties in poor neighborhoods have an option this couple did not have. They can simply abandon a property when the potential rent no longer justifies the maintenance and tax costs. Of the occupied units in ghetto neighborhoods, about three-fourths are rental units; one-quarter comprises owner-occupied units. In comparison, in low-poverty neighborhoods, two-thirds of occupied housing units are owner-occupied.

Thus, the low proportion of homeowners in ghettos and barrios makes them susceptible to rapid disinvestment if the neighborhood declines. Homeownership rates in neighborhoods with high poverty rates do not vary much by race: 30 percent for non-Hispanic whites, 27 percent for non-Hispanic blacks, and 30 percent for Hispanics.[6] In the other two categories of neighborhoods, however, non-Hispanic whites are much more likely to own their homes than are blacks or Hispanics.

Economic Characteristics

It is neither surprising nor illuminating to discover that other indicators of economic distress reach disproportionate levels in high-poverty neighborhoods. But the exact pattern of economic discrepancies across metropolitan areas can provide insight into why some neighborhoods are so poor. For example, if high-poverty neighborhoods have the same labor force participation and employment rates but much lower wage rates, one would explain neighborhood poverty differently than if the reverse pattern were found. This section provides a cross-sectional economic snapshot of metropolitan neighborhoods, including labor force participation, employment, hours, wages, industry, occupation, and sources of household income, by neighborhood poverty level. Given the large difference in poverty levels between the neighborhoods, some of the similarities on economic measures are surprising.

Employment and Labor Force Participation

Table 4.3 details the distribution of adults aged sixteen and over in terms of gender and labor force status (excluding members of the armed forces). Striking differences in labor force participation by neighborhood poverty level are evident. Men in ghettos, barrios, and slums are nearly twice as likely to be out of the labor force— not even looking for work. Only about one-third of adult women are employed and more than half are not in the labor force. In low-poverty neighborhoods, three of every four males are employed, compared with less than half in high-poverty areas. The proportion of *all* adult males who are unemployed is much higher in the poorest neighborhoods: 11 percent compared with 4 percent in low-poverty neighborhoods. The disparity in unemployment rates—the proportion of adult males *in the labor force* who are unemployed— is even greater: 18 percent compared with 5 percent.

Disaggregating by race reveals that the differences described above cannot be attributed to differences in neighborhoods' racial composition. Blacks in wealthier tracts are similar to the whites in those areas: two-thirds of black males are employed compared with 74 percent of white males. Employment rates are actually higher for black women than for white women in those areas. Similarly, in the poorest neighborhoods, all three groups—whites, blacks, and Hispanics—have much lower percentages of adults employed and higher percentages not in the labor force. About the same proportion of white and black men were out of the labor force, although white men have a small advantage when it comes to being

Table 4.3   Labor Force and Employment Status by Gender and
Race/Ethnicity, by Neighborhood Poverty Level, 1990

	All Metropolitan Neighborhoods	Neighborhood Poverty Level		
		0–19.9%	20–39.9%	40–100%
Total men (000s)	70,627	58,341	9,481	2,805
Employed	70.8%	73.5%	61.1%	46.3%
Unemployed	4.7	3.9	8.0	10.5
Not in Labor Force	24.5	22.6	30.9	43.3
White men (000s)	56,901	50,525	5,246	1,130
Employed	72.4%	73.9%	63.0%	49.4%
Unemployed	3.9	3.6	6.3	7.1
Not in Labor Force	23.7	22.5	30.7	43.4
Black men (000s)	7,929	4,017	2,667	1,245
Employed	58.4%	66.7%	54.0%	40.9%
Unemployed	9.4	7.0	11.0	13.5
Not in Labor Force	32.3	26.3	35.1	45.6
Hispanic men (000s)	6,797	3,939	2,203	655
Employed	71.7%	76.2%	68.6%	55.4%
Unemployed	7.7	6.1	9.4	11.2
Not in Labor Force	20.6	17.7	22.0	33.5
Total women (000s)	78,108	64,263	10,561	3,284
Employed	54.6%	56.9%	46.4%	36.0%
Unemployed	3.5	2.9	5.8	7.6
Not in Labor Force	41.9	40.2	47.7	56.4
White women (000s)	62,440	55,629	5,659	1,152
Employed	55.0%	56.3%	45.7%	38.4%
Unemployed	2.8	2.6	4.3	4.8
Not in Labor Force	42.3	41.2	50.0	56.8
Black women (000s)	9,756	4,677	3,389	1,689
Employed	53.4%	63.5%	48.5%	35.2%
Unemployed	7.2	5.7	7.9	9.6
Not in Labor Force	39.5	30.8	43.6	55.1
Hispanic women (000s)	6,757	3,936	2,125	696
Employed	50.2%	56.7%	43.9%	32.9%
Unemployed	6.2	5.3	7.5	7.5
Not in Labor Force	43.6	38.0	48.6	59.5

Source: 1990 census, Summary Tape File 3A (CD-ROM), tabulations by the author.
Notes: Includes persons 16 years and over, excluding members of the armed forces.
Hispanics may be of any race. Percentages may not add to 100 because of rounding.

employed. Hispanics were out of the labor force less and worked more than either whites or blacks. The sharpest contrasts, however, are not among racial and ethnic groups within neighborhoods but across neighborhood poverty levels.

Hours and Wages

Employment is only part of the story. The quality of jobs—their pay, stability, working conditions, and on-the-job training—compound the differences in employment. As shown in table 4.4, residents of poor neighborhoods are less likely to hold full-year, full-time jobs. More than half the men in wealthier neighborhoods hold these "family breadwinner" jobs, whereas less than one-fourth of ghetto and barrio males do. During 1989, about 40 percent of males in poor neighborhoods worked either part of the year or part time, and nearly as many did not work at all.[7] Similarly, only 15 percent of women in ghetto neighborhoods worked at full-year, full-time jobs compared with 24 and 32 percent in the mid- and low-poverty areas, respectively.

Perhaps the most important attribute of a job is its wage. Unfortunately, wages are not reported in the tract-level data, only total

Table 4.4   Distribution of Adults by Gender and Weeks and Hours Worked, by Neighborhood Poverty Level, 1990

	All Metropolitan Neighborhoods	Neighborhood Poverty Level		
		0–19.9%	20–39.9%	40–100%
Male (000s)	71,823	59,465	9,545	2,813
Full year and full time	51.1%	54.6%	37.6%	23.7%
Part year or part time	28.7	27.3	34.5	39.6
No work during year	20.2	18.1	27.9	36.7
Female (000s)	78,261	64,404	10,572	3,286
Full year and full time	30.0%	31.7%	24.1%	15.4%
Part year or part time	33.2	33.3	32.0	33.6
No work during year	36.8	35.0	44.0	51.0

Source: 1990 census, Summary Tape File 3A (CD-ROM), tabulations by the author.
Notes: Includes persons 16 years and older. Percentages may not add to 100 because of rounding.

wage and salary income. Approximate average wages can be calculated by estimating the total hours worked. First, the number of full-year, full-time workers is multiplied by 2,000, on the assumption that such workers worked fifty weeks and forty hours per week. Assume that, on average, part-time and part-year workers worked half that, or 1,000 hours. Then the aggregate reported wage and salary income is divided by the estimated total number of hours worked. The estimated wage is $13.00 an hour in the low-poverty neighborhoods, $8.21 an hour in the mid-poverty neighborhoods, and only $5.72 an hour in the high-poverty areas. Full-time work at the average ghetto, barrio, or slum wage would yield $11,440—not enough to lift a family of four above the 1989 poverty line ($12,674).

Industry and Occupation

Table 4.5 profiles adult workers by industrial sector and occupation for the three neighborhood types. Interestingly, workers in high-poverty neighborhoods work in roughly the same industries as other workers. Slightly fewer are in manufacturing industries and in finance, insurance, and real estate; somewhat more work in service industries. But the similarities in industrial structure are more striking than the differences, especially in light of the vast differences in employment and hours.

Despite the similarity in *industry* of employment, the *occupational titles* of workers in poor neighborhoods differ markedly from those of their counterparts in better-off neighborhoods. Far fewer ghetto and barrio workers are managers and professionals. More than twice as many are employed in service occupations. Many more have low-skill occupations—operator, assembler, inspector, driver, and manual laborer. Similarly, a smaller share of workers in high-poverty (28 percent) and mid-poverty (29 percent) neighborhoods are in technical, sales, and administrative support positions than are workers in low-poverty neighborhoods (34 percent). It seems reasonable to assume that a more detailed breakdown would show a larger skill disparity between neighborhoods, with more of the technical support jobs in wealthier neighborhoods and more clerical and sales support jobs in poor neighborhoods.

Table 4.5   Employed Persons by Industry and Occupation, by
              Neighborhood Poverty Level, 1990

	All Metropolitan Neighborhoods	Neighborhood Poverty Level		
		0–19.9%	20–39.9%	40–100%
All employed persons (000s)	92,640	79,470	10,691	2,479
Industry				
Agri., forestry, fishing	1.7%	1.6%	2.6%	2.2%
Mining	0.4	0.4	0.5	0.3
Construction	6.1	6.1	6.0	5.3
Manufacturing	16.9	16.9	17.2	14.1
Trans., comm., util.	7.3	7.4	6.9	6.1
Wholesale and retail trade	21.5	21.4	21.8	22.5
FIRE	7.6	8.0	5.4	4.5
Service industries	33.6	33.2	35.0	40.7
Public administration	4.9	4.9	4.6	4.4
Occupation				
Managers, prof. specialty	28.0%	29.8%	17.7%	15.4%
Tech., sales, admin. support	33.2	34.0	28.8	28.4
Service occupations	13.0	11.7	19.7	25.2
Farming, forestry, fishing	1.6	1.4	2.5	2.3
Production, craft, repair	10.8	10.8	11.1	8.6
Operators, assemblers, inspectors	6.0	5.4	9.6	9.1
Transportation, moving	3.7	3.5	4.9	4.7
Helpers, cleaners, laborers	3.7	3.3	5.7	6.2

Source: 1990 census, Summary Tape File 3A (CD-ROM), tabulations by the author.
Notes: Includes employed persons, 16 years and older. Percentages may not add to
100 because of rounding. FIRE stands for finance, insurance, and real estate.

That the *industrial* classifications of jobs are similar but the *occupational* profiles differ raises several points. The labor market in which ghetto and barrio residents compete is similar in structure to the metropolitan area as a whole. Ghetto and barrio residents are not restricted to narrow segments of the labor market, such as services or retail. They compete in the same labor market as everyone else. They do, however, tend to get jobs in the lower-skilled occupations across all the industrial sectors. For a more definitive argument, one would need to know about the access to firms and establishments within industrial groups, but it appears that ghetto and barrio residents are not shut out of entire segments of the labor market. Instead, they tend to get the least rewarding jobs in all sectors.

Sources of Income

One of the most persistent images in American politics and, to a certain extent, the academic literature, is the notion of people inside ghetto and barrio neighborhoods shunning the world of work and passively collecting welfare payments. The veracity of this image can be examined through the use of census data on the sources and amounts of household income in 1989 for different neighborhoods, as shown in table 4.6.

The *relative* contribution of each income source differs little among the neighborhood types. About three-quarters of total neighborhood income in all three categories comes from wages and salaries. The proportion of households with income from wages and salaries declines as the neighborhood poverty rate increases from 81 percent down to 63 percent. Yet considerably more than half of the households in the poorest category of neighborhood receive at least some income from wages and salaries (although the average amount received per household is less than half that of households in better-off neighborhoods).

Not surprisingly, the proportion receiving public assistance differs markedly across the neighborhood types.[8] Fewer than one in twenty receive public assistance in the more affluent neighborhoods, compared with six in twenty in the poorest. But the amounts received are very low, about $4,000 regardless of neighborhood type. As a result, even in ghettos and barrios, public assistance contributes little to the total income of the neighborhood—only 6.9 percent of the neighborhood's total income.

Table 4.6   Household Income by Source, by Neighborhood Poverty Level, 1990

	All Metropolitan Neighborhoods	Neighborhood Poverty Level		
		0–19.9%	20–39.9%	40–100%
Total households (000s)	71,854	59,578	9,532	2,744
Households receiving[a]				
Wages and salaries	78.8%	80.5%	72.9%	62.6%
Self-employment	11.6	12.6	7.5	4.9
Farm income	1.2	1.3	0.8	0.4
Interest and dividends	41.8	46.2	22.8	13.5
Social security	24.8	24.7	25.8	25.6
Public assistance	7.2	4.8	16.0	29.4
Other pensions	15.6	16.2	13.1	10.3
Other income	9.8	9.8	10.2	10.2
Average amount per household[b]				
Wages and salaries	$87,510	$42,452	$25,822	$19,235
Self-employment	$46,364	$22,619	$13,300	$10,445
Farm income	$24,406	$8,720	$8,749	$6,937
Interest and dividends	$16,095	$7,436	$4,837	$3,822
Social security	$20,913	$8,230	$6,807	$5,876
Public assistance	$12,607	$4,394	$4,278	$3,935
Other pensions	$23,218	$9,961	$7,179	$6,078
Other income	$11,636	$4,437	$3,728	$3,471
Percent of total neighborhood income[c]				
Wages and salaries	76.1%	76.2%	76.0%	72.0%
Self-employment	6.1	6.3	4.0	3.0
Farm income	0.3	0.3	0.3	0.2
Interest and dividends	7.3	7.7	4.5	3.1
Social security	4.8	4.5	7.1	9.0
Public assistance	0.8	0.5	2.8	6.9
Other pensions	3.6	3.62	3.8	3.7
Other income	1.0	1.0	1.5	2.1

Source: 1990 census, Summary Tape File 3A (CD-ROM), tabulations by the author.
[a] Since households can receive income from more than one source, percentages add to more than 100.
[b] Includes only those households with at least some income from that source.
[c] Percentages may not add to 100 because of rounding.

Although a much smaller percentage of households in low-poverty neighborhoods receive public assistance, the base number of such households is far greater. The number of households receiving public assistance is actually greatest in the neighborhoods with the lowest poverty rates. Table 4.7 shows the actual number of households receiving income from each source; in contrast to table 4.6, it shows the percentages across rather than within neighborhood types. More than half of all households receiving public assistance are in neighborhoods with relatively low poverty rates, and only one in six households on public assistance are in ghetto neighborhoods. These findings negate the impression that only residents of inner-city ghettos receive public assistance—a notion that erodes public support for such programs. It also suggests that geographic targeting of services aimed at welfare recipients may miss many of its intended beneficiaries.[9]

Wealth, as opposed to income, is not reported in the census. Interest and dividend income, however, is correlated with wealth at least in terms of financial assets. Here the disparity between

Table 4.7   Households by Source of Income, by Neighborhood Poverty Level, 1990

	All Metropolitan Neighborhoods	Neighborhood Poverty Level		
		0–19.9%	20–39.9%	40–100%
Total households	71,854,000	82.9%	13.3%	3.8%
Households receiving[a]				
Wages and salaries	56,644	84.7%	12.3%	3.0%
Self-employment	8,355	89.8	8.6	1.6
Farm income	868	90.1	8.5	1.4
Interest and dividends	30,063	91.5	7.2	1.2
Social security	17,851	82.3	13.8	3.9
Public assistance	5,190	55.0	29.4	15.6
Other pensions	11,208	86.4	11.1	2.5
Other income	7,076	82.4	13.7	4.0

Source: 1990 census, Summary Tape File 3A (CD-ROM), tabulations by the author.
[a] Since households can receive income from more than one source, numbers may add to more than totals. Percentages may not add to 100 because of rounding.

neighborhood types is great. Table 4.6 shows that nearly half the households in the wealthiest group of neighborhoods received interest and dividend income averaging $7,400 per household, whereas only about one in eight households in the poorest neighborhoods got any interest or dividends, and the average for those households that did was $3,800. Although interest and dividend income in that range indicates substantial income-generating assets for some households, 86.5 percent of ghetto and barrio households reported no interest or dividend income at all. Thus, the average interest and dividend income for all households in the ghettos and barrios is $512, with a highly skewed distribution.

Obstacles to Employment

Residents of high-poverty areas have lower labor force participation, higher unemployment, more part-time jobs, and lower wages than residents of other neighborhoods, yet they receive approximately the same proportion of their total income from wages and salaries and tend to work in the same industries as residents of other neighborhoods. Undoubtedly, differences in educational attainment, racial discrimination in hiring, and other factors contribute to the poorer economic status of ghetto and barrio residents. In this section, I address several other factors that help to explain why they fare so poorly in the labor market.

Disability

One important obstacle to economic self-sufficiency is disability. Disability is a multifaceted concept that resists simple categorizations. The census asks people whether they have a "work disability," that is, a disability that limits the amount of work they can do or prevents them from working entirely. The answers are subjective, and people with the same physical disability might answer the question differently. In part, the answer will depend on an individual's skills and abilities. For example, people confined to wheelchairs are readily employable, but not for all kinds of work. The census reveals many people who say they have a work disability and yet report they are employed or looking for work.

To focus on those for whom disability is a bar to self-sufficiency, table 4.8 shows the number and percentage of working-age men who are prevented from working by a disability, as well as the group's contribution to overall nonparticipation in the labor force. One in twelve working-age males living in high-poverty areas reported being disabled to this extreme degree—nearly triple the rate for men in nonpoor neighborhoods. Many more may be partially disabled in ways that limit the type or amount of work they are able to do.

Although 8.5 percent of working-age males in high-poverty neighborhoods are prevented from working by disabilities, their numbers do not appear to explain the higher relative proportion of males in ghettos and barrios who are not in the labor force (see table 4.3). Those prevented from working because of disabilities make up about the same proportion of nonelderly males outside the labor force as one would find in low-poverty neighborhoods. The implication is that while disability as a source of labor force non-participation in high-poverty neighborhoods is nearly triple that in low-poverty ones, other reasons for not being in the labor force—such as caring for dependents, attending school, engaging in the underground economy—are similarly elevated.

Choice of Transportation

Assuming people can work, how do they get to their destination? The answers have potentially important implications for public pol-

Table 4.8   Nonelderly Males Prevented from Working by a Disability, by Neighborhood Poverty Level, 1990

	All Metropolitan Neighborhoods	Neighborhood Poverty Level		
		0–19.9%	20–39.9%	40–100%
Prevented from working by a disability (000s)	2,236	1,522	509	205
As a percentage of total males, 16–64	3.7%	3.0%	6.2%	8.5%
Not in the labor force	25.0	24.2	28.1	24.1

Source: 1990 census, Summary Tape File 3A (CD-ROM), tabulations by the author.

icy. The primary mode of transportation in ghettos and barrios is the same as in other neighborhoods: cars, trucks, and vans. The *degree* of reliance on motor vehicles differs by neighborhood type, however. Nationally, in more affluent neighborhoods, close to nine in ten people use motor vehicles to get to work, compared with about two-thirds in poor neighborhoods. The difference is made up by greater reliance on public transportation (19.5 percent) and on motorcycles, bicycles, walking, and other means (15.5 percent). As one might expect, the figure for public transportation is much higher in the Northeast, where more than 45 percent of ghetto residents use public transportation to get to work. This confirms Hughes's observation that the changing spatial distribution of jobs may be more of an issue in older industrial cities where residents are more dependent on an outmoded transportation system (Hughes 1989b).

Travel Time

The "spatial mismatch hypothesis" (Ellwood 1986, Kain 1968) argues that job growth has centered on the urban periphery, which limits employment possibilities for inner-city residents in several ways. One aspect of the theory is that long commutes discourage people from working by lowering their effective wage. Yet table 4.9 shows that the journey to work does not differ much by neighborhood poverty, except in the Northeast. The commute for employed people is 23.2 minutes, with little variation by neighborhood poverty level. This finding is especially surprising given the differences in modes of transportation to work.

Regions of the country and metropolitan areas vary greatly in terms of spatial organization and transportation networks. Repeating the calculation of travel times separately by region and city, I find that the national pattern is replicated in all regions but the Northeast, where commutes averaged 29.5 minutes for workers in high-poverty neighborhoods compared with 24.9 minutes for workers in low-poverty neighborhoods. New York and Chicago are noteworthy for having much longer travel times in general and relatively large "penalties" for workers in high-poverty neighborhoods. Several other large cities have longer commutes for ghetto and barrio residents (see table 4.9), but more than three hundred

Table 4.9 Commuting Times and Penalties for Workers in High-Poverty
Neighborhoods, by Region and Metropolitan Area, 1990

	Average Commute from High-Poverty Areas (minutes)	Difference from Low-Poverty Areas (minutes)	Rank[a]
All metropolitan areas	22.5	−0.28	—
Northeast	29.5	+4.58	—
Midwest	20.5	−1.25	—
South	20.9	−1.83	—
West	21.4	−2.25	—
Selected metro. areas			
Chicago, IL	33.4	+5.4	5
New York, NY	36.9	+3.4	11
Baltimore, MD	28.9	+3.0	16
Milwaukee, WI	22.3	+2.4	24
Los Angeles, CA	28.1	+1.9	30

Source: 1990 census, Summary Tape File 3A (CD-ROM), tabulations by the author.
[a] Rank among metropolitan areas with respect to the difference in average travel times for workers 16 or older in high-poverty neighborhoods compared with low-poverty neighborhoods.

metropolitan areas have commuting differentials of less than two minutes.

To be fair, there are a few reasons why the commuting data may understate the issue of job accessibility. First, it would be more appropriate to study travel times for "marginal workers." In other words, the *average* travel time may reflect an earlier era when jobs were generated in a pattern more favorable to inner-city residents. New jobs, in contrast, may be farther away and, hence, less accessible to those seeking employment. Second, the figures reflect only people who are working. Someone who never heard about a job or could not get out to interview for one because it was too far away is not employed, and so we do not know what the travel time would have been. Still, the data on travel time at least suggest that distance in itself does not prevent ghetto and barrio residents from being employed, although travel time may be a problem in selected cities.

Social Characteristics

The social pathologies of the ghetto, as they are called, are deeply disturbing to some analysts, who view them as the symptoms of "a much more general deterioration of American Society and culture." In this view, "a spreading underclass culture is undermining the country's productive capacity, family life, social integration, and, ultimately, its political stability" (as summarized by Peterson 1991, 9). Many Americans feel uncomfortable reading articles such as "The Code of the Streets," by Elijah Anderson, which describes an "oppositional culture" among urban black youth (Anderson 1994). This culture seems alien, and its adherents seem locked in an unbreakable cycle of alienation, conflict, and failure.

At the same time, Anderson points out that many ghetto families "tend to accept mainstream values . . . and attempt to instill them in their children. . . . They are generally 'working poor.' . . . They value hard work and self-reliance and are willing to sacrifice for their children" (Anderson 1994, 82–83). The "decent" culture and the "street" culture, Anderson argues, are part of a continuum, and "many people in the community slip back and forth between decent and street behavior" (p. 94).

The key question is whether the observed deviations from mainstream norms are caused to some degree by the prevailing economic or social conditions of the neighborhoods. Merely observing that "social pathologies" are disproportionately represented in poor neighborhoods is not sufficient, in itself, to prove the existence of neighborhood effects because spatial concentrations of social problems could well arise through selective migration (Tienda 1991). The best way to control for selection of this sort is to use longitudinal data with rich controls for family background. Census data satisfy neither of these criteria. Thus, my purpose in this section is not to try to prove or disprove the existence of neighborhood effects but to show the extent to which residents of high-poverty neighborhoods differ from other metropolitan area residents on a number of social dimensions.

Family Structure

One of the sharpest divisions between high-poverty areas and the rest of society is the prevalence of single-parent families. Table 4.10

Table 4.10   Female-Headed Families as a Percent of All Families with
Children by Race and Income Level, by Neighborhood Poverty
Level, 1990

	All Metropolitan Neighborhoods	Neighborhood Poverty Level		
		0–19.9%	20–39.9%	40–100%
All female-headed				
families with children	19.4%	14.9%	35.5%	56.6%
Above poverty line	12.2	11.2	19.7	23.9
Below poverty line	60.9	55.2	62.4	73.1
White female-headed				
families with children	14.2	13.0	24.9	33.8
Above poverty line	10.2	9.9	13.4	12.9
Below poverty line	52.7	52.8	52.7	51.5
Black female-headed				
families with children	48.4	35.7	55.7	71.9
Above poverty line	29.9	26.8	35.4	36.3
Below poverty line	80.2	74.4	79.8	85.3
Hispanic female-headed				
families with children	22.7	17.4	26.6	38.7
Above poverty line	12.2	11.7	13.2	13.3
Below poverty line	48.1	45.5	47.2	53.8

Source: 1990 census, Summary Tape File 3A (CD-ROM), tabulations by the author.
Notes: Figures shown are the percentage of all families with children headed by a
single female. Percentages of families headed by single males or married couples are
not shown separately. Thus, the percentages do not add to 100 in any direction.

shows the percentage of all families with children that are headed
by a single woman, by race, poverty status, and neighborhood
type.[10] Female-headed families constitute less than 15 percent of the
families with children in low-poverty neighborhoods. That proportion is nearly double in neighborhoods with mid-levels of poverty.
In high-poverty neighborhoods, more than half of families with children were headed by women as were more than seven in ten black
families with children.

The widely noted breakdown of the family *is* characteristic of
poor neighborhoods, particularly ghettos. But to ascribe all of the

difference in family structure to the effects of living in a ghetto (that is, "concentration effects" or "neighborhood effects") would be incorrect. The dearth of married-couple families in high-poverty neighborhoods could result from two sources that have nothing to do with "ghetto culture":

> Female-headed families tend to be poor no matter where they live. Where large numbers of female-headed families are clustered, perhaps because of public housing patterns or low rents, the poverty rate will be high. The poverty status of the neighborhood may, however, simply be a reflection of families' marital status rather than a cause of it.

> High-poverty neighborhoods are disproportionately composed of members of minority groups, who have higher rates of female-headed families than whites no matter where they live, even after controlling for family income.

Table 4.10 partially addresses these issues.[11] The overall difference in the percentage of female-headed families between the poorest and the least poor neighborhoods is more than 40 percentage points (56.6 percent less 14.9 percent). As noted above, black families are more likely than white or Hispanic families to be headed by a single woman. Among whites and Hispanics, the difference between the two neighborhood types is 20 percentage points. Among blacks, it is 35 percentage points. Thus, at least part of the 40-point difference is an artifact of racial composition.

Poverty status is even more important. Are the poor in ghettos and barrios different from the poor in other neighborhoods? If not, then the case for neighborhood effects and a social milieu that fosters single parenthood is weakened. Table 4.10 speaks to this issue. Poor families have high rates of female-headed households regardless of the neighborhood's poverty status. In fact, 55.2 percent of poor families with children are headed by females, even in the most affluent neighborhoods. The difference in rates of female-headship among neighborhoods is less than 20 percentage points for both poor and nonpoor families. In other words, controlling for poverty status accounts for nearly half the disparity in the proportion of female-headed households across neighborhoods.[12]

Simultaneously controlling for race and poverty yields dramatic results. The differences in female-headship across neighborhoods are sharply reduced. Poor white families in low-poverty neighborhoods are actually slightly more likely to be headed by a single mother than in slum neighborhoods. Nonpoor white and Hispanic families are only slightly more likely to be headed by a woman if they live in high-poverty neighborhoods. For poor Hispanic families, the difference is 8.3 percentage points. For blacks, it is 9.5 and 10.9 percentage points for nonpoor and poor families, respectively.

The point here is not to deny the possibility of neighborhood effects. Rather, it is to show that it is unwise to assume that social problems observed in a ghetto or barrio are caused by the culture of the neighborhood, such as an increased tolerance of out-of-wedlock births. Some of the social characteristics are common to poor people or minority groups *wherever* they live. They simply happen to be most visible in ghettos and barrios because people who share the characteristic are concentrated there.

Educational Attainment

Schools in poor inner-city neighborhoods, with some notable exceptions, are dangerous, overcrowded, and ineffective. Moreover, children in those schools, seeing the unemployment and poor earnings of the adults in their neighborhood, may conclude that education has little value. As a result, the educational attainment of adults is far below that in other neighborhoods. Whereas only one in five residents of low-poverty neighborhoods are high school dropouts, more than half of the residents of poor neighborhoods do not complete high school (see table 4.11). More than 30 percent of the residents of better-off neighborhoods earn a college degree (associate, bachelor's, or higher), and another 20 percent have some college experience, bringing the total with college experience to half. In contrast, fewer than one in eight residents of poor neighborhoods has a degree, and only one in four has any exposure to college.

These figures are likely to underestimate the educational disparities across different neighborhood types. On average, inner-city schools have far lower standards, and potential employers may view a degree from a notorious inner-city high school quite differently

Table 4.11   Educational Attainment of Adults, by Neighborhood Poverty
Level, 1990

	All Metropolitan Neighborhoods	Neighborhood Poverty Level		
		0–19.9%	20–39.9%	40–100%
Persons, 25 and older (000s)	124,228	104,293	15,678	4,256
Educational attainment				
High school dropout	23.0%	19.2%	40.7%	51.7%
High school graduate	28.7	29.1	27.3	23.9
Some college	19.5	20.4	15.6	12.7
Two-year degree	6.4	6.8	4.6	3.4
Four-year degree	14.4	15.8	7.5	5.0
Grad. or prof. degree	8.0	8.8	4.3	3.2

Source: 1990 census, Summary Tape File 3A (CD-ROM), tabulations by the author.
Notes: Includes adults age 25 and older. Percentages may not add to 100 because of rounding.

than one from a suburban high school. Both the real and perceived
disparities in educational quality may mean that a degree from an
inner-city high school or community college is worth less than comparable degrees from other institutions. In effect, the low quality of
inner-city education devalues one of the principal routes out of
poverty and punishes those who attempt to play by the rules and
stay in school.

School, Work, and Idleness

The high number of dropouts is cause for concern given the economy's increasingly technological orientation. Some argue, however,
that students who drop out do so to work and support a family, and
that work is as valid a means of building human capital as school.
Unfortunately, in ghettos and barrios, those who drop out often are
not working. Table 4.12 shows the activities of older teenagers
(youths 16–19 years old). Most are in school, regardless of neighborhood type. In fact, youths in poor neighborhoods are almost as
likely to be in school as those in low-poverty neighborhoods and
more likely than those in mid-poverty neighborhoods.

Table 4.12   Educational and Labor Force Status of Teenagers by
Race/Ethnicity, by Neighborhood Poverty Level, 1990

	All Metropolitan Neighborhoods	Neighborhood Poverty Level		
		0– 19.9%	20– 39.9%	40– 100%
Total teenagers (000s)	10,828	8,258	1,793	777
In school	78.2%	79.5%	72.3%	78.4%
Not in school— H.S. graduate				
Employed	7.3	8.2	5.5	2.8
Unemployed	1.2	1.1	1.6	1.2
Not in labor force	1.9	1.7	2.6	2.4
Not in school—Dropout				
Employed	4.6	4.4	6.3	3.3
Unemployed	1.9	1.5	3.3	2.8
Not in labor force	4.8	3.6	8.4	9.0
White teenagers (000s)	7,910	6,733	839	338
In school	79.2%	79.6%	72.5%	86.6%
Not in school— H.S. graduate				
Employed	8.3	8.7	6.7	2.4
Unemployed	1.1	1.1	1.3	0.6
Not in labor force	1.6	1.5	2.3	1.3
Not in school—Dropout				
Employed	4.6	4.4	6.9	2.6
Unemployed	1.6	1.5	3.2	1.6
Not in labor force	3.6	3.1	7.2	4.9

In low-poverty neighborhoods, more of those not in school are
high school graduates than dropouts (11 percent compared with 9.5
percent, obtained by adding up the shares for the three categories
of labor force status). In poor neighborhoods, nearly twice as many
teens not in school are dropouts (15 percent), compared with graduates (6 percent). Whether graduates or not, teens in ghettos and
barrios are much more likely to be unemployed or not in the labor
force. But most teenagers in these neighborhoods were in school,
in contrast to the stereotype.

Table 4.12   *(continued)*

	All Metropolitan Neighborhoods	Neighborhood Poverty Level		
		0–19.9%	20–39.9%	40–100%
Black teenagers (000s)	1,717	797	599	321
In school	75.8%	78.9%	73.9%	71.9%
Not in school— H.S. graduate				
Employed	5.1	6.0	4.9	3.3
Unemployed	2.1	1.9	2.3	2.1
Not in labor force	3.1	2.7	3.3	3.7
Not in school—Dropout				
Employed	3.0	2.8	3.3	2.8
Unemployed	2.8	1.9	3.4	3.9
Not in labor force	8.1	5.8	8.9	12.3
Hispanic Teenagers (000s)	1,422	767	486	169
In school	69.4%	71.7%	65.7%	69.8%
Not in school— H.S. graduate				
Employed	5.4	6.5	4.4	3.1
Unemployed	1.1	1.1	1.2	1.0
Not in labor force	2.0	1.9	2.2	2.0
Not in school—Dropout				
Employed	9.8	9.3	11.5	7.2
Unemployed	3.4	2.7	4.2	3.9
Not in labor force	9.0	6.8	11.0	13.0

Source: 1990 census, Summary Tape File 3A (CD-ROM), tabulations by the author.
Notes: Includes 16- to 19-year-olds not in the armed forces. Percentages may not add to 100 because of rounding.

Economic Conditions of Children

Economic disadvantage and the high degree of family breakup combine to create dreadful conditions for the children in poor neighborhoods. Nearly six in ten of these children live in a female-headed family. And although all family types in the high-poverty areas have high rates of poverty, as one would expect, the rate for children in female-headed families is a shocking 78.4 percent, as shown in table 4.13. Female-headed families have high rates of poverty

Table 4.13   Poverty Rates of Children by Age and Family Structure, by
Neighborhood Poverty Level, 1990

	All Metropolitan Neighborhoods	Neighborhood Poverty Level		
		0–19.9%	20–39.9%	40–100%
Children, 0–4 years				
Married couple	8.8%	5.5%	24.6%	44.6%
Male-headed	26.2	18.1	38.0	54.4
Female-headed	59.1	45.0	68.6	82.8
Children, 0–17 years				
Married couple	8.0%	4.9%	23.1%	42.6%
Male-headed	21.8	14.2	35.8	51.7
Female-headed	47.9	33.2	62.0	78.4

Source: 1990 census, Summary Tape File 3A (CD-ROM), tabulations by the author.

regardless of neighborhood type, but in ghettos and barrios their poverty rate is more than twice that in low-poverty neighborhoods. Even children in married-couple families have a high rate of poverty in the poorest census tracts—42.6 percent. The poverty rates for younger children aged 0 to 4 years are even higher. There is never a good time to be in a poor family, but the consequences may be worse for very young children. Poor nutrition, a harsh and unstimulating environment, exposure to lead, and other concomitants of poverty in the earliest years may have lasting effects on a child's development.

The Complex Reality of Life in America's Poor Neighborhoods

The extreme poverty of ghettos and barrios notwithstanding, the popular and politically exploitable image of ghettos and barrios as places where everyone drops out of school, no one works, and everyone receives welfare is a gross distortion of reality. Many of their residents work, albeit at lower-skill occupations for fewer hours and lower wages. Earnings account for about the same proportion of total income in ghettos and barrios as elsewhere.

Although households on public assistance are more common in these high-poverty neighborhoods, most residents receive no government assistance. Most of the teenagers are in school. People who work tend to be employed in the same industries as residents of other neighborhoods and spend about the same time commuting to their jobs. Although census data do not allow for analysis of such aspects of ghetto life as the levels of crime or drug use, the picture that emerges is not the popular image of ghetto neighborhoods as otherworldly, a class apart.

The major exception is the rather complete breakdown of the married-couple family as the childrearing unit. Yet even here, the high levels of mother-only families are mostly due to the composition of the neighborhoods. Ghettos have high proportions of poor and minority families, who have high rates of female-headship wherever they live. If there is a neighborhood effect on family structure, working through a ghetto culture, it appears to be small compared with the effects that operate through race and poverty. Ghetto and barrio neighborhoods cannot, then, be understood in isolation from "the general social and economic trends evident to some degree in the whole society which have more adversely affected the most disadvantaged members of the society, the inner-city minority poor" (Jackson 1993, 436).

Elliot Liebow (1967) in *Talley's Corner*, reached a similar conclusion: "[The ghetto] does not appear as a self-contained, self-generating, self-sustaining system or even sub-system with clear boundaries marking it off from the larger world around it. It is in continuous, intimate contact with the larger society—indeed, is an integral part of it—and is no more impervious to the values, sentiments and beliefs of the larger society . . ." (p. 209).

Liebow found that most of the "streetcorner men" he studied held many mainstream values, attitudes, and goals, but were unable to succeed by middle-class criteria. Much has changed in the thirty years since Liebow did his fieldwork, but the 1990 data on conditions in high-poverty areas remain consistent with Liebow's conclusions. There are some ghetto and barrio residents, particularly gang-involved young males, who behave in antisocial and self-destructive ways, but they are hardly the whole story.

Chapter 5

Theory and Evidence on Inner-City Poverty

The widespread physical expansion of blighted urban neighbor-hoods is a troubling phenomenon for neighborhood residents and policymakers alike. We have seen, particularly in the analysis of Milwaukee's ghetto expansion, that such neighborhoods are the result of complex interactions between the economy, racial segre-gation, and economic segregation. Despite widespread agreement that economic changes and settlement patterns both have impor-tant roles in ghetto and barrio formation, there is no consensus on the relative roles of economic change, racial and ethnic segregation, and economic segregation. Even less agreement exists about whether an entrenched neighborhood culture, having arisen as a reaction to economic impoverishment or the incentive effects of government assistance programs, now acts to sustain and expand the ghetto (Mead 1987; Murray 1984).

A growing body of literature attempts to formulate and test hypotheses about the causal determinants of concentrated urban poverty and related phenomena, such as the underclass. These hypotheses may be divided into those which principally concern metropolitan-scale economic changes; those which emphasize the spatial patterning of persons of different races and incomes; and those which focus on how neighborhoods affect values, behavior, or outcomes. In this chapter, I focus on the first two types of hypotheses: structural economic transformations and segregation by race and income.

Any discussion of this literature is complicated by researchers' use of different dependent variables, as noted in chapter 1. For example, the causal structure of neighborhood poverty, defined on a geographic basis, is not necessarily the same as the causal structure of the underclass, defined as spatial concentrations of deviant behaviors. Moreover, a related literature exists on the determinants of metropolitan poverty rates without regard to the geographic distribution of that poverty within metropolitan areas. Although the determinants of changes in spatial patterning are not necessarily the same as the forces driving the overall level of poverty, this literature is also relevant given the obvious connection between overall poverty and the concentration of poverty. Because each approach contributes to an understanding of the forces that have converged to increase the size of poor neighborhoods and the concentration of poverty, I will discuss research based on several conceptually distinct dependent variables.

The focal point for research on the growth of neighborhood poverty is Wilson's *The Truly Disadvantaged* (1987). He identifies a complex interaction of economic, spatial, and social forces leading to the deterioration of Chicago's ghettos. In particular, he focuses on structural economic transformations and the flight of the black middle class. By contrast, in a series of articles and a recent influential book, *American Apartheid,* Massey and his colleagues argue that Wilson's analysis underplays the importance of racial segregation, both in its general effects on the black community's economic status and its role in creating and sustaining ghetto neighborhoods. In this chapter, I discuss these hypotheses and the evidence for them that has been presented by Wilson, Massey, and others. I present my own analysis of neighborhood poverty in chapter 6.

Structural Economic Transformations

Wilson (1987), whose work pertains mainly to poor black neighborhoods, summarizes the economic conditions contributing to ghetto growth as follows:

[U]rban minorities have been particularly vulnerable to structural economic changes, such as the shift from goods-producing to service-producing industries, the increasing polarization of the labor market into high-wage and low-wage sectors, technological innovations, and the relocation of manufacturing industries out of the central cities. (p. 39)

In other words, several simultaneous changes in the metropolitan labor markets have adversely affected the economic situation of urban blacks. Wilson's statement, implicitly or explicitly, embodies three distinct hypotheses about why poor neighborhoods in inner cities have been expanding:

Ghetto poverty is caused by *deindustrialization*: a decrease in the share of metropolitan jobs in the manufacturing sector;

Ghetto poverty is caused by *employment deconcentration*: a decrease in the share of all jobs (or in some formulations, of manufacturing jobs) located in the central city versus the suburban ring;

Ghetto poverty is caused by *occupational bifurcation:* changes in production technology in all sectors that result in fewer middle-income jobs.

This following section takes up each of these hypotheses. The cumulative effects of these economic trends on black income distribution are then discussed.

Deindustrialization

For evidence concerning deindustrialization, Wilson primarily cited the work of Kasarda (1989):

[America's major cities] have transformed . . . from centers of the production and distribution of goods to centers of administration, finance, and information exchange. In the process, many blue-collar jobs that once constituted the economic backbone of cities and provided employment opportunities for their poorly educated residents have either vanished or moved. These jobs have been replaced, at least in part, by knowledge-intensive white-collar jobs with educational requirements that exclude many with substandard education. (p. 28)

Many large cities, especially in the North, experienced declines in the proportion of their jobs in the manufacturing sector. Between 1970 and 1985, the percentage of nonagricultural employees in manufacturing declined from 25.8 to 15.5 percent in New York, and by similar amounts in Philadelphia, Baltimore, and St. Louis (Kasarda 1988, 170–71). All of these cities had large increases in neighborhood poverty between 1970 and 1980 (Jargowsky and Bane 1990, appendix I).

Such declines, however, were part of a general trend away from manufacturing toward services. Despite the similar timing of the expansion of poor neighborhoods and deindustrialization, a more systematic attempt to test the relationship between deindustrialization and neighborhood poverty is needed. For example, Boston experienced a decline in manufacturing of similar magnitude and had a large *decrease* in ghetto poverty over the same period. Figure 5.1 shows that almost all metropolitan areas experienced declines in their share of manufacturing jobs. At the same time, neighborhood poverty increased in the majority of metropolitan areas. But there does not appear to be any relationship between the extent of manufacturing job loss and the size of the increase in neighborhood poverty among blacks—that is, in ghetto poverty. The bivariate correlations between changes in the share of jobs in manufacturing and changes in ghetto poverty are not impressive: −0.31 in the 1970s and −0.02 in the 1980s. At best, the plots suggest a weak relationship in the 1970s, particularly in the South, and no relationship at all in the 1980s.

Neither Wilson, whose analyses were confined to Chicago, nor Kasarda attempt an econometric test of the hypothesis that changes in the share of manufacturing employment are responsible for increases in ghetto poverty. Hughes (1989) estimates a regression in which the dependent variable is the change in the number of "impacted ghetto" tracts in thirty-eight of the largest metropolitan areas. He includes a variable for deindustrialization, defined as "the percentage change in manufacturing employment in the central county," and an interaction term (deindustrialization multiplied by a dummy variable for the North) to test the hypothesis that the effect of deindustrialization on ghetto poverty was worse in that region.[1] When adding these variables to a base

Figure 5.1 Neighborhood Poverty and Manufacturing Employment

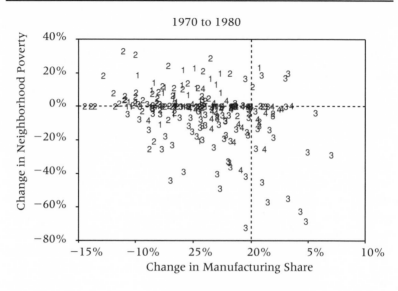

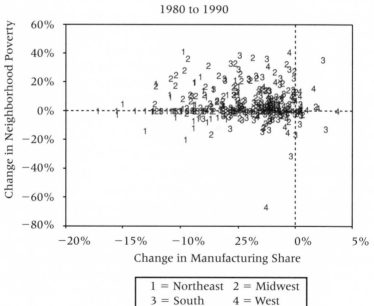

1 = Northeast   2 = Midwest
3 = South   4 = West

regression that includes only population, percent black, and a North dummy variable, the explanatory power of the model increases by only 5 percent. Only the coefficients on population size and the interaction term are statistically significant. Hughes interprets his results as lending only modest support to the deindustrialization hypothesis, although he favors the deconcentration hypothesis (see below).

It is curious, however, that deindustrialization per se does not appear to play a role in increasing ghetto poverty. The coefficient on deindustrialization is not statistically significant. But the *interaction* between the deindustrialization variable and a dummy variable for location in the North is significant, implying that deindustrialization only leads to ghetto increases in northern metropolitan areas. Hughes does not explore why changes in manufacturing employment are more important in the North. It may be, however, that the industrial jobs outside the North paid less well to begin with primarily because of different rates of unionization, and hence are less different from the jobs that subsequently replaced them. This suggests the possibility that the interaction of deindustrialization with a North dummy may actually be measuring the decline of union jobs rather than deindustrialization. Moreover, it would be useful to look at the change in share of jobs in manufacturing at the metropolitan level, rather than the central-city level. Doing so would eliminate the possibility of confounding the effect of movements of jobs to the suburban ring with the effect of changing industrial structure.

The impact of deindustrialization has also been evaluated by other researchers whose main concern is not neighborhood poverty but overall metropolitan poverty rates or the general trend in wages. Eggers and Massey (1991) found only minor effects of deindustrialization on metropolitan poverty rates for blacks and Hispanics in a series of recursive structural equation models using cross-sectional data from 1980. In contrast, they found that prevailing wage rates in both manufacturing and services were the most important variables in determining minority poverty. Eggers and Massey (1992) did find support for the deindustrialization hypothesis in a similar model, however, one that employed data on *changes* in the black poverty rate between 1970 and 1980.

In an attempt to account for the stagnation of wages and increases in inequality, Bound and Johnson (1992) decompose the impact of international trade, deindustrialization, technological change, and cohort shifts. They find little support for the theory that deindustrialization affected the distribution of wages. They conclude that the most important factor was an increase in the demand for skills, stemming from a general change in workplace technology, which cut across industrial sectors.

Bound and Holzer (1993) found somewhat more support, however, for the importance of industrial shifts. This study may be more relevant to the ghetto poverty issue than Bound and Johnson's research because the former exploits variation among metropolitan areas in employment and wages, whereas the latter focuses solely on the time trend at the national level. Bound and Holzer conclude that "while the decline in manufacturing appears to explain only fairly small fractions of the overall declines in black or white employment during the 1970s, for the young and less-educated the magnitudes are more substantial" (p. 395). They characterize the employment effects of industrial shifts as "generally small," but in the case of young black high school dropouts, they estimate that "as much as one-third to one-half of the large employment declines . . . can be thus explained" (p. 395).

All things considered, the early emphasis of researchers on manufacturing may have been misplaced. There is, at best, only modest evidence to support the notion that the shift from manufacturing to services is important to the overall poverty rate of blacks, and almost no direct evidence that it contributes to the growth of poor neighborhoods. The general stagnation of wages and the growth of inequality seem driven more by changes in the demand for skills than by changes in the sectoral composition of employment. On the other hand, there is some evidence that sectoral shifts may have had a disproportionate impact on the less-well educated, so the possible impact of deindustrialization on the growth of ghettos and barrios cannot be entirely dismissed.

Employment Deconcentration

The decline in central-city manufacturing jobs between 1970 and 1980 was part of a long-term trend. The proportion of total metropolitan manufacturing employment located in central cities declined from 63.3 percent in 1950 to 46.2 percent in 1980.[2] To some extent, this decline merely reflects a general spreading out of metropolitan areas over historically fixed central-city borders. For example, the proportion of the total metropolitan population in central cities declined only 3 percent faster than did manufacturing employment between 1950 and 1980. Central cities' share of service employment fell at the same rate as manufacturing. The same equivalence between rates of decline for manufacturing and services held for 1970–80 as well, although by then employment was dropping faster than population.

Kasarda (1989) argues that "confinement of poorly educated blacks in cities rapidly losing jobs . . . poses another serious impediment to lowering their unemployment rates. As . . . jobs expanded in the suburbs, whites were able to relocate much more easily than blacks" (p. 35). The employment deconcentration hypothesis is a version of Kain's spatial mismatch hypothesis (1968). Christopher Jencks and Susan Mayer (1990b), in a review of the spatial mismatch literature, stated the issue succinctly:

> In 1968 John Kain published a seminal paper in which he argued that the high level of joblessness among urban blacks was partly attributable to the fact that a growing fraction of urban jobs—especially blue-collar manufacturing jobs—had moved to the suburbs while exclusionary housing practices had kept blacks penned up in central cities. Kain argued that the resulting "spatial mismatch" reduced both employers' willingness to hire black workers and black workers' ability to find jobs that were in principle open to them. (p. 187)

Note that the deconcentration of jobs matters only if two conditions hold: physical distance affects access to jobs;[3] and blacks cannot readily pursue jobs that move to the suburbs. The second proposition is true: outside the South, blacks live predominantly in central cities because of historical patterns of racial segregation, ongoing racial discrimination in housing markets, and zoning practices that keep suburban housing out of reach for low-income households. Given that employment deconcentration is well established and that the majority of blacks are likely to live in central cities for the foreseeable future, the empirical issue is the extent to which the first condition holds. In other words, does distance from areas of employment growth affect employment?

Most research on spatial mismatch does not attempt to test the hypothesis that deconcentration of employment is related to poor neighborhoods per se. But a significant spatial mismatch effect on employment or wages would translate into more black poverty and, other things equal, more ghetto poverty. As Jencks and Mayer note above, the spatial mismatch effect might result from demand-side or supply-side factors, or both. We need not distinguish them here but instead ask what the net effect of the spatial mismatch is on the employment and earnings of segregated blacks.

In a well-known study, David Ellwood showed that proximity to jobs made little impact on black adolescents' employment rates. Residential proximity "matters only slightly—about as much as would be expected from a slightly lower real wage caused by extra commuting time" (Ellwood 1986, 182). This and other studies led Jencks and Mayer (1990b) to conclude that "the support [for spatial mismatch] is so mixed that no prudent policy analyst should rely on it. . . . There is as much evidence against such claims as for them" (p. 219).

Kain (1992), in an exhaustive review of the literature spawned by his 1968 article, has criticized many of these studies on methodological grounds. In particular, many studies critical of the spatial mismatch hypothesis use racial segregation as the spatial mismatch measure. Racial segregation is typically measured by the dissimilarity index, which is a measure of the evenness of the spatial distribution of two distinct groups (Duncan and Duncan 1955a; Massey and Denton 1988). Kain argues that studies using dissimilarity as the mismatch variable are misspecified because this variable does not measure the spatial *proximity* of segregated areas to areas of employment growth.[4] Other studies comparing "suburban" blacks to central-city blacks have a similar problem in that many areas technically considered suburbs may actually be just as far from employment growth as central-city ghettos.

More recent empirical work has been supportive of a spatial mismatch effect. Price and Mills (1985), using 1978 data from the Current Population Survey (CPS), found that central-city residence could explain 6 percentage points of a 34 percent difference in the wages of black and white male full-time workers. There may be uncontrolled differences, however, between blacks who have moved to the suburbs and those who have not, potentially leading to an overstatement of the effect of location (Holzer 1991). Ihlanfeldt and Sjoquist (1989) studied youth employment in Chicago and several other cities using more recent data, providing a counterpoint to Ellwood's research. They find that differences in job access can explain a significant proportion of the difference in employment for black and white youths.

Analysis of quasi-experimental data from the Gautreaux housing program in Chicago indicates that program participants who relocated to the suburbs were 13 percent more likely to be employed than those who relocated within the central city (Popkin, Rosenbaum, and Meaden 1993; Rosenbaum 1995; Rosenbaum and Popkin 1991). Program participants were selected for suburban or central-city locations virtually randomly, thereby largely controlling for unobserved individual differences. Thus, the Gautreaux findings provide strong evidence for the spatial mismatch hypothesis. Holzer's reading of these studies leads him to conclude that "the preponderance of evidence from data of the last decade shows that spatial mismatch has a significant effect on black employment" (Holzer 1991, 118).

Thus, a growing body of evidence supports Kain's theory that spatial mismatch affects the employment and earnings of minorities in central cities. The effect seems to be growing over time, as metropolitan areas continue to move toward a more decentralized paradigm (Kain 1992). Hughes (1989) attempted to statistically test the impact of employment deconcentration on the ghetto formation process and contrasted it with deindustrialization:

> The [deindustrialization] hypothesis is that the extent of impacted ghetto formation is related to the site conditions of the ghetto, and, in particular, to the level of manufacturing employment loss in the central city. . . . The essence of the competing deconcentration hypothesis is that the . . . extent of impacted ghetto formation is related to the level of deconcentration of manufacturing employment from the center toward the periphery of the metropolitan area, particularly in the northeastern MSAs. . . . A maintained hypothesis of

> this analysis is that the implications of deconcentration in northeast-
> ern MSAs are more severe because of segregation and accessibility.
> (p. 200)

Hughes concludes that deconcentration has been a more important determinant of increasing ghetto poverty than deindustrialization. He bases this conclusion on regression results, using the
change in the number of ghetto tracts as the dependent variable
and with data for thirty-eight of the largest metropolitan areas. As
noted above, adding variables for deindustrialization—separately
and interacted with the North dummy—did little to increase the
explanatory power of the regression, and only the interaction
term was statistically significant. In contrast, adding deconcentration (also separately and interacted with a dummy for the North)
to the same regression increased the explanatory power of the
regression by more than 20 percentage points (1989, table 2,
p. 201).[5]

Unfortunately, Hughes's use of the number of ghetto tracts as the
measure of ghetto poverty probably biases his results in favor of
deconcentration. Most cities were losing residents as well as jobs to
the suburbs. In some metropolitan areas, the number of high-
poverty tracts increased even though there was no change in population-weighted measures of neighborhood poverty. In essence,
there were more, but less dense, poor neighborhoods in these cities.
If these cities had job decentralization as well, as seems likely, then
we would expect the results Hughes obtained. Nevertheless,
Hughes's results remain the only attempt to test the employment
deconcentration hypothesis and provide the strongest empirical evidence to date that deconcentration has been a contributor to
increasing neighborhood poverty.

Occupational Bifurcation

Wilson, as quoted earlier, refers to the polarization of the labor market into high-wage and low-wage sectors. Other analysts also see a
trend toward a splitting of occupations into two tiers, resulting from
both deindustrialization and changing occupational profiles within
industrial sectors (Stanback and Noyelle 1983). According to Harrison and Bluestone (1988), the upper tier includes "managers,

lawyers, accountants, bankers, business consultants, and other technically trained people." The lower tier comprises

> . . . the other, less fortunate pool of urban residents whose collective function is to provide services to the workers in the upper tier. They are the ones who wait tables, cook meals, sell everything from office supplies to clothing, change bed and bath linen in the dozens of new hotels, provide custodial service and child care, and find lower-level employment in the city's hospitals, health clinics, schools, and municipal government itself. (p. 69–70)

Although the case is frequently overstated, some evidence suggests a trend toward a greater degree of heterogeneity in the skill requirements of jobs. Levy (1987) grouped occupations into five broad groups, roughly by the type and amount of skill required: professional and managerial workers; other white-collar workers; blue-collar workers; service workers; farmers and farm-related occupations. Between 1950 and 1980, the proportion of white men in white-collar occupations increased from 34 percent to 43 percent; the blue-collar proportion declined from 47 percent to 43 percent; and the service proportion increased from 6 percent to 9 percent (Levy 1987, table 7.3).[6]

Occupational bifurcation could contribute to neighborhood poverty in two ways. First, members of minority groups could have seen a decline in average occupational status, at least relative to whites, because they more often fall into the lower tier of jobs. Second, to the extent that some blacks make it to jobs in the upper tier and the rest are confined to the lower tier, upward pressure could be exerted on income inequality among blacks. These effects on the mean and variance of black socioeconomic status could then contibute to neighborhood poverty. A changing occupational structure, however, is only one of many factors affecting income distribution.

Structural Economic Transformations and Black Income Distribution
The common thread among these "structural economic transformations" is that they keep the average income of blacks lower than it would have been in the absence of such changes. Moreover, by selectively disfavoring those with the least education and skills,

they increase inequality *among* blacks. These economic changes increase black poverty in general and therefore help explain the increasing levels of ghettoization, given the relation between overall poverty and ghetto poverty. As Wacquant and Wilson (1989) have argued, it is the net effect of several types of economic change and their possible interactions that ought to concern us. The expansion of ghetto neighborhoods, they argue, has been the result of "a set of mutually reinforcing spatial and industrial changes in the country's urban political economy . . . marking large numbers of inner-city blacks with the stamp of economic redundancy" (pp. 11–13).

Much recent literature has focused on changes in income distribution in the United States. Most of it, however, does not explicitly address the connection to neighborhood poverty. It is important to keep in mind, however, the most important *long-run* trend with regard to the economic status of blacks is the dramatic improvement in black wages and income, both in absolute terms and compared to whites (Jaynes and Williams 1989). In 1940, the average hourly wage rate for black males was only 43 percent of the average wage of white males. By 1970, average black male wages had risen to 64 percent of the white male wage. The gap between average black and white wage rates for men continued to narrow through the 1970s, with black wages rising to 73 percent of white earnings by 1980 (Smith and Welch 1989). Moreover, the ratio of black to white *annual earnings*—which incorporates both wage rates and hours worked—increased from 44 percent in 1939 to 66 percent in 1979, but then dropped slightly by 1984 (Jaynes and Williams 1989, table 6-5).

As a result of these trends, white and black income distributions now overlap to a significant degree:

> In 1940, three quarters of all blacks were below the white middle class. . . . The real story of the period from 1940 to 1980 has been the emergence of the black middle class, whose income gains have been real and substantial. . . . As a group it outnumbers the black poor. . . . For the first time in American History, a sizable number of black men are economically better off than white middle-class America. (Smith and Welch 1989, 525)

The gains noted by Smith and Welch have been across a broad spectrum of the income distribution. The 1940 to 1980 gain of the tenth percentile of the black income distribution was 48 percent, compared to 46 percent for the ninetieth percentile.

Smith and Welch do note, however, that increases in black wages (calculated on the basis of employed persons) need to be viewed in the context of decreasing levels of labor force participation and higher levels of unemployment, especially for young black men (Smith and Welch 1989, 548). Bound and Freeman (1990), for example, found a deterioration in earnings of young black men relative to young white men since 1973. Employment also declined for both black and white young men. The decline was greater in absolute terms for blacks, but the ratio of black and white employment rates remained constant. The hourly wage rate for black males of all ages declined from $10.55 in 1979 to $8.35 in 1984 (in 1984 constant dollars) after steady increases since 1939; the ratio of white to black male wages also declined over the same period (Jaynes and Williams 1989, table 6-5).

The *ratio* of black unemployment to white unemployment has not changed over the past several decades, although the absolute increase was greater for blacks (Jencks 1991, 46). So despite the positive trends for employed black males, the proportion of black men who report zero annual earnings rose from 15 percent in 1940 to 21 percent in 1980 (Danziger and Gottschalk 1987, 211).

Income inequality, after a long period of decline, has been rising since about 1977 (Juhn, Murphy, and Pierce 1989; Karoly 1990; Levy 1987), although the exact year of the turnaround depends on the measures of inequality and income used and the subgroup studied. For example, the change in income for the bottom quintile of families between 1979 and 1989 was −4.3 percent (adjusted family income weighted by persons) (Committee on Ways and Means 1991, 1184). All other quintiles had gains, with larger gains accruing to the higher quintiles. Moreover, inequality has risen faster among blacks than whites between 1940 and 1980, whether measured by the Gini coefficient, the coefficient of variation, or the variance of log earnings (Danziger and Gottschalk 1987).[7]

All of these figures are national averages. Yet neighborhood poverty is measured at the metropolitan level. Even if there had been no change in the black income distribution *on average*, the pattern of increases and decreases in ghetto poverty *at the metropolitan level* could still reflect metropolitan-level variations in income trends. In the first study to systematically test the elements of Wilson's theory, Massey and Eggers (1990) provided measures of black income for sixty metropolitan areas, including the fifty largest and ten others with large Hispanic populations. Median family income among blacks fell between 1970 and 1980 in twenty-nine of the sixty metropolitan areas, and all but nine of the declines were in the Northeast or North Central regions (pp. 1166–67). In contrast, only four had a decline for whites.

Massey and Eggers also found evidence for a splitting of the income distribution among minorities. In the North, the proportions of black and Hispanic families in "upper-middle" and "lower-middle" brackets decreased, with corresponding increases in the proportions of families in the "poor" and "affluent" income brackets (Massey and Eggers 1990, table 1). Whites generally and blacks in the South and West did not display a trend toward bifurcation. In 1980, the interquartile ratio in the sixty metropolitan areas was 2.39 for whites and 3.39 for blacks. Between 1970 and 1980, the ratio increased by 9 percent for whites and 23 percent for blacks. For blacks, the highest levels and largest changes were in the Northeast and North Central regions.

Massey and Eggers therefore find strong evidence for a deterioration of black income and greater black income inequality in the 1970s. Moreover, the regional pattern of changes in the black income distribution corresponds to the regional pattern of changes in ghetto poverty in that period. As shown in figure 5.2, a positive correlation exists between changes in the overall black poverty rate (measured at the metropolitan level) and changes in ghetto poverty. Massey and Eggers also provide an econometric test of the relationship between blacks' income distribution and their measure of poverty concentration.[8] The black poverty rate, which reflects both the mean and variance of black income, is strongly significant. (Other variables in their regressions reflect economic and racial segregation.) Korenman, Sjaastad, and Jargowsky (1995) find that similar regressions for the 1980s also show a powerful relationship between changes in the black poverty measured at the metropoli-

Figure 5.2   Neighborhood Poverty and Overall Poverty

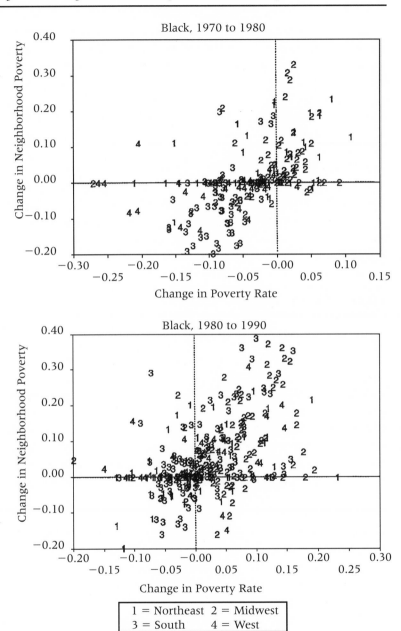

1 = Northeast 2 = Midwest
3 = South   4 = West

tan level and ghetto poverty, as does my analysis presented in the next chapter.

Thus, even though the forces behind the structural economic transformations to which Wilson referred in *The Truly Disadvantaged* are still a matter of debate, a key determinant of ghetto poverty is the pattern of change in the black income distribution. Saying that, of course, begs the question of exactly what factors underlie the stagnation of black family income and the increase in wage inequality among blacks, and the even more complex question of why such effects were worse in some metropolitan areas than others. Whatever their exact source, however, almost all researchers in the field concur with Wilson's emphasis on the importance of changes in the overall opportunity structure of the minority community. His other hypotheses—on the flight of the black middle class and social isolation as causes of the concentration of poverty—have been more controversial.

Flight of the Black Middle Class

The second major causal factor identified by Wilson in *The Truly Disadvantaged* was the flight of the black middle class from inner-city neighborhoods. Reductions in housing discrimination enabled middle-income blacks to move out of ghetto neighborhoods, where they had previously been confined despite their economic successes. Selective outmigration of the nonpoor would then leave these areas poorer.[9] This proposition is true by definition, but the key empirical issue is whether this outmigration was large enough to have a measurable impact on ghetto poverty. A second issue is the importance of black middle-class flight relative to other determinants of neighborhood poverty.

There is prima facie evidence that the spatial organization of people, and not just overall poverty rates, affect levels of neighborhood poverty. For example, thirteen metropolitan areas with more than one million residents in 1990 had black poverty rates of 25–30 percent.[10] Despite similar overall poverty rates, the black concentration of poverty in these cities ranged from 12 percent in Fort Lauderdale to 45 percent in Chicago. Something about the spatial organization of the black poor in Chicago resulted in a far greater proportion of them living in high-poverty census tracts. The two key aspects of spatial organization relevant to ghetto formation are economic segregation, discussed in this section, and racial segregation, the subject of the next.

As we have seen, differential outmigration of the nonpoor increases a neighborhood's poverty rate, leading marginal tracts to become ghettos. This phenomenon was very common in mixed-income census tracts near the edge of the older ghettos in Milwaukee. Jargowsky and Bane (1991), in an examination of tract-level changes between 1970 and 1980, also found that differential outmigration of nonpoor blacks from mixed-income areas was an important factor in the creation of new ghetto areas in Cleveland and Philadelphia.

Wilson's black-middle-class-flight hypothesis has been criticized by Douglas Massey and his colleagues. They argue that economic segregation, although in principle a possible contributing factor to ghetto poverty, has in fact played almost no role (Massey and Eggers 1990; Massey and Denton 1993; Massey, Gross, and Shibuya 1994). Massey and Denton (1993) summarize the debate as follows:

> Wilson also argues that concentrated poverty arose because the civil rights revolution allowed middle-class blacks to move out of the ghetto. Although we remain open to the possibility that class-selective migration did occur, we argue that concentrated poverty would have happened during the 1970s with or without black middle-class migration. (p. 8)

The primary evidence marshaled in defense of this position are the models estimated in Massey and Eggers (1990), the metropolitan area simulations presented in *American Apartheid* and in Massey (1990), and an analysis of the geocoded PSID in Massey, Gross, and Shibuya (1994).

Massey and Eggers (1990) found an increase in the level of economic segregation among blacks using a variant of the dissimilarity index. The index of dissimilarity measures the evenness of the distribution of discrete groups—usually whites and blacks. Income, however, is a continuous variable. To surmount this problem, they divided all families into four income classes in 1980 and created roughly similar divisions for 1970.[11] A separate index of dissimilarity can be calculated for each distinct pairing of the two income groupings, and there are six such combinations. The six measures were averaged.[12] "Spatial dissimilarity between black income groups," Massey and Eggers (1990) report, "increased over the 1970s, often quite sharply, and this trend was opposite to those of other racial/ethnic groups" (p. 1170).

Massey and Eggers, despite finding increasing interclass segregation by their measure, question the relevance for explaining the concentration of poverty for several reasons. First, economic segregation increased even where their measure of ghetto poverty decreased. Second, the level of economic segregation among blacks is low compared to other minority groups that experience lower levels of ghetto poverty. Third, the levels they observe for blacks show relatively low levels of segregation in an absolute sense. They conclude that "interclass segregation plays a secondary role in promoting concentrated poverty among Hispanics and Asians, but it has *no detectable effect whatsoever among blacks*" (Massey and Eggers 1990, 1183, emphasis added).

Such a strongly worded conclusion does not seem to be supported by the regressions they present. Included in their model were the group poverty rate, racial segregation, and their measure of class segregation. In a model on levels of the concentration of poverty for blacks only, the coefficient on interclass dissimilarity very nearly attains statistical significance. The t ratio is 1.71, which is significant at the 0.10 level in a two-tailed test or at the 0.05 level for a one-tailed test. Although it is not significant in a two-tailed test at the 0.05 level—the usual standard in social science research—it provides at least *some* evidence of a role for economic segregation. Moreover, in models for Hispanics, Asians, and a pooled model, economic segregation is highly significant ($p < 0.01$) (see table 4 in Massey and Eggers 1990). The coefficients in the other equations are similar in magnitude and significance to those on the racial segregation measure, so the designation of the effect as "secondary" also seems questionable.

As further evidence against a role for economic segregation, Massey (1990) and Massey and Denton (1993) in *American Apartheid* report the results of a series of simulation models. The models consist of a grid of sixteen "neighborhoods" into which a population is assigned based on certain rules. The levels of poverty concentration[13] that result from different combinations of racial and economic segregation and different underlying poverty rates are then measured. Table 5.1 partially reproduces a table from *American Apartheid* that presents the results of the models. Massey and Denton argue that racial segregation acts to amplify the effects of any increase in the black poverty rate by confining it to a limited number of segregated neighborhoods. In their simulation, an increase in overall black poverty from 20 percent to 30 percent, in the context of no economic segregation, causes an increase in poverty concentration of only 2.5 percentage points when no racial segregation is present and 10 percentage points when racial segregation is total.

The effect is even more dramatic when economic segregation is present: the increase in black poverty results in a 5-percentage-point increase in poverty concentration if there is no racial segregation and in 20 percentage points if racial segregation is total. In conclusion, Massey and Denton (1993) argue that the simulations show that

> [T]he effect of class segregation is to heighten and reinforce the poverty-concentrating effects of racial segregation. . . . With or without class segregation, residential segregation between blacks and whites builds concentrated poverty into the residential structure of the black community. (p. 125)

Table 5.1   Simulation of the Concentration of Poverty

	Concentration of Poverty (Massey and Eggers Measure)		
	20%	30%	% Change
No class segregation			
No racial segregation	12.5%	15.0%	2.5%
Complete racial segregation	20.0	30.0	10.0
With class segregation			
No racial segregation	25.0	30.0	5.0
Complete racial segregation	40.0	60.0	20.0

Source: Massey and Denton (1993), table 5.1.
Note: Intermediate levels of racial segregation and concentration of poverty for poor white families are omitted.

This reading of the simulation results is unpersuasive. Indeed, using the same logic, the simulation results could be read the opposite way. In the absence of racial segregation, the increase in overall black poverty from 20 to 30 percent increases poverty concentration by 2.5 percentage points if there is no economic segregation and by 5 points if there is class segregation; if racial segregation is complete, the increase in black poverty increases the poverty concentration by 10 points if there is no class segregation but by 20 if there is.

Based on this simulation, one could just as well conclude that the effect of *racial* segregation is to heighten and reinforce the poverty-concentrating effects of *economic* segregation. The effect could be even larger than the table indicates, since the degree of economic segregation used in the simulation is not as extreme as the simulated level of racial segregation. In the simulations with economic segregation, Massey (1990) reports that the interclass index of dissimilarity is 0.625. In the models with no economic segregation, it presumably is zero. In contrast, the simulations test racial segregation levels from zero up to one.

Massey, Gross, and Shibuya (1994) use a geocoded version of the PSID to analyze movements into and out of different types of neighborhoods.[14] They, too, find "little support for the view that the geographic concentration of black poverty is caused by the out-migration of non-poor blacks" (p. 425). Oddly, this study misstates the findings of Massey and Eggers:

> Massey and Eggers (1990) reasoned that if poor and nonpoor African-Americans had moved selectively to different neighborhoods during the 1970s, then we should have observed an increase in black segregation by income over the decade; but they detected no such increase in the degree of class segregation among blacks. (p. 427)

Yet, as noted earlier, Massey and Eggers (1990) actually found that "spatial dissimilarity between black income groups increased over the 1970s, often quite sharply" (p. 1170).

In the 1994 study, Massey, Gross, and Shibuya calculated the probabilities of moving from one type of neighborhood to another. They focus on black neighborhoods (where blacks constitute at least 60 percent of the population) with poverty rates in the 20–39 percent range. These are the mixed-income or "borderline" neighborhoods that often become high-poverty areas over time. The key question is: Does selective out migration operate to increase the poverty rate in these neighborhoods? Massey, Gross, and Shibuya reported that in 1970–73, nonpoor blacks were slightly more likely (0.23 compared to 0.20) to move out of their neighborhood than poor blacks—which supports Wilson's hypothesis. But in 1979–84, the pattern is sharply reversed: the probability of leaving is 0.14 for nonpoor and 0.24 for poor (table 2).[15] They conclude, "The highlighted coefficients do not support Wilson's view that black nonpoor out-migration is the driving force of poverty concentration" (p. 431).[16]

Nonetheless, the tables in Massey, Gross, and Shibuya (1994) also provide some support for Wilson's middle-class-flight hypothesis. First, a substantial portion of the blacks in the sample (23.4 percent) live in "racially/socioeconomically mixed" areas. These are also borderline neighborhoods, both economically and racially. Massey et al. say little about outmigration from these neighborhoods, focusing only on the "poor black areas" where 33.3 percent of blacks in their sample reside. Combining both time periods, nonpoor blacks have a greater propensity to leave mixed neighborhoods than poor residents—0.14 compared to 0.11 (Massey, Gross, and Shibuya 1994, table 2).

Second, many moves constitute "churning," or moving from one neighborhood to another neighborhood of similar social status. For example, if a person moved from one poor tract to another, then back to the original tract, both moves are counted. Table 3 of their paper examines this issue by showing the destination neighborhood of those who moved. Of those who moved out of poor black areas, 59 percent of the poor movers moved to a neighborhood with the same or lower status, compared to 49 percent of the nonpoor movers. Of those who moved out of mixed areas, 58 percent of the poor movers moved to a neighborhood with the same or lower status compared to 38 percent of the nonpoor movers.

A direct answer to the main question—how selective outmigration affected neighborhood poverty rates in borderline areas—is difficult to derive from the tables in Massey, Gross, and Shibuya (1994). The transition matrices give neighborhoods of origin by their poverty rates in year t, while destination neighborhoods are classified by their poverty rates in year $t + 1$. This is related to the nature of the PSID, which is a household-based survey with some neighborhood identifiers grafted on after the fact.

To illustrate how selective outmigration affects neighborhood poverty transitions, it would be preferable to classify neighborhoods at a fixed point in time as borderline, poor, very poor, and so on, and then hold those designations constant. Then, to eliminate the effect of churning, a move should only be counted when a person moves from one neighborhood type to another (either up or down), ignoring moves that are merely horizontal. Finally, the net affect of all recorded moves over the whole period on the overall poverty level in the borderline tracts would provide a direct test of Wilson's middle-class-flight hypothesis. In the absence of such a calculation, and given the partial support for Wilson's hypothesis that can be found in their tables 2 and 3, it seems that Massey, Gross, and Shibuya's blanket rejection of a role for increasing economic segregation in ghetto formation based on the PSID analysis is overstated.

Thus, the critique of Wilson's economic segregation hypothesis presented by Massey and his colleagues is not altogether persuasive. The tract/neighborhood level results presented by Wilson (1987) and Jargowsky and Bane (1991), and my tract-level analysis for Milwaukee (chapter 3) indicate an important role for economic segregation. Economic segregation must have played a role in the general increase in neighborhood poverty between 1970 and 1990, given that racial segregation *declined* over that period, and, on average, poverty rates in metropolitan areas changed very little.

Massey and Eggers (1990) did find a significant and positive coefficient on economic segregation in their equation on levels of poverty concentration, but they discounted the importance of the finding because the coefficient was small and because it was insignificant in the black subsample. Korenman, Sjaastad, and Jargowsky (1995), in a replication and extension of the Massey and Eggers paper, find support for economic segregation in some models and not others. The answer seems to be sensitive to the way in which the variable is measured and the specification of the relationship, an issue that is further addressed in chapter 6.

Segregation by Race

Three decades after the passage of landmark civil rights and fair housing legislation, racial segregation between blacks and whites in U.S. metropolitan areas remains extremely high (Farley and Frey 1994; Massey and Denton 1987, 1989). The highest levels are found in the Northeast and North Central regions. Between 1970 and 1980, however, racial segregation declined in several cities. The significance of these declines seems to be in the eye of the beholder. Massey and Denton (1987) stressed that most large U.S. cities continue to have very high levels of segregation (index of dissimilarity above 0.70). Farley (1991), in contrast, stressed that the declines of the 1970s reversed a long-term trend toward greater segregation.

In the 1980s, racial segregation declined even further. The population-weighted average level of racial segregation for 318 metropolitan areas declined from 0.70 to 0.66.[17] As shown in table 5.2, there were declines in every major region of the country. They were not limited to cities with few black residents, where whites might

Table 5.2   Changes in Racial Segregation (Index of Dissimilarity) by Region and Quartile of Percent Black, 1980–90

	Metropolitan Areas		Black-White Dissimilarity		
	Total	Decreases	1980	1990	Change
United States	318	260	0.70	0.66	−0.05
Region					
Northeast	63	42	0.74	0.72	−0.02
Midwest	81	65	0.77	0.74	−0.04
Overlapping	8	8	0.72	0.68	−0.04
South	114	100	0.69	0.62	−0.07
West	52	45	0.63	0.57	−0.07
Percent black					
1st quartile	80	66	0.75	0.72	−0.03
2nd quartile	79	67	0.75	0.69	−0.06
3rd quartile	79	68	0.64	0.58	−0.06
4th quartile	80	59	0.56	0.50	−0.06

Source: Census tract data for 1980–90 (See Appendix A), tabulations by the author.

be expected to have less fear of integration. The lower panel of table 5.2 divides metropolitan areas into quartiles based on the percentage black. Metropolitan areas with the highest percentage of blacks had declines—albeit small—in racial segregation, as did a substantial majority of cities in each quartile.

The number of census tracts with zero blacks has fallen precipitously (Kain 1992). Although one or two black families per tract are not sufficient to change the aggregate segregation figures, Kain (1992) sees the reduction in all-white tracts as a hopeful sign:

> Suburban communities with *no* Afro-American residents are much less common than in the past. . . . This is a very important change. It is much easier to prevent or discourage a single Afro-American household from moving into a community with *no* Afro-American residents than it is to monitor and limit the numbers of black households that move into a community that has a small number of Afro-American residents. In addition, if small numbers of Afro-American households move into a large number of suburban communities, the likelihood that continued nonwhite entry will cause any of these communities to become completely, or predominantly, black is small. (p. 62)

Despite a trend in the right direction, racial segregation in the United States remains extremely high by any standard.

As noted above, Massey argues that underclass scholars have systematically failed to recognize the importance of racial segregation in the ghetto formation process. In *American Apartheid*, he and Denton state their position:

> Geographically concentrated poverty is built into the experience of urban blacks by racial segregation. Segregation, not middle-class out-migration, is the key factor responsible for the creation and perpetuation of communities characterized by persistent and spatially concentrated poverty. Concentrated poverty is created by a pernicious interaction between a group's overall rate of poverty and its degree of segregation in society. When a highly segregated group experiences a high or rising rate of poverty, geographically concentrated poverty is the inevitable result, and from this geographic concentration of poverty follow a variety of other deleterious conditions. (p. 118)

Massey, Denton, Eggers, and others are entirely correct about racial segregation being a necessary precondition for the existence of ghetto poverty. If a poor minority group lived in a residentially integrated society with a wealthier majority group, high-poverty areas would be unlikely to exist in any significant number. The majority group would, in effect, water down the higher poverty of the minority group. Yet it is just as true to say that without black poverty, there would be no concentration of poverty problem. And since the overall black poverty rate in most metropolitan areas is less than 40 percent, without some degree of economic segregation, there would be no ghettos. In this purely definitional sense, racial segregation is a fundamental reason that ghettos exist.

A related question is whether differences among metropolitan areas in the degree of racial segregation explain differences in ghetto poverty. But even if such a relationship could be demonstrated empirically, it would not explain the recent *increases* in ghetto poverty, because racial segregation declined in most metropolitan areas over the last two decades.

A second level of Massey's argument is that differences among metropolitan areas in racial segregation contribute to ghetto poverty, in that they interact with impoverishment. In other words, Massey argues that increases in overall black poverty rates lead to relatively greater increases in ghetto poverty in metropolitan areas with higher levels of racial segregation. Massey and Eggers (1990) postulate this effect and present evidence for it, as discussed below.

A third, and in some ways more fundamental, level of Massey's argument concerns the cumulative effects of racial segregation and the centrality of segregation—as well as the institutional arrangements that support and sustain it—for understanding the status of black Americans on a range of dimensions. In his view, residential segregation has dynamic feedback effects on the acquisition of human capital by blacks, helps to sustain white racism and discrimination, and keeps blacks isolated from job networks and community supports that whites can take for granted. Repeatedly, Massey and Denton (1993) identify this as their principal thesis; for example: "Our fundamental position is that racial segregation—and its characteristic institutional form, the black ghetto—are the key structural factors responsible for the perpetuation of black poverty in the United States" (p. 9).

In this view, the total effect of racial segregation on high levels of black poverty and the concentration of that poverty is the sum of many indirect effects operating through such mechanisms as educational attainment of blacks, human capital, labor market functioning, and the resulting black income distribution. The thesis that racial segregation is a key determinant of black poverty—and therefore indirectly helps to create and sustain ghetto poverty—is conceptually distinct from the two arguments presented above: that racial segregation contributes directly to the formation of ghettos and that racial segregation interacts with changes in poverty rates to produce ghettos.

It is, therefore, important to distinguish among the different levels of the arguments of Massey and his colleagues concerning the impact of racial segregation on ghetto poverty. In order to determine the sources of the growth of concentrated poverty, the right question to ask is whether racial segregation has any statistically significant effects on the levels of or changes in ghetto poverty, including any interaction effects. Alternatives to the racial segregation arguments of Massey and others include black economic status and economic segregation. It may well turn out that *these* determinants of ghetto poverty are themselves functions of past or current racial segregation. Indeed, many of Massey's arguments about the effects of racial segregation on the current economic status of blacks are very convincing. Understanding both sets of linkages is important to a full understanding of the "urban poverty nexus" (Galster and Keeney 1988).

The most straightforward test of the hypothesis that racial segregation has an impact on ghetto poverty, as opposed to black poverty more generally, is presented in Massey and Eggers (1990). They hypothesize that "changes in class structure interact with patterns of racial/ethnic segregation to produce the unusual concentrations of poverty observed among blacks and Hispanics during the 1970s" (p. 1180). To test this thesis, Massey and Eggers estimate regressions in which the dependent variable is their measure of poverty concentration, the exposure of the black poor to poverty, for sixty large metropolitan areas. In the model for levels of poverty concentration in 1980 for blacks, Asians, and Hispanics, the group's poverty rate, racial segregation, and economic segregation are all positive and significant.[18] Thus, metropolitan areas with more racial segregation have more concentrated poverty.

Massey and Eggers's hypothesis, however, is that there is an interaction between racial segregation and poverty. Thus, they estimate a model that includes the interaction term. However, "because of multicollinearity among the regressors, the interactive and main effects are not estimated in the same model" (p. 1183). The coefficient on the interaction term is 5.1 ($t = 11.8$). Their interpretation is that "segregation is the key factor accounting for variation in the concentration of poverty" (p. 1183). This conclusion is highly questionable, however. By their own admission, the interaction term is highly collinear with an omitted variable: the black poverty rate, which in the black model had a coefficient of 4.9 ($t = 10.6$). The interaction term clearly picks up most of the effect of this omitted variable. And even in the absence of multicollinearity issues, it is impossible to determine which of the two variables that make up an interaction term is the "key" factor.

Without question, racial segregation in the United States is a pernicious evil. Efforts to reduce racial segregation are probably among the most important public policies that could be pursued to reduce poverty. And the concentration of poverty among blacks would not be nearly as high today were it not for levels of racial segregation for blacks that dwarf those ever experienced by any other racial or ethnic group in U.S. history. But the role of racial segregation or an interaction between segregation and changes in poverty in explaining trends in concentrated poverty is a conceptually distinct empirical question. It is hard to see how racial segregation could explain much of the recent increases in ghetto poverty, since it has been declining. It is possible, as Massey and Eggers argue, that racial segregation interacts with increases in black poverty to create ghettos; in that case, it is not so much the recent small declines in racial segregation that matter but the continued high levels. Yet the evidence to support the interaction effect comes mostly from a badly flawed econometric model.

The Forces Behind Growing Neighborhood Poverty

The debate continues over why neighborhood poverty has increased since 1970. Many Americans feel economically insecure in this time of increasing internationalization of the labor market, economic restructuring, and sectoral shifts. Minorities with little education are probably most vulnerable to these forces and stand the risk of becoming socially and economically marginalized. In the remainder of this book I explore why ghetto neighborhoods have spread and possible policy responses. Based on the literature and evidence discussed thus far, however, a few preliminary conclusions may be drawn.

First, though the exact mechanisms are somewhat murky, structural changes in the economy have worked to the disadvantage of those with lower levels of education and job skills, resulting in slow or negative wage growth for such persons. Because of the poor quality of inner-city schools and the correlation between socioeconomic background and educational attainment, the decline in demand for low-skill labor has had a disproportionate impact on inner-city minorities, particularly young men. At the same time, employment deconcentration creates a spatial mismatch between available jobs and inner-city residents and reduces the probability of finding any job, let alone one with high wages. These underlying economic trends are reflected in the stagnation of black wages and an increase in inequality within the black income distribution. Second, though hotly disputed, tract-level evidence supports an important role in the growth of neighborhood poverty for the flight of the black middle class—that is, economic segregation within a minority group. Third, racial segregation is fundamental to high poverty levels among blacks. Yet the empirical evidence to support a direct role for racial segregation in recent decades is mixed at best. Indeed, the possibility exists that neighborhood poverty among blacks is lower than it otherwise would have been as a result of the recent declines in the level of black/white segregation.

I will show, in the next chapter, that changes in the overall opportunity structure, as measured by the mean income of all metropolitan residents, are by far the most important determinants of ghetto poverty. Racial and economic segregation play secondary roles, and their importance varies depending on whether we are examining the *levels* of ghetto poverty in 1970, 1980, and 1990 or the *changes* in ghetto poverty in recent decades. Taken together, the macrostructural explanations of neighborhood poverty—which hold that ghettos and barrios are the result of larger, metropolitan-level processes—can explain about four-fifths of the variance in ghetto poverty. Although the importance of these metropolitan processes does not preclude a role for the culture or values of ghetto residents, it does suggest that such factors play a secondary role at best.

Chapter 6

An Analysis of Neighborhood Poverty

Given the rapid expansion of ghetto and barrio neighborhoods, there is a great desire among policymakers, especially at the state and local level, to design policies to combat urban blight. Often, attention is focused on programs in the most distressed neighborhoods. Yet a primary finding of my research is that the extent of ghetto and barrio poverty within a metropolitan area and the changes in it over time are largely determined by dynamic metropolitan-wide processes. The most important of these is the functioning of the metropolitan economy, as reflected in the overall level of income and the inequality in its income distribution. Beyond the economy, spatial segregation, along both racial and class lines, also affects neighborhood poverty. In the end, I conclude neighborhood factors—such as location relative to available jobs or a local culture of poverty—play a more limited role than is commonly believed.

Hypotheses about the causal factors underlying the growth of ghettos and barrios are controversial. There is little agreement on how to explain their growth and the relative importance of various factors in the process. Part of the difficulty in resolving these issues lies in the lack of a clearly specified model of how high-poverty neighborhoods are related to their metropolitan areas. In this chapter, I outline such a model and then test the hypothesis that neighborhood poverty is largely the result of metropolitan-wide processes of income generation and neighborhood sorting. To the extent possible, I try to indicate the relative importance of different factors.

Structural Links

Hughes (1989) has argued that "we cannot understand changes in the ghetto without understanding changes in its metropolitan context." Indeed, one problem with much public policy discussion of ghetto neighborhoods is its narrow focus on the residents' social and economic characteristics. There are at least two problems with this. First, these characteristics are often highly exaggerated because they are based on the most deviant neighborhoods or the most deviant individuals. As chapter 4 showed, poor neighborhoods have a great diversity of social and economic characteristics. Second, such a focus treats poor neighborhoods as if they were self-perpetuating islands within the metropolitan area. Looking narrowly at ghettos leads naturally to a focus on the attitudes, values, choices, and behaviors of ghetto residents (or at least assumptions and preconceptions about these matters) as a means of explaining the size or growth of ghetto neighborhoods.

For example, in a *Newsweek* column that is fairly typical of commentary about urban poverty, Joe Klein (1994) wrote,

> The problem in the Fort Greene projects isn't the absence of jobs. It's the culture of poverty. It's the pattern of dependent, irresponsible, antisocial behavior that has its roots in the perverse incentives of the welfare system, and the legacy of white racism, and the general, societal obsession with sex, materialism and violence and—yes—the departure of manufacturing jobs as well. (p. 57)

Although he acknowledges a role for the economy (almost as an afterthought), it is seen as secondary to the neighborhood culture, in this case, that of the Fort Greene projects.

Mickey Kaus (1994) provides another example of how poor neighborhoods and the conditions within them are viewed in isolation. In comparing welfare reform to a pending crime bill, he asked, "What . . . will make the streets safer: creating fifty-eight new federal death penalties, or shrinking the culture of poverty and broken families that welfare subsidizes?" (p. 6). Implicit in Kaus's question is the view that welfare and social programs lead to the conditions found in poor neighborhoods, so that cutting cash assistance to the poor will actually lower crime. His statement is remarkable in not recognizing that reducing public assistance will almost certainly *increase* crime in the short run, even if he is right about the role of welfare in shaping cultural attitudes within poor neighborhoods. But when such neighborhoods are viewed in isolation, analysts must locate within them both the presumed cause (welfare receipt) and the observed effects (social pathologies and ghetto expansion).

My point is not to deny the existence of social problems in ghetto and barrio neighborhoods. But acknowledging the realities of life in ghettos and barrios does not automatically lead to the conclusion that a culture of deviance from mainstream norms causes or sustains neighborhood poverty. Hicks (1994) notes that it is a common mistake to observe a preponderance of social problems in certain locations and conclude that the locations caused the problems. In our highly mobile society, the possibility must be acknowledged that people with economic and social problems from throughout a metropolitan area (and indeed beyond) tend to gravitate to neighborhoods where there are low rents, public housing, or targeted service provision (Hicks 1994; Tienda 1991).

Poor neighborhoods are dynamically linked to metropolitan labor markets, housing markets, and social networks. People—both poor and nonpoor—are constantly moving in and out of ghettos and barrios (Gramlich, Laren, and Sealand 1992; Massey, Gross, and Shibuya 1994). To appreciate fully the causes of the increases in neighborhood poverty that have been so prevalent in the 1980s, these connections to the larger metropolis must be clearly understood.

Distribution of Neighborhoods

Descriptive terms like "ghetto" or "underclass neighborhood"—and the research based on them—often contribute to the impression that there is a hard and fast division between ordinary neighborhoods and troubled ones. The same is true of poverty studies: scholars and the public become fixated on "the poor": families with incomes below the federal poverty line. Meanwhile, families with one dollar of income in excess of the poverty line are technically not poor, even though their quality of life may be indistinguishable from that of many "poor" families. Indeed, given idiosyncratic family circumstances (sickness of a family member, debt problems, poor household management skills), the latter family may be worse off in many cases. While there is a great value to operationalizing concepts in ways that can be measured consistently across time and space, such definitions oversimplify reality to a certain extent.

Nevertheless, the term *high-poverty area* does obscure the reality of a continuous range of neighborhoods rated by their economic status, just as there is a continuous range of households by income. In other words, there is a distribution of neighborhoods—defined by some measure of each neighborhood's income—with a broad middle area that includes most neighborhoods. It also has an upper tail composed of the very wealthiest neighborhoods and a lower tail composed of ghetto and barrio neighborhoods. Most research on neighborhood poverty analyzes the lower tail rather than the factors that shape the distribution of neighborhoods as a whole.

To be more specific, the *neighborhood distribution of income* is the distribution of households by the mean household income of the neighborhood in which they live. The neighborhood distribution of income is analogous to the more familiar household distribution of income. The only difference is that when the households are tallied up, each household is sorted by the average income for the neighborhood, rather than its own income. Equivalently, one could say the neighborhood distribution of income is the distribution of neighborhoods by the mean income of the neighborhood, weighting each neighborhood by the number of households it contains. Weighting by households is necessary because of the large variation in the size of census tracts. Since ghettos and barrios are among the poorest neighborhoods, they are represented by the neighborhoods at the extreme right of the distribution.[1]

Figure 6.1 compares the household and neighborhood income distributions for four major metropolitan areas. (The household distributions are shown as line graphs whereas the neighborhood distributions are shown as bar graphs to enhance readability.) In the Chicago metropolitan area, for example, approximately one million households live in neighborhoods with average household incomes of $35,000 to $50,000 (the tallest bar). Only about four hundred thousand households, however, had individual household incomes in that range. Indeed, the household distribution of income is much

Figure 6.1 Distribution of Household Income and Neighborhood Income, Four Metropolitan Areas, 1990

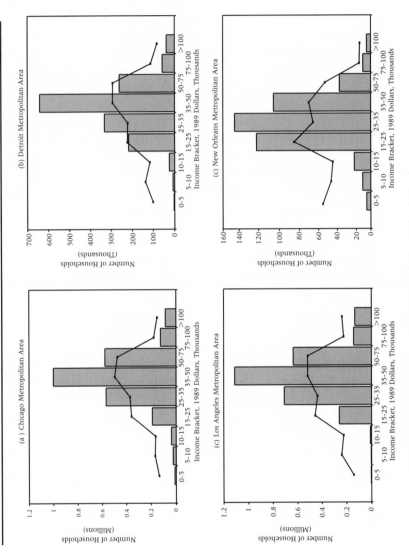

Source: 1990 census, Summary Tape File 3A (CD-ROM), tabulations by the author.

broader (that is, flatter) in all four metropolitan areas. One can see that in all four areas, a household is more likely to live in a neighborhood with a mean income in the $25,000–$50,000 range than to have its own income fall in that range.

Although the official poverty threshold varies by family size, assume that households with incomes below $15,000 are poor and that neighborhoods with *average* incomes below $15,000 are ghettos and barrios. Using these crude rules of thumb, the households falling below the threshold in the household income distribution (the lowest three income brackets in figure 6.1) would be poor, and the proportion of the distribution below the line would be the analog of the poverty rate. Similarly, the households below the cutoff point in the neighborhood distribution would be considered to reside in high-poverty areas, and the proportion of such households would be analogous to the level of neighborhood poverty. In these four metropolitan areas, several points stand out:

The number of poor households is well above the number of households in high-poverty areas, so most poor households reside outside such areas;

The poverty rate exceeds the level of neighborhood poverty in all four areas;

A much larger proportion of New Orleans households are located in poor neighborhoods, whereas Los Angeles appears to have the lowest rate of neighborhood poverty (consistent with the findings in chapter 3).

The distributions in figure 6.1 include households of all races and ethnicities. Figure 6.2 shows the analogous distributions for black households only. Both the household and neighborhood distributions are shifted to the left, relative to the overall distributions, so that there is a greater proportion of poor households and a greater proportion of households residing in ghettos. This shift is particularly noticeable in New Orleans, which has the highest ghetto poverty level of the four areas. The disparity between the proportion of poor households and ghetto households is also smaller, since black poor households are more likely to live in the ghetto. As

Figure 6.2   Distribution of Black Household Income and Black Neighborhood Income, Four Metropolitan Areas, 1990

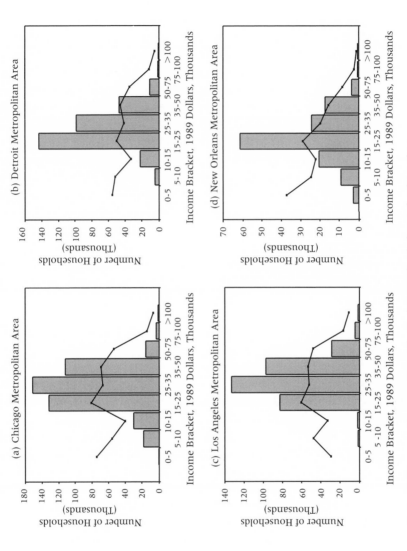

Source: 1990 census, Summary Tape File 3A (CD-ROM), tabulations by the author.

noted earlier, however, only about one-third of poor blacks in metropolitan areas lived in ghetto neighborhoods.

Parameters of the Neighborhood Distribution

If high-poverty areas may be conceptualized as that segment of the
distribution of neighborhoods below a threshold level, one cannot
look only within ghettos and barrios for an explanation of neighborhood poverty. Although a causal role for within-neighborhood
factors is not by any means ruled out, a logical reaction to thinking of poor neighborhoods as part of a larger distribution of neighborhoods is to ask what factors shape this larger distribution. In
other words, neighborhood poverty *could* increase because of
changes occurring mainly in the neighborhoods that make up the
lower tail of the neighborhood distribution, for example, a culture
of poverty that develops only in poor neighborhoods. Yet, when
there is a change in the proportion of a distribution below some
threshold, changes in the parameters of the distribution itself are
obvious suspects. The relative magnitude of macro-level forces and
neighborhood-specific forces in determining the size of and change
in neighborhood poverty is, therefore, an open question. The
empirical task is to evaluate the extent to which changes in the
parameters of the neighborhood distribution cause or sustain poor
neighborhoods, in contrast to factors unique to the lower portion
of the distribution.

Figure 6.3 is a schematic outline of the forces shaping the neighborhood distribution of income. The first set of forces—the income-
generation process—is the primary determinant of the distribution
of household income. The income-generation process primarily
reflects the macroeconomic and institutional functioning of the
labor market. It also includes transfer payments and other sources
of income. Moreover, changes in family structure and the decisions
of individuals to participate in the labor force also affect income distribution among households. These processes interact in complex
ways to produce the distribution of household income.

Typically, analysts are concerned with two aspects of household
income distribution: its overall level and its degree of inequality.
The overall level is typically measured by either the mean or
median. A wide variety of measures of income inequality have

Figure 6.3   Neighborhood Poverty and Its Relation to the Metropolitan
Context: Schematic Diagram with Short-Run Causal Links

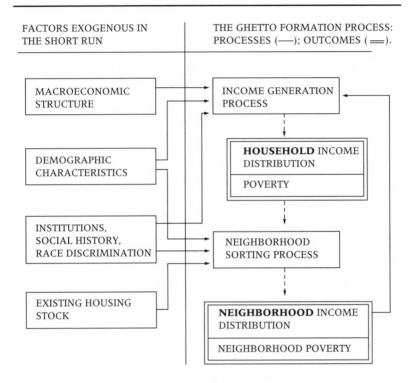

been proposed; one of the most common is the *coefficient of variation*, which is simply the standard deviation of household income divided by the mean: a measure of how spread out household incomes are after controlling for the mean income level. Controlling for the mean level is important when making comparisons across metropolitan areas, because our intuitive sense of what we mean by inequality implies that a metropolitan area with a standard deviation of household income of $20,000 and mean of $20,000 has more inequality than a metropolitan area with the same standard deviation but a mean of $100,000. In the following analyses, I refer to the former variable as *MSAMEAN* and the latter as *INEQUALITY*.

Neighborhood sorting processes—the functioning of the housing market, housing discrimination, and individual preferences regarding desirable neighborhood characteristics—determine how segregated households of different incomes are from one another. By far, the most powerful influence on this process in the United States is racial segregation. Since whites, on average, earn more than blacks, and since whites and blacks are highly residentially segregated from one another, residential sorting along the income dimension is partly a result of sorting along racial lines. But there is also economic segregation *within* each race (see chapter 5). The actual levels of economic segregation within racial groups are relatively low (Massey and Eggers 1990, 1993; White 1987), but they are rising (Jargowsky 1996, table 2).

In figure 6.3, a feedback loop leads from the neighborhood distribution of income to the household distribution of income. This pathway simply represents the possibility that the average income of a neighborhood has an independent effect on an individual's income, after controlling for individual characteristics and local labor market characteristics (Corcoran and others 1992). This is a separate issue from the effect of the neighborhood's physical location. Although neighborhoods probably have a direct effect on wages and employment, these effects are secondary compared with factors composing the income-generation process.

Table 6.1 shows the means and standard deviations of the household and neighborhood distributions for the four metropolitan areas in figures 6.1 and 6.2. The means of the two distributions for each area are identical; this is a mathematical necessity.[2] The standard deviation of the household income distribution is greater, however, than the standard deviation of the neighborhood income distribution. This is a logical consequence of the diversity of incomes within each neighborhood and the numerical representation of the fact that the household distribution is broader and flatter than the neighborhood distribution. At one theoretical extreme, if there were absolutely no segregation by income, all neighborhoods would have the same mean income and the standard deviation of the neighborhood distribution would be zero. At the other, if there were complete economic segregation, all households would live in neighborhoods with mean incomes that approximate their own income. In that case, the standard deviation of the neighborhood distribution would begin to approach the standard deviation of the household distribution.

These properties of the standard deviation of the neighborhood distribution of income suggest that a useful measure of economic segregation is the ratio of the neighborhood-income standard deviation to the household-income standard deviation. In table 6.1, this ratio ranges from 0.377 in New Orleans to 0.535 in Detroit. I refer to this ratio as the Neighborhood Sorting Index (Jargowsky 1995, 1996). When there is almost no economic segregation, NSI approaches zero because its numerator—the standard deviation of the neighborhood distribution—approaches zero. That is, each neighborhood shares the same economic mix of households as the metropolitan area as a whole, and so the neighborhood means are tightly clustered around the overall mean. When economic segregation is nearly complete, the NSI approaches one as the two standard deviations converge, because there is little difference between a household's income and the mean income of its neighborhood.

Table 6.1   Comparison of Household and Neighborhood Income Distributions, Four Metropolitan Areas, 1990

Distribution	Chicago	Detroit	Los Angeles	New Orleans
Household income				
Mean	$45,977	$42,293	$47,253	$32,659
Standard deviation	$51,564	$39,258	$54,936	$41,307
Coefficient of variation (income inequality)	1.122	0.928	1.163	1.265
Neighborhood income				
Mean	$45,977	$42,293	$47,253	$32,569
Standard deviation	$22,240	$20,999	$26,437	$15,573
Ratio of standard deviations (Neighborhood Sorting Index)	0.431	0.535	0.481	0.377
Proportion of variance between neighborhoods	0.186	0.286	0.232	0.142

Source: 1990 U.S. Census on Population and Housing, STF 3A (CD-ROMs), tabulations by the author.
Note: For estimator of the standard deviation of household income from census data, see Jargowsky (1995), appendix A.

This measure is very useful for comparisons across cities and over time. The square of NSI, also shown in table 6.1, is the ratio of the variance of the neighborhood distribution to the variance of the household distribution. Those familiar with analysis of variance (ANOVA) will recognize that NSI-squared is the proportion of the total variance in household income among rather than within neighborhoods.[3]

Just three variables therefore can completely represent the information about the household and neighborhood income distributions shown in table 6.1: mean income (*MSAMEAN*), income inequality (*INEQUALITY*), and the degree of economic segregation (*NSI*). The first two are primarily determined by the income-generation process. The third variable measures economic segregation arising from the neighborhood sorting process. The next step is to use these parameters to derive the mathematical relationship between the parameters of income generation and neighborhood sorting and the resulting levels of ghetto and barrio poverty. In so doing, the precise relationship between poor neighborhoods and their metropolitan areas will be clarified.

Predicting Ghetto Poverty from Metropolitan Parameters

From measures of the mean and standard deviation of the neighborhood distribution, the expected neighborhood poverty rate (NPR) in a metropolitan area can be calculated, if certain assumptions are made about the shape of that distribution. As a basic test of the neighborhood distribution hypothesis, these predictions, based on metropolitan-level parameters, can be compared with levels of neighborhood poverty calculated directly from census tract data.

Figures 6.1 and 6.2 suggest that it is plausible to assume that neighborhood distributions are approximately normal. To calculate the proportion of a normal distribution below a given level, only the relevant standardized score (represented by z) needs to be calculated and then translated into a cumulative normal probability (typically represented mathematically by the symbol Φ). Thus,

$$6.1 \quad NPR = \Phi(z) = \Phi\left(\frac{T - MSAMEAN}{\sigma_N}\right)$$

where T represents a threshold income level that identifies high-poverty areas and σ_N is the standard deviation of the neighborhood distribution. However, the relationships described above suggest that σ_N can be rewritten in terms of the metropolitan mean income, inequality, and neighborhood sorting. From the definition of *NSI* can be derived an expression for σ_N:

6.2 $\sigma_N = \sigma_H * NSI$

In this expression, σ_H is the standard deviation of the household distribution of income. From the definition of *INEQUALITY*, which is σ_H divided by the metropolitan mean, one gets an expression for σ_H:

6.3 $\sigma_H = MSAMEAN * INEQUALITY$

From these two substitutions, the expression for the neighborhood poverty rate can be written as

6.4 $NPR = \Phi\left(\dfrac{T - MSAMEAN}{MSAMEAN * INEQUALITY * NSI} \right)$

Equation 6.4 suggests three conceptually distinct reasons why a metropolitan area's neighborhood poverty level might increase:

Mean household income could decrease. Holding income inequality and neighborhood sorting constant, a *decrease* in mean income would shift both distributions down and *increase* the percentage of households in neighborhoods below the high-poverty threshold (top panel of figure 6.4).

Income inequality could increase. Holding mean income and neighborhood sorting constant, an *increase* in income inequality would result in more neighborhood poverty by "spreading out" both distributions (bottom panel of figure 6.4), so that more households are in neighborhoods that fall below the threshold. (The relative spread of the two distributions does not change if the NSI is held constant.)

Figure 6.4   Changes in Neighborhood Poverty Resulting from Changes in
            Income Generation

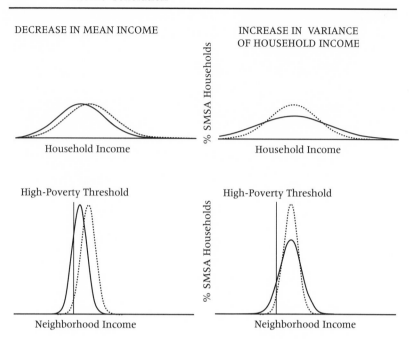

DECREASE IN MEAN INCOME

INCREASE IN VARIANCE
OF HOUSEHOLD INCOME

% SMSA Households

Household Income

Household Income

High-Poverty Threshold

High-Poverty Threshold

% SMSA Households

Neighborhood Income

Neighborhood Income

Neighborhood sorting could increase. Even if the metropolitan mean
income and the degree of income inequality were held constant,
an increase in the degree of economic segregation would lead to
an increase in the spread of the neighborhood distribution, as
shown in figure 6.5, again resulting in more neighborhoods
below the threshold.

Specifying the links used twice between metropolitan-level processes
and neighborhood poverty makes it easier to identify the links in the
causal chain. Consider the oft-cited transformation from manufacturing to services (Kasarda 1989). The shift from manufacturing to
service-sector jobs could create ghettos and barrios in several conceptually distinct ways. It could simply make people poorer—that is,
lower the mean of the household income distribution, so that more

Figure 6.5 Changes in Neighborhood Poverty Resulting from Changes in Neighborhood Sorting

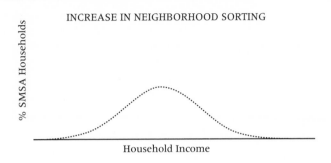

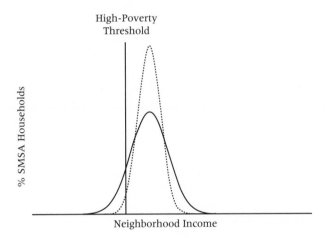

of the distribution was below the threshold. Alternatively, it could increase the inequality of household income if middle-income manufacturing jobs are replaced by low- and high-paying jobs in the service sector. The increase in inequality, holding the mean constant, would shift more households over the threshold and therefore increase neighborhood poverty. Finally, the distribution of income could be unaffected, but the location of the new service-sector jobs in the peripheral areas could affect the neighborhood sorting process. Better educated persons, able to obtain good employment in the service sector, might follow jobs out of the downtown area, with the result that economic segregation would increase.

A Single-Group Model of Ghetto Formation

If the hypothesis advanced above—namely, that neighborhood poverty is largely the result of metropolitan-wide processes of income generation and neighborhood sorting—is correct, then the model should accurately predict the level of neighborhood poverty in a metropolitan area simply from metropolitan parameters of income generation and neighborhood sorting. If the hypothesis is false, and the extent of neighborhood poverty is strongly influenced by neighborhood-level variables, then the three metropolitan-level parameters (*MSAMEAN, INEQUALITY*, and *NSI*) are inadequate in themselves to predict the level of neighborhood poverty. In other words, if neighborhood poverty is created and sustained by forces that originate or operate in or near ghettos and barrios, then information about specific neighborhoods is needed to predict the level of neighborhood poverty in a metropolitan area, in addition to information about the metropolitan area as a whole.

I first test the hypothesis empirically by seeing how well it can predict the level of ghetto poverty—that is, the black neighborhood poverty rate—in 1990 and the changes in ghetto poverty between 1980 and 1990.[4] As in figure 6.2, I consider data for black households only; in other words, the household distribution of income will include only black households, and the neighborhood distribution will be based on the mean black household income in each neighborhood. This is a simplifying assumption, since the mean income of a neighborhood is actually the weighted average of the mean incomes of the different racial and ethnic groups that share the neighborhood. (In the next section, I specifically allow for interactions among different racial groups.) Thus, the methodology here treats metropolitan areas as if they were completely segregated by race.

To make use of equation 6.4, I must specify a threshold level for mean household income. An income cutoff of $17,092 in 1989 dollars is comparable to the 40 percent poverty level employed earlier. In previous research, this level was selected to maximize the metropolitan-level correlation with ghetto poverty as measured by the standard definition, based on census tracts with poverty rates of 40 percent or more (Jargowsky 1991).[5] Then, for each metropolitan area, the actual level of ghetto poverty using the income criterion is calculated from tract-level data and a prediction of the level of ghetto poverty is calculated, based solely on metropolitan-level parameters and equation 6.4.

The predicted poverty levels for 1990 are plotted against the actual ghetto poverty figures calculated from the tract-level data in figure 6.6. The correspondence between the predicted values and the actual values is extremely strong, with a correlation coefficient of more than 0.95. In one sense, the close correspondence between predictions based on the model and the actual values is impressive, given that only three parameters were used, all of which are calculated at the metropolitan level with no special emphasis or weighting given to ghetto neighborhoods. Clearly, ghetto poverty, at least defined in this way, is almost entirely a function of income generation and neighborhood sorting at the metropolitan level,

Figure 6.6   Predicted Versus Actual Levels of Neighborhood Poverty Among Blacks, 1990

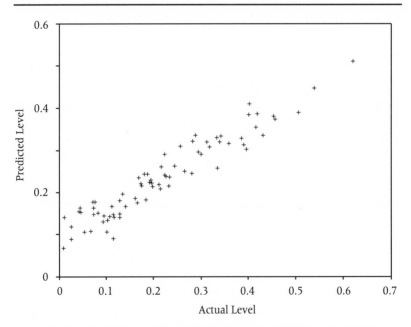

Source: 1990 census, Summary Tape File 3A (CD-ROM), tabulations by the author.

both in cross-section and over time. On the other hand, one could argue that the model is true by definition, which is not entirely true since the predicted values could be in error to the extent that actual neighborhood distributions do not conform to a normal distribution. Given how the variables are defined, it is not surprising that the model is effective in predicting cross-sectional variation.

A more useful application of the conceptual framework is to see how well the model explains changes over time in ghetto poverty. If neighborhood-specific factors create and sustain ghettos, then the ability to predict change in ghetto poverty merely from metropolitan parameters would be limited. To examine this issue, I used the model to predict ghetto poverty levels for 1980 and 1990, and the change between 1980 and 1990. These predicted changes are plotted against the actual changes calculated from the tract-level data in figure 6.7. Again, the model predicts the changes with great precision. The changes in ghetto poverty—at least in this simplified model—seem driven largely by metropolitan-level processes that shift the entire household and neighborhood income distributions and not by local factors that would show up as changes in one tail of the distribution.

As noted above, there are at least three ways that ghetto poverty could increase—through a decline in mean income, through an increase in income inequality, and through an increase in neighborhood sorting. Of these, changes in the metropolitan mean have the largest impact on ghetto poverty by far. Changes in mean income alone account for more than 72 percent of the variance in ghetto poverty between 1980 and 1990.[6] When all three variables are used, the variance explained rises to 80 percent. The same pattern is seen when the changes in ghetto poverty between 1970 and 1980 are analyzed. Changes in mean household income alone explain about 84 percent of the variation in ghetto poverty; adding the information on income inequality and neighborhood sorting increases the variance only slightly, to 88 percent (Jargowsky 1991). Interestingly, when the 1970–80 analysis is run separately for different regions, the relative importance of income generation and neighborhood sorting is partly reversed. When the analysis is limited to cities in the Northeast and Midwest, income-generation factors account for at best 41 percent of the variance. When neighborhood sorting is added, the

Figure 6.7   Predicted Versus Actual Changes in Neighborhood Poverty
Among Blacks, 1980 to 1990

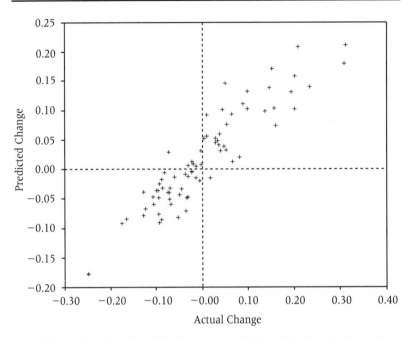

Source: Census tract data for 1970–90 (see appendix A), tabulations by the author.

percentage of the variance rises to 79 percent. (A similar pattern
is not observed for 1980–90.)

These analyses, however, are based on a highly simplified model.
Because this version of the model considers only black households,
it cannot be used to assess the role of racial segregation (or, for that
matter, integration) in ghetto poverty. Clearly, the effects of racial
segregation, both in themselves and in their influence on other
variables, are important questions that need to be addressed. Hence,
the following analysis does take account of residential interactions
between blacks and other groups.

Expanding the Model

The previous section indicated the power of thinking about ghettos
as part of a larger distribution of neighborhoods, which itself is
shaped by income-generation and neighborhood sorting processes.

The analysis can be broadened to include multiple racial and ethnic groups and to allow for residential sorting along economic and racial lines by using additional variables.

Additional Variables

Despite high levels of racial segregation, very few neighborhoods are either all white or all black. The mean income of any given neighborhood will be a weighted average of the mean incomes of the racial and ethnic groups in it. In addition to overall mean household income, a way to measure the economic status of each subgroup is needed. The mean household income of the group is a possible measure but suffers from a high degree of collinearity with the overall mean income. Instead, I retain the *MSAMEAN* variable and add the *ratio* of black mean household income to the overall mean income ($INCRATIO_{blk}$), when analyzing ghetto poverty, and the ratio of Hispanic mean household income to the overall mean ($INCRATIO_{hsp}$), when analyzing barrio poverty. Further, I add two variables to represent the extent of income inequality within the black and Hispanic income distributions ($INEQUAL_{blk}$ and $INEQUAL_{hsp}$) to supplement the overall measure of income inequality ($INEQUALITY$). Taken together, these variables capture the essential aspects of the income-generation process for metropolitan areas. The overall mean establishes the center of the distribution for both household and neighborhood income, and the two mean-income ratios locate black and Hispanic household income distributions in relation to that center. The inequality variables then measure the dispersion of the overall and subgroup income distributions.

Additional variables are also needed to characterize the neighborhood sorting process when more than one group is involved. In the previous analysis, the neighborhood sorting index was the only variable needed because only one group was involved. With more than one group and sorting along both economic and racial/ethnic lines, several new variables must be added. Residential segregation by race and ethnicity can be measured by the index of dissimilarity ($DISSIM_{wht/blk}$ and $DISSIM_{wht/hsp}$). This index measures only one dimension of segregation—the evenness of the spatial distribution of two distinct groups (Massey and Denton 1988). It is not sensitive to the relative size of the two groups. Yet the impact of black or Hispanic incomes on neighborhood mean incomes will depend not only on how evenly they are spread out among neighborhoods but also on the proportion of the neighborhood's population they constitute. Thus, the percentage of metropolitan blacks (*PCTBLACK*) and percentage of Hispanics (*PCTHISPANIC*) are added to the analysis. In addition to the overall NSI, measures of the economic segregation within the black and Hispanic communities are added (NSI_{blk} and NSI_{hsp}).

All variables are drawn from the same data sources used in chapters 2 and 3. The following key variables are employed in the analysis:

Income-Generation Variables

MSAMEAN: Metropolitan mean household income;

INEQUALITY: The coefficient of variation (the standard deviation of the household income distribution divided by the mean);

$INCRATIO_{blk}$: Ratio of black mean household income to metropolitan mean household income;

$INEQUAL_{blk}$: Standard deviation of black household income divided by the black mean household income;

$INCRATIO_{hsp}$: Ratio of Hispanic mean household income to metropolitan mean household income;

$INEQUAL_{hsp}$: Standard deviation of Hispanic household income divided by the Hispanic mean household income.

Neighborhood Sorting Variables

PCTBLACK: Percentage black of total metropolitan area population;

PCTHISPANIC: Percentage Hispanic of total metropolitan area population;

$DISSIM_{wht/blk}$: Index of dissimilarity of blacks from whites;

$DISSIM_{wht/hsp}$: Index of dissimilarity of Hispanics from whites;

NSI: Economic segregation (neighborhood sorting index, as defined previously);

NSI_{blk}: Economic segregation among blacks;

NSI_{hsp}: Economic segregation among Hispanics.

Implications for Functional Form

Another implication of the conceptual model is that the relationships between neighborhood poverty and the variables that shift the household and neighborhood income distributions are not linear. For example, consider the effect of decreases in metropolitan mean household income on neighborhood poverty, assuming a starting level near zero. If the shape of the neighborhood distribution is approximately normal, as it appears to be in figure 6.1, decreases in the mean will at first cause only small increases in neighborhood poverty, as the tail of the distribution crosses the threshold. Once the more central portion of the distribution begins to cross the threshold, however, increases in neighborhood poverty will be much larger per dollar of decrease in mean household income.

A graph of the neighborhood poverty level versus mean income would approximate the shape of the cumulative normal distribution. A standard linear regression model would therefore be inappropriate, since the effects of the independent variables on the dependent variable are not constant. If the dependent variable is transformed into log-odds form, however, the model will be specified correctly. Letting *NPR* represent the neighborhood poverty rate, defined as the percentage of the population (of whatever racial or ethnic group) that resides in high-poverty census tracts, the transformed variable is given by

$$6.5 \quad NPR' = \ln\left(\frac{NPR}{1-NPR}\right)$$

The log-odds of a percentage graphed against the original percentage has a shape very similar to the cumulative normal distribution, as shown in figure 6.8. It has the desired functional form in that variables that shift the log-odds of ghetto poverty in a linear way will shift the level of ghetto poverty in a nonlinear way. As a further advantage, the log-odds ratio is a continuous variable, whereas the untransformed level of ghetto poverty is restricted to

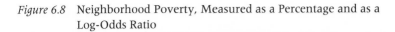

Figure 6.8   Neighborhood Poverty, Measured as a Percentage and as a Log-Odds Ratio

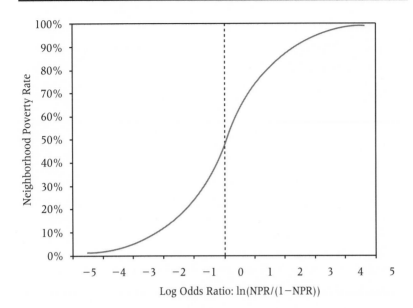

the range of zero to one. A restricted range variable violates several of the underlying assumptions of linear regression. For these reasons, the dependent variable in all these regression models is the log-odds ratio of the neighborhood poverty rate or changes in the log-odds ratio. The interpretation of the regression coefficients is slightly less straightforward when the dependent variable is transformed in this way, but a positive sign on a coefficient still implies that increases in the variable increase neighborhood poverty, and a negative sign still implies that increases in the variable decrease neighborhood poverty. The difference is that the exact magnitude of the impact varies depending on the starting point.

One further econometric issue concerns the variance of the error term in these regression models. Because the dependent variable is based on a proportion, its variance is inversely proportional to the size of the population, implying that the model is heteroskedastic. Thus, all models are weighted by the square root of the metropolitan area population (Maddala 1977, 268). For the regressions using changes over time, the weight is the average of the weights from the beginning and ending points of the period in question.

Ghetto Poverty in 1990

Table 6.2 presents several regression models for ghetto poverty in 1990. The dependent variable is the log-odds of the black neighborhood poverty rate. Model 1 includes three dummy variables representing different regions. In addition, the percentage of jobs in manufacturing industries (*PCTMANUF*) and the percentage of jobs in professional and managerial occupations (*PCTPROF*) are included. If deindustrialization is an important contributor to ghetto poverty, then metropolitan areas with lower levels of manufacturing jobs should have higher ghetto poverty; a larger share of high-skill jobs should be associated with higher levels of ghetto poverty, since a smaller share of jobs would be available for persons with lower skill levels. These variables are included to illustrate how their effect, if any, operates indirectly through the parameters of income generation; after illustrating this point, they are dropped from the final model.

Although the coefficient on *PCTMANUF* in model 1 has the expected sign, it is statistically insignificant. The coefficient on *PCTPROF* is significant but negative indicating that a higher share of high-skill jobs is actually associated with lower levels of ghetto poverty. In the absence of a control for the metropolitan income level, however, the *PCTPROF* variable may be acting as a proxy for economies that have been growing in recent years. Model 1 also indicates that ghetto poverty levels are higher in metropolitan areas in the Midwest, Northeast, and South than in the reference category—in this case, metropolitan areas in the West.

Model 2 introduces the variables for the income-generation process that were discussed above. These include metropolitan mean household income (*MSAMEAN*) and the ratio of black mean income to the overall mean (*INCRATIO$_{blk}$*). Both of these variables are strongly significant. The standardized coefficients (found in the column labeled "beta") indicate that a one-standard-deviation decrease in the metropolitan mean income increases the log-odds of ghetto poverty by more than one-half of a standard deviation; this is the largest standardized effect of any of the variables included

Table 6.2   Analysis of Cross-Sectional Variation in Neighborhood Poverty, Black 1990

DEPENDENT VARIABLE: Level of neighborhood poverty (log-odds), 1990

	Model 1				Model 2				Model 3			
	Coeff.	Beta	Std. Err.	t	Coeff.	Beta	Std. Err.	t	Coeff.	Beta	Std. Err.	t
Intercept	0.334	0.000	0.828	0.40	1.622	0.000	1.608	1.01	−0.159	0.000	1.438	0.11
MIDWEST	1.205***	0.519	0.280	4.31	0.731***	0.315	0.182	4.02	0.380**	0.164	0.183	2.07
NORTHEAST	0.684**	0.288	0.273	2.50	0.559***	0.236	0.170	3.29	0.432**	0.182	0.170	2.54
SOUTH	0.641***	0.352	0.233	2.75	0.063	0.034	0.169	0.37	−0.025	−0.013	0.177	0.14
Industry and occupations												
PCTMANUF	−0.887	−0.052	1.766	0.50	0.721	0.042	1.124	0.64				
PCTPROF	−9.446***	−0.392	2.277	4.15	−0.607	−0.025	2.027	0.30				
Income generation												
MSAMEAN					−0.071***	−0.531	0.013	5.65	−0.095***	−0.712	0.009	10.57
INCRATIO$_{blk}$					−5.995***	−0.344	1.104	5.43	−4.391***	−0.252	1.034	4.25
INEQUALITY					1.178***	0.164	0.441	2.68	0.886**	0.123	0.395	2.24
INEQUAL$_{blk}$					2.197**	0.166	0.927	2.37	1.762**	0.133	0.826	2.13
Neighborhood sorting												
PCTBLACK									0.877	0.091	0.663	1.32
DISSIM$_{wht/blk}$									1.646***	0.206	0.595	2.77
NSI									2.655***	0.169	1.042	2.55
NSI$_{blk}$									0.265	0.028	0.593	0.45
N	116				116				116			
R^2	0.286				0.740				0.799			
Adj R^2	0.253				0.718				0.777			

Note: Significance levels: ***p < 0.01; **p < 0.05; *p < 0.10.

in the model. Both overall income inequality and income inequality among blacks (*INEQUALITY* and *INEQUAL$_{blk}$*) are statistically significant and have the expected effect, increasing ghetto poverty. The two variables have nearly identical standardized coefficients, suggesting similar contributions to ghetto poverty.

The model's explanatory power is far greater when the income-distribution parameters are added, indicated by an increase in R^2 from 0.29 in model 1 to 0.74 in model 2. Thus, nearly half of the variance (0.45) in the dependent variable is explained by the income-generation variables. But this is a lower bound on the explained variance because of an inherent ambiguity in the concept (Farkas 1974). A regression including only the income-distribution parameters—one that omits the region dummies and the two job-share variables—has an R^2 of 0.65 (regression not shown). The total variance in the dependent variable explained by the income distribution parameters is therefore between 45 and 65 percent, depending on how one thinks about the covariance between the two sets of variables. Variables added in later models may further complicate efforts to allocate the variance, but in any case the basic opportunity structure, as represented by the overall distribution of metropolitan income, income inequality, and the ratio of black average income to the total, is the key determinant of ghetto poverty among blacks.

Model 2 also shows that once these measures of income generation are taken into account, neither the share of manufacturing jobs nor that of high-skill jobs has any influence on ghetto poverty. In other words, holding the level of income and income inequality constant, it does not matter whether jobs are in manufacturing or other sectors, or whether more jobs are in professional and managerial occupations.[7] The coefficient on the dummy variable for the southern region also becomes insignificant once the income distribution is controlled, and the size of the coefficients on the Northeast and Midwest fall substantially. The higher levels of ghetto poverty for their metropolitan areas compared with the West are partly explained—and in the case of the South, fully explained—by differences in the regions' income distributions.

Model 3 adds the variables representing neighborhood sorting processes.[8] These are the percentage of blacks in a metropolitan area

(*PCTBLACK*), residential segregation by race as measured by the index of dissimilarity (*DISSIM*$_{wht/blk}$), and two measures of economic segregation—the overall Neighborhood Sorting Index (*NSI*) and the neighborhood sorting index among blacks (*NSI*$_{blk}$). The percentage black coefficient is not statistically significant, suggesting that the process of ghetto formation works the same in metropolitan areas regardless of the relative size of the black population.[9] The segregation of whites from blacks is strongly significant and positive; in other words, higher levels of racial segregation are associated with higher ghetto poverty.

The two economic segregation variables tell an interesting story. When the black NSI is included alone, it attains borderline statistical significance ($t = 1.674$) and has the expected positive sign (regression not shown). This is consistent with the black-middle-class-flight hypothesis advanced by Wilson (1987). But when both the overall NSI and black NSI are included, as in model 3, only the overall NSI is statistically significant. The insignificance of the black NSI is not the result of a multicollinearity problem, since the bivariate correlation between them is below 0.40.[10] Rather, the interpretation is substantive: the overall neighborhood sorting process contributes more to the level of ghetto poverty than the economic segregation of blacks from each other. On the other hand, the middle-class-flight hypothesis is implicitly about changes over time; the regression on changes in ghetto poverty discussed below may be a better test of Wilson's hypothesis; the black NSI does perform better in a regression based on changes in ghetto poverty between 1980 and 1990.

Also of interest is the fact that despite the inclusion of income-generation and neighborhood sorting variables, the coefficients on the dummy variables for the Northeast and the Midwest remain positive and statistically significant. Metropolitan areas in these regions have more ghetto poverty than do those in the South and West, even after controlling for the theoretically relevant variables. A reason for the differences cannot easily be determined. For example, if racial discrimination in housing is more acute in these regions, presumably the index of dissimilarity would have picked up this effect. One possibility is that a greater proportion of Hispanics in the South and West, who may share neighborhoods with blacks, might decrease the poverty rate in such tracts. To test this hypothesis, I ran an additional model that included all the variables in model 3 and added the percent Hispanic, Hispanic relative income, the segregation of whites from Hispanics, and the segregation of blacks from Hispanics. None of these variables was significant, nor did they have much effect on either the size or statistical significance of the Northeast and Midwest regional dummies.

Model 3 has an R^2 of 0.80, only a small improvement over the percentage of the variance explained by model 2 ($R^2 = 0.74$). The standardized coefficient of the overall income level of the metropolitan area (-0.71) indicates it has by far the largest effect of any individual variable; the next largest standardized coefficient is the black/total income ratio (-0.25), followed by residential segregation by race (0.21). This analysis, then, of the complex interactions among racial and ethnic groups bears out the basic conclusion of my earlier simplified single-race analysis—that household income distribution is the most powerful predictor of ghetto poverty.

Ghetto Poverty in 1970 and 1980

Table 6.3 applies model 3 from the previous table to ghetto poverty in 1970 and 1980. The 1990 coefficients and significance levels for model 3 are repeated to allow for comparisons. On the whole, a similar picture emerges, though there are some important differences in the details. Income-generation parameters are consistently significant, with the single exception of inequality among blacks in 1970; the magnitudes of the coefficients vary little across the decades.

In contrast, the neighborhood sorting parameters are quite different in the earlier years. The percent black, which was not significant in the 1990 regression, has larger and statistically significant positive coefficients in 1970 and 1980. Metropolitan areas with relatively larger black populations had higher levels of ghetto poverty in 1970 and 1980 after controlling for income-generation processes and the other neighborhood sorting parameters. Another important difference is that racial segregation has a much larger coefficient in the 1980 regression. Inspecting the standardized coefficients shows

Table 6.3 Regression Analyses of Neighborhood Poverty, Black 1970 and 1980

DEPENDENT VARIABLE: Level of neighborhood poverty among blacks in given year (log-odds)

	1970				1980				1990
	Coeff.	Beta	Std. Err.	t	Coeff.	Beta	Std. Err.	t	Coeff.
Intercept	5.033**	0.000	2.495	2.02	1.634	0.000	2.313	0.71	-0.159
MIDWEST	0.085	0.029	0.390	0.22	0.581*	0.204	0.311	1.87	0.380**
NORTHEAST	-0.450	-0.138	0.368	1.22	0.418	0.143	0.283	1.47	0.432**
SOUTH	-0.294	-0.122	0.399	0.74	0.412	0.183	0.289	1.43	-0.025
Income generation									
MSAMEAN	-0.091***	-0.299	0.034	2.72	-0.182***	-0.672	0.026	7.05	-0.095***
$INCRATIO_{blk}$	-9.812***	-0.446	2.400	4.09	-8.993***	-0.339	1.872	4.80	-4.391***
INEQUALITY	1.074*	0.177	0.623	1.73	-1.258*	-0.152	0.681	1.85	0.886**
$INEQUAL_{blk}$	-0.952	-0.100	1.070	0.89	3.006***	0.312	0.992	3.03	1.762**
Neighborhood sorting									
PCTBLACK	4.775***	0.325	1.555	3.07	3.388***	0.275	1.072	3.16	0.877
$DISSIM_{wht/blk}$	1.227	0.116	1.044	1.18	5.182***	0.469	0.980	5.29	1.646***
NSI	0.488	0.082	0.463	1.06	1.081	0.055	2.167	0.50	2.655**
NSI_{blk}	0.299	0.040	0.601	0.50	5.753***	0.397	1.692	3.40	0.265
N	74				103				116
R^2	0.664				0.704				0.799
Adj R^2	0.605				0.669				0.777

Notes: 1990 coefficients from table 6.2, model 3. (Shown for comparison purposes.)

that it has the second-largest effect, after *MSAMEAN*. And contrary to the 1990 regression, economic segregation among blacks is statistically significant, whereas overall economic segregation is not. Neither measure of economic segregation has a statistically significant effect in 1970. Perhaps this pattern of coefficients reflects the fact that economic segregation has been increasing over time, and therefore contributing more to the cross-sectional variations in neighborhood poverty in recent years.

Neighborhood Poverty Among Hispanics

Cross-sectional regressions for the percentage of Hispanics in high-poverty neighborhoods in 1970, 1980, and 1990 are shown in table 6.4. The indicated relationships between metropolitan-level income generation and neighborhood sorting are fairly consistent with those observed for blacks. Metropolitan mean income is strongly significant and has the largest standardized coefficient at all three points in time. The ratio between Hispanic mean household income and the overall mean household income is also significant—in all three regressions. Inequality does not appear to have an effect on the percentage of Hispanics in high-poverty neighborhoods, except for inequality among Hispanics in 1970.

The aspect of barrio formation among Hispanics that most differentiates them from blacks, according to these regressions, is residential segregation. Residential segregation of Hispanics from whites is not significant in any time period, whereas it did have a statistically significant coefficient for blacks in both 1980 and 1990. Economic segregation, however, does play a measurable role in the extent to which they live in high-poverty neighborhoods, as it did for blacks. In 1990, both the overall degree of economic segregation and economic segregation among Hispanics were significant; in the earlier years, only the latter was significant. As in the black regressions, the models explain nearly four-fifths of the variance. What is striking about these regressions is that despite the vastly different history of Hispanic poverty in the United States and despite Hispanics' unique language and culture, the conceptual framework presented in this chapter explains barrio poverty about as well as it does ghetto poverty.

Table 6.4 Regression Analyses of Neighborhood Poverty, Hispanics 1970 to 1990

DEPENDENT VARIABLE: Level of neighborhood poverty among Hispanics in a given year (log-odds)

	1970				1980				1990			
	Coeff.	Beta	Std. Err.	t	Coeff.	Beta	Std. Err.	t	Coeff.	Beta	Std. Err.	t
Intercept	-2.451	0.000	4.836	0.51	6.721	0.000	4.628	1.45	-1.653	0.000	3.115	0.53
MIDWEST	-1.911**	-0.241	0.870	2.20	1.940***	0.268	0.704	2.76	0.543	0.073	0.590	0.92
NORTHEAST	1.314	0.176	1.110	1.18	0.286	0.059	0.604	0.47	0.626	0.126	0.540	1.16
SOUTH	-0.595	-0.143	0.446	1.33	0.740*	0.193	0.400	1.85	-0.400	-0.099	0.353	1.13
Income generation												
$MSAMEAN$	-0.241***	-0.615	0.058	4.16	-0.251***	-0.714	0.052	4.82	-0.190***	-0.812	0.024	7.97
$INCRATIO_{hsp}$	-5.766**	-0.293	2.594	2.22	-10.158***	-0.453	3.157	3.22	-4.749*	-0.219	2.613	1.82
$INEQUALITY$	-0.080	-0.009	0.806	0.10	1.175	0.106	1.547	0.76	1.877	0.129	1.437	1.31
$INEQUAL_{hsp}$	5.660***	0.605	1.141	4.96	1.334	0.097	1.762	0.76	1.841	0.115	1.837	1.00
Neighborhood sorting												
$PCTHISPANIC$	3.299	0.355	2.147	1.54	1.446	0.164	1.870	0.77	2.923**	0.323	1.202	2.43
$DISSIM_{whit/hsp}$	1.074	0.087	2.556	0.42	0.754	0.057	2.909	0.26	2.175	0.164	2.225	0.98
NSI	-0.136	-0.013	0.712	0.19	3.013	0.109	4.450	0.68	6.564**	0.202	3.232	2.03
NSI_{hsp}	14.167***	0.490	3.496	4.05	5.250*	0.297	2.696	1.95	4.554***	0.289	1.645	2.77
N	26				42				56			
R^2	0.9481				0.8275				0.8165			
Adj R^2	0.9100				0.7664				0.7716			

Note: Significance levels: ***p < 0.01; **p < 0.05; *p < 0.10.

Changes in Neighborhood Poverty Between 1980 and 1990

Policymakers may be more concerned with what causes changes in neighborhood poverty over time than what explains variations among metropolitan areas at a given point in time. This section therefore focuses on recent changes in ghetto poverty. To start, I discuss some of the econometric issues involved in the transition from regressions on levels of a variable to regressions on the changes over time.

It is a fairly common practice to estimate regressions on both levels of a variable and changes in the same variable over time. In theory, if the relationships being estimated are based on fundamental economic and social relationships whose parameters do not change over time, regressions on levels and changes provide two different estimates of the same underlying parameters. For example, take two variables Y and X for 1990 and 1980; the coefficient on X can be estimated from a model using the 1980 levels or the 1990 levels:

6.6 $Y_{90i} = \beta_0 + \beta_1 X_{90i} + \mu_i + \epsilon_i$

6.7 $Y_{80i} = \beta_0 + \beta_1 X_{80i} + \mu_i + \delta_i$

The error term in this regression is broken into two parts: one part (μ_i) that is random across cities but is constant for a given metropolitan area regardless of the time period, and another part (ϵ_i, δ_i) that is random with respect to both city and time. One equation can be subtracted from the other to get the following:

6.8 $(Y_{90i} - Y_{80i}) = \beta_1(X_{90i} - X_{80i}) + \xi_i$

Here both the constant and the city-specific (fixed) part of the error term drop out. Yet this equation can be used to estimate the same parameter (the coefficient on X) as the two equations based on cross-sectional levels. In practice, however, one often gets quite different coefficients from the two approaches. Such differences may occur because the underlying process has changed over time, or because implicitly controlling for the city-specific error term removes a source of bias, or simply because of sampling variation.

Hanushek (1986, 1157) criticizes equation 6.8 because it assumes that the change over the decade is independent of the starting level. He suggests that the beginning level, in this case Y_{80}, can be shifted to the right-hand side of the equation and be treated as another independent variable:

6.9 $Y_{90i} = \alpha Y_{80i} + \beta_1(X_{90i} - X_{80i}) + \xi_i$

If the change over the decade is independent of the starting level, then the value of α is 1 and equations 6.8 and 6.9 are identical. But if cities with already high levels at the beginning of the period have larger increases after controlling for changes in the other X variables, then α will be greater than 1. If cities with high levels at the beginning of the period have smaller increases, other things being equal, then α will be less than 1. If, for whatever reason, α is not 1 and it is constrained to be 1 by estimating a regression equation like 6.8, then the coefficients on the other variables could be biased.[11]

In any case, the actual value of α is an empirical question, and so Hanushek's form of the equation was used, with the 1990 neighborhood poverty level as the dependent variable and the 1980 neighborhood poverty level entered as an independent variable. All the other variables are expressed as changes over the decade. Even though the dependent variable is the level of neighborhood poverty in 1990, the coefficients on the independent variables measure their contribution to the change in neighborhood poverty over the decade because the starting level is controlled for. Because the regional dummies are constant over the period, they drop out when the regression is converted to a changes form. Taking model 3 from table 6.2 as a point of departure, the basic model is

6.10 $NPR_{90} = f(NPR_{80}, \Delta MSAMEAN, \Delta INCRATIO_{blk}, \Delta INEQUALITY,$
$\Delta INEQUAL_{blk}, \Delta PCTBLACK, \Delta DISSIM_{wht/blk}, \Delta NSI,$
$\Delta NSI_{blk})$

In this equation, the symbol Δ represents the change in the variable between 1980 and 1990.

Changes in Neighborhood Poverty Between 1980 and 1990

Table 6.5 presents the regressions on changes in neighborhood poverty during the decade of the 1980s.[12] Results for ghetto poverty are shown in the top half of the table and those for barrio poverty in the bottom half. Comparable cross-sectional results are shown for comparison. The coefficient on ghetto poverty at the beginning of the period is substantially less than 1.[13] The pattern of coefficients on substantive variables is very similar to the corresponding cross-sectional model (model 3 from table 6.2), with many of the coefficients in the changes equation matching their counterparts in the cross-sectional equation in both sign and general order of magnitude.

The parameters representing the level of income, *MSAMEAN* (metropolitan mean household income) and *INCRATIO* (ratio of black mean household income to *MSAMEAN*) are strongly significant. As in the cross-sectional regressions, these coefficients have the largest effects (of those variables entered in a changes form) as measured by standardized regression coefficients. One area of difference between the cross-sectional and change regressions concerns the role of income inequality. In contrast to the cross-sectional regression, overall income inequality is not statistically significant in explaining the increases in ghetto poverty between 1980 and 1990. Black income inequality has a smaller coefficient and achieves only a borderline level of statistical significance ($p = 0.091$).

Differences are also apparent in terms of the variables measuring neighborhood sorting processes. The overall neighborhood sorting index (*NSI*) is insignificant in the changes regression, whereas the NSI for blacks becomes significant. Although economic segregation helps to explain differences among metropolitan areas, economic segregation *among* blacks contributed to changes in ghetto poverty in the 1980s. (Hence, Wilson's hypothesis of black middle-class flight is directly supported in the changes analysis, if not in the cross-section.) In addition, increases in residential segregation by race lead to increases in ghetto poverty, consistent with the cross-sectional regression.

By far, the most important difference between the cross-sectional findings and the changes analysis is that the variable for percent black in metropolitan areas increases dramatically and becomes sta-

Table 6.5   Analysis of Changes in Neighborhood Poverty, 1980–90

	Coeff.	Beta	Std. Err.	t	Coefficients from Cross-sectional Models, 1990
	Change in Neighborhood Poverty (Blacks)				
Intercept	−0.807***	0.000	0.207	3.90	
NPR_{80}	0.473***	0.559	0.043	10.95	
Income generation					
MSAMEAN	−0.062***	−0.288	0.012	5.07	−0.095***
$INCRATIO_{blk}$	−8.523***	−0.306	1.825	4.67	−4.391***
INEQUALITY	−0.330	−0.034	0.849	0.39	0.886**
$INEQUAL_{blk}$	0.745*	0.102	0.437	1.71	1.762**
Neighborhood sorting					
PCTBLACK	11.145***	0.171	3.285	3.39	0.877
$DISSIM_{wht/blk}$	2.395**	0.102	1.157	2.07	1.646***
NSI	0.250	0.010	2.089	0.12	2.655**
NSI_{blk}	1.356**	0.108	0.662	2.05	0.265
N	103				116
R^2	0.803				0.799
Adj R^2	0.784				0.777
	Change in Neighborhood Poverty (Hispanics)				
Intercept	−0.182	0.000	0.684	0.27	
NPR_{80}	0.735***	0.668	0.121	6.08	
Income generation					
MSAMEAN	−0.125***	−0.331	0.039	3.25	−0.190***
$INCRATIO_{hsp}$	0.707	0.013	6.308	0.11	−4.749*
INEQUALITY	1.883	0.102	3.397	0.55	1.877
$INEQUAL_{hsp}$	1.950	0.078	2.402	0.81	1.841
Neighborhood sorting					
PCTHISPANIC	1.669	0.029	6.377	0.26	2.923**
$DISSIM_{wht/hsp}$	1.381	0.027	5.685	0.24	2.175
NSI	12.149	0.241	9.475	1.28	6.564**
NSI_{hsp}	−0.424	−0.017	3.053	0.14	4.554***
N	42				56
R^2	0.762				0.8165
Adj R^2	0.695				0.7716

Note: Significance levels: ***$p < 0.01$; **$p < 0.05$; *$p < 0.10$.

tistically significant. The change in ghetto poverty over the decade, after controlling for changes in the income-generation variables and the other neighborhood sorting variables, is greater in cities where the black percentage is increasing. In the cross-sectional model, the level of the percent black variable was much smaller in magnitude (0.877 compared with 11.145 in the changes model) and not statistically significant. This is the only coefficient with a different order of magnitude when the variable is measured as a change rather than a level. One possible interpretation is that it represents a disequilibrium condition: in cities with rapidly growing black populations, housing market discrimination forces more black families to reside in poor neighborhoods. The effect is quite large, though the coefficient by itself is misleading, given the measurement scale of the variables. The standardized coefficient shows that the change in the percent black is the third most important of the income-generation and neighborhood sorting variables. Only the metropolitan mean household income and the ratio of the black mean household income to the overall figure have larger standardized impacts.

The regression on changes in barrio poverty in the 1980s, also shown in table 6.5, has few significant coefficients. Of the variables for the income-generation process, only the metropolitan mean household income is statistically significant. None of the neighborhood sorting variables is significant. Despite the lack of significant coefficients, the overall R^2 for the regression is reasonably high (0.76).[14] The lack of significant results may stem from the smaller number of observations (forty-two) included in the regressions. Another possibility is that the barrio poverty numbers actually represent distinct subgroups (see chapter 2). The relationships among income generation, neighborhood sorting, and Hispanic barrios may be dissimilar for Puerto Ricans in the Northeast, Mexicans in the South and West, and Cubans in Florida. Lumping together the data for these groups may tend to obscure the causal relationships. Nevertheless, the results on changes in barrio poverty are consistent with the findings on ghetto poverty, to the extent that the income-generation process, and in particular the mean level of metropolitan household income, is the key determinant of neighborhood poverty.

Interactions with Racial Segregation

As noted in chapter 5, Massey and Eggers (1990) stress the role that the interaction between racial residential segregation and changes in the black income distribution plays in increasing the concentration of poverty. I encountered the same difficulty as did Massey and Eggers in attempting to test the hypothesis of an interaction between residential segregation and changes in the income distribution: the interaction term constructed by multiplying the two variables is highly collinear with the main effects. As an alternative approach, I divided the metropolitan areas into thirds based on the level of black/white segregation in 1980. Then two dummy variables are introduced: *HIGHSEG*, which equals 1 if the metropolitan area is in the most segregated third of metropolitan areas and zero if otherwise; and *MIDSEG*, which equals 1 if the area is in the middle third and zero if otherwise. The lowest third of metropolitan areas is the reference group. The parameters representing the income-generating process are then interacted with the two dummy variables. A significant coefficient on any of these interaction terms would indicate that the change in ghetto poverty associated with the variable was dependent on the level of racial segregation. Massey and Eggers's hypothesis is that the more segregated metropolitan areas should have larger (more negative) coefficients on the variables measuring black economic status.

Table 6.6 shows the results of this analysis for 1970–80. For comparison, the coefficients and significance levels from the comparable regression with no interaction terms are shown (from table 6.5). There is no evidence for any interaction between the level of segregation and changes in the income-generation parameters. The highest *t* score for any of the interaction terms is 1.128 ($p = 0.263$), on the coefficient for change in black income inequality. The magnitudes of the slope coefficients are little affected by including the interactions with the segregation category. The coefficient on changes in black income inequality becomes insignificant, however, as does the coefficient on changes in racial segregation. The coefficient on economic segregation among blacks remains significant, but at a lower level ($p < 0.10$ compared with $p < 0.05$). There is little change in the R^2 for the regression, despite the addition of

Table 6.6   Changes in Neighborhood Poverty and Interactions Between Racial
Segregation and Black Income, 1980–90

	Regression Without Interactions	Regression Allowing Interaction With Level of Racial Segregation, 1980			
	Coeff.	Coeff.	Beta	Std. Err	t
Intercept	−0.807***	−0.683***	0.000	0.226	3.03
NPR_{80}	0.473***	0.465***	0.550	0.047	9.82
Income generation					
MSAMEAN	−0.062***	−0.084***	−0.394	0.032	2.65
*HIGHSEG		−0.013	−0.044	0.032	0.42
*MIDSEG		0.031	0.145	0.028	1.09
$INCRATIO_{blk}$	−8.523***	−11.560***	−0.415	3.399	3.40
*HIGHSEG		3.904	0.090	4.183	0.93
*MIDSEG		3.331	0.112	3.835	0.87
INEQUALITY	−0.330	0.150	0.016	1.583	0.10
*HIGHSEG		−0.649	−0.049	1.585	0.41
*MIDSEG		−1.257	−0.080	1.712	0.73
$INEQUAL_{blk}$	0.745*	0.861	0.117	0.870	0.99
*HIGHSEG		−1.249	−0.090	1.108	1.13
*MIDSEG		0.548	0.045	1.126	0.49
Neighborhood sorting					
PCTBLACK	11.145***	10.103***	0.155	3.423	2.95
$DISSIM_{wht/blk}$	2.395**	1.946	0.083	1.306	1.49
NSI	0.250	−1.212	−0.048	2.322	0.52
NSI_{blk}	1.356**	1.220*	0.097	0.668	1.83
N	103	103			
R^2	0.803	0.826			
Adj R^2	0.784	0.791			

Notes: F-test on restriction that all interaction terms = 0: $F_{8,85}$ = 1.404, F_{crit} = 2.049, p = 0.207.
Significance levels: ***p < 0.01; **p < 0.05; *p < 0.10.

eight variables. An *F* test fails to reject the null hypothesis that the
coefficients on all the interaction terms are simultaneously zero.

The lack of evidence for any interaction between the level of
racial segregation and changes in black economic status may be
attributed to the similarity among the cities analyzed in terms of the
black/white index of dissimilarity. The dividing lines between the

three groups, the 33rd and 67th percentiles, are 0.673 and 0.754, respectively. If racial segregation varied more among metropolitan areas, the hypothesized interaction might have greater importance. Although the interaction is logical conceptually and theoretically, I conclude that the effect either does not exist or is too subtle to be demonstrated with the available data. Of course, the lack of evidence for an interaction effect does not contradict the findings presented earlier about the direct effects of racial segregation, which were statistically significant both in terms of explaining the cross-sectional variation in ghetto poverty and the changes between 1980 and 1990. And none of the analyses presented here addresses the role of historical patterns of racial segregation in terms of its cumulative effects on the black income distribution as discussed by Massey and Denton in *American Apartheid* (1993).

Implications of the Empirical Analysis

My main goals in this chapter were, first, to formulate a conceptual framework for the relationship between ghettos and their metropolitan areas: ghetto neighborhoods should be thought of as the most impoverished part of a larger distribution of neighborhoods, which in turn is shaped by metropolitan-wide processes of income generation and neighborhood sorting. Second, I used this conceptual framework to analyze the determinants of ghetto and barrio poverty, in particular the determinants of the recent growth in ghetto and barrio poverty.

The empirical model strongly suggests that economic opportunities at the metropolitan level largely determine ghetto poverty and barrio poverty. Neighborhood sorting processes also play an important role. In particular, the overall level of economic segregation helps explain ghetto poverty levels in 1990, and the changes in economic segregation among blacks—Wilson's "flight of the black middle class"—plays a role in the changes in ghetto poverty between 1980 and 1990. Racial segregation has a direct impact on both changes and levels, although I found no evidence to support the interaction effect between segregation level and changes in the parameters of income generation. Racial segregation does have indirect effects through its impact on black income distribution—for example, by making it harder for people to accumulate capital and by keeping blacks at a far remove from the areas of rapid job creation.

Abstract econometric analyses may seem removed from grim urban realities, as detailed by ethnographers and portrayed vividly in movies, such as Spike Lee's *Do the Right Thing*. And neighborhood poverty, as I have defined it, does not capture all of the social and behavioral dimensions of high-poverty areas. For my research to be relevant to policymakers who are concerned about the prevalence of underclass behaviors, I need to discuss the relationship of high-poverty neighborhoods to the deterioration of social conditions within such neighborhoods. I therefore take up this question more directly, and its implications for public policy, in the next and final chapter.

Chapter 7

Chaos or Community? Directions for Public Policy

High-poverty neighborhoods, be they black ghettos, Hispanic barrios, or even poor white neighborhoods, have been growing at an alarming rate. Between 1970 and 1990, the number of persons living in ghettos, barrios, and slums in the U.S. grew by 92 percent, and the number of poor people living in them grew by 98 percent. The size of the blighted areas of most metropolitan areas increased even faster. For nearly four million poor people who now live in these neighborhoods, reduced economic opportunities and social isolation add insult to the injury of being poor. Within some of these communities, the deprivation does irreparable harm.

These trends have profoundly negative consequences for our society. The injuries to the residents of high-poverty neighborhoods are apparent in their lower levels of employment and earnings, and in their higher dropout and out-of-wedlock birth rates, even after controlling for individual characteristics and family background. The growth and spread of ghettos and barrios also have more subtle costs, which have to do with the fragile social fabric that keeps anarchy at bay and makes it possible for cities to be communities and not just agglomerations of fearful strangers.

In the last chapter, I argued that the primary factors behind the increasing concentration of poverty are metropolitan economic growth and the general processes that create and sustain segregation by race and class. Metropolitan-level variables for economic opportunity and segregation can explain about four-fifths of the variation among metropolitan areas and about the same proportion of the changes in neighborhood poverty over time. Although such factors as spatial location, neighborhood culture, and social policy may play a role, they are secondary to income generation and neighborhood sorting, which together explain most of the observed variations in ghetto and barrio poverty.

The corollary to this finding on the policy side is that neighborhood poverty cannot be "solved" with programs in ghettos and barrios alone. Specifically, the idea that such neighborhoods have become self-sustaining enclaves—with a "culture of poverty" and a separate, totally disconnected underclass—is not supported by the data. A self-sustaining neighborhood culture implies that levels of neighborhood poverty would respond slowly, if at all, to increased economic opportunity. Chapter 2, however, documented that ghettos and barrios can decrease sharply in regions experiencing economic booms, as in the Southwest in the 1970s and the Northeast in the 1980s. And the multivariate analysis in chapter 6 showed that neighborhood poverty declines as the overall metropolitan mean income rises.

There are a number of implications in this research for ways to reduce neighborhood poverty. Policies that increase productivity and reduce inequality are fundamental to doing so in the long run. Policies that affect the spatial organization of metropolitan areas and reduce racial and economic segregation will also affect the formation of ghettos and barrios. In contrast, policies that aim to alter the culture, values, and behavior of ghetto residents are unlikely to make much difference without larger changes in the metropolitan economy and in rates of segregation. In the context of actual improvements in the opportunity structure, such policies may do some good and help specific individuals. Other policies, such as enterprise zones and local economic development projects that target specific neighborhoods need to be evaluated and implemented carefully, or they too will be ineffective.

Social Costs of Poverty Concentration

The focus of this study has been high-poverty neighborhoods, most but not all of which are black ghettos or Hispanic barrios.

The strategy I chose—to include all poor neighborhoods in the analysis, regardless of racial and ethnic composition and regardless of any indicators of social problems commonly associated with poor neighborhoods—arose from a concern that concentrated economic deprivation provides the *context* for the development of an "underclass" (Van Haitsma 1989; Wacquant and Wilson 1989; Wilson 1987). The appropriate way, then, to investigate this phenomenon was to identify all extremely poor neighborhoods (those with poverty rates 40 percent or higher) and study whether the social problems identified as underclass behaviors were more common in such neighborhoods after individual characteristics were taken into account. It soon became evident, however, that documenting the extent of high-poverty neighborhoods, their characteristics, and their growth over time, as well as investigating the explanation for the growth of ghetto poverty, was a substantial project in itself.

Yet, the public, as well as many analysts and most policymakers, are much more concerned about the dramatic social deterioration in urban poverty areas than with their existence and prevalence. Indeed, the term *underclass* is now used far more often to refer to inner-city poverty than terms like *ghettos, barrios,* or *high-poverty areas.* Given this focus of public debate, I discuss the links between the economic and social characteristics of poor neighborhoods to show how my approach of defining ghetto poverty in economic terms is relevant to public policy.

A Culture of Poverty?

David Ellwood (1988) notes that the public image of severe poverty has changed from the forlorn, isolated poverty of Appalachia to the "more foreign and more menacing" images of the urban ghetto:

> Now the [public's image of poverty] is the inner city. The values, culture, and attitudes seem distorted and perverse. On camera, young men brag about how many children they have fathered out of wedlock. Young women act as though having children outside of marriage is inevitable and acceptable. Occasionally, murder is justified as an appropriate response by gangs whose honor was somehow challenged. Drugs and alcohol seem to be everywhere. (p. 191)

Such images are powerful and make a lasting impression.

Other observers go a step further, arguing that the *cause* of neighborhood poverty is a self-sustaining "culture of poverty" found in poor neighborhoods. Conservative spokesman and presidential candidate Pat Buchanan has bluntly articulated an extreme form of this view:

> The real root causes of the crisis in the underclass are twofold. First, the old character-forming, conscience-forming institutions—family, church, and school—have collapsed under relentless secular assault; second, as the internal constraints on behavior were lost among the black poor, the external barriers—police, prosecutors, and courts— were systematically undermined. . . . What the black poor need more than anything today is a dose of truth. Slums are the products of the people who live there. . . . The first step to progress, for any group, lies in the admission that its failures are, by and large, its own fault, that success can come only through its own efforts, that, while the well-intentioned outsider may help, he or she is no substitute for personal sacrifice. (Quoted in Edsall and Edsall 1991, 80)

Lawrence Mead and Charles Murray argue (with considerably less vitriol) that well-intentioned but misguided public policies are at the core of the "relentless secular assault" on values and values-forming institutions. Mead (1986) argues that the "permissive character of social programs" has eroded the functioning and competence of the poor (p. 23). Murray (1984) takes a more economic approach, analyzing the effects of government programs on the incentive structure facing the poor. Government policy, he argues, has resulted in the "destruction of status rewards." Both would agree that "poverty often arises from the functioning problems of the poor themselves, especially difficulties in getting through school, working, and keeping their families together" (Mead 1986, ix).

Nicholas Lemann (1991), while calling for a broad range of progressive social policies that the conservative authors cited above would not support, nevertheless echoes the same fundamental analysis of the problem:

> [T]he overall concept is simple and direct: the government should be trying to break the hold on individuals of those aspects of ghetto culture that work against upward mobility, by providing a constant, pow-

erful force that encourages the people of the gettos to consider themselves part of the social structure of the country as a whole. (p. 351)

The key policy implication of the "ghetto culture" notion is that a significant subgroup of the residents of poor neighborhoods are so alienated and damaged that they would not be able to take advantage of an objective improvement in economic conditions, were one to occur.

The notion of a culture of poverty was first articulated in academic literature by Oscar Lewis (1966, 1968). At various times repudiated and revived, the culture of poverty thesis became an anathema to the left. Indeed, after the furor over the Moynihan Report on the black family, the topic of the values and culture of poor people became virtually off-limits to academics, especially white academics, who exercised a form of self-censorship in order to avoid being charged with "blaming the victim."[1] To the extent that the issues were discussed at all, Ellwood (1988) notes, "the policy debate that surrounded these issues has been exceptionally simplistic. Conservatives seemed to blame all poverty on bad values. . . . Liberals blamed poverty entirely on racism and the lack of opportunity" (p. 197).

This impasse was finally breached by William Julius Wilson, who meticulously documented deteriorating social conditions in Chicago's ghettos (Wilson 1987). Wilson explicitly rejected the culture of poverty thesis, emphasizing instead the social isolation of such neighborhoods. There is a conceptual distinction between Wilson's and Lewis's analyses. Wilson tried to raise the level of the discussion by placing the evolution of ghetto social conditions in the context of the changes in a metropolitan area's opportunity structure. Since publication of *The Truly Disadvantaged*, however, Wilson's work has often been misinterpreted as a culture of poverty analysis (Wilson 1988).

Wilson argued, that "cultural values emerge from specific circumstances and life chances and reflect an individual's position in the class structure" (1987, p. 158). According to Wilson, several things happened at about the same time to objectively change the conditions of inner-city neighborhoods. Most important, economic transformations of the metropolitan economy marginalized inner-city residents, reducing their potential employment and earnings. Second, the relaxation of restrictive racial covenants made it possible for employed blacks to escape the worst neighborhoods. Their exodus reduced the effectiveness of "social buffers"—churches, civic and neighborhood groups, and informal social hierarchies—just at the time they were most needed to cushion the stresses of economic hard times. The result was, according to Wilson (1987), "concentration effects": a dramatic deterioration in social conditions over and above what would have been predicted from economic and demographic changes alone.

For Wilson, concentration effects include some ghetto residents' adoption of self-destructive lifestyles and value systems that deviate from mainstream expectations. Even if there are objective changes in economic conditions, he believes that not all ghetto residents will be fully able to take advantage of them, as argued by Lewis. Wilson's concept of social isolation differs, however, from the culture of poverty thesis in two ways. First, the strong form of the culture of poverty thesis as stated by Lewis denied the possibility of change, or at least measured the time it would take in generations. In contrast, Wilson (1987) argues that concentration effects slow down the reaction of people enmeshed in ghetto culture, but "as economic and social situations change, cultural traits, created by previous situations, likewise *eventually* change even though it is possible that some will linger on and influence behavior for a period of time" (emphasis in the original, p. 138). Although it is not stated explicitly, Wilson is talking about years, not generations, and certainly within the current generation's lifetime.

The second way in which Wilson's concept of social isolation differs from the culture of poverty thesis is in the recommended response:

> [T]he key conclusion from a public policy perspective is that programs created to alleviate poverty, joblessness, and related forms of social dislocation should place primary focus on changing the social and economic situations, not the cultural traits, of the ghetto underclass. (1987, p. 138)

So, even though Wilson has done more than anyone to call attention to the "tangle of pathology" in the ghetto, he does not advocate policies that attempt to address those pathologies directly:

If ghetto underclass minorities have limited aspirations, a hedonic orientation toward life, or lack of plans for the future, such outlooks ultimately are the result of restricted opportunities and feelings of resignation originating from bitter personal experiences and a bleak future. Thus the inner-city social dislocations emphasized in this study . . . should be analyzed not as cultural aberrations but as symptoms of racial-class inequality. It follows, therefore, that changes in the economic and social situations of the ghetto underclass will lead to changes in cultural norms and behavior patterns. (1987, pp. 158–59)

Thus, Wilson's concept of social isolation goes beyond the simplistic "culture" versus "opportunity" argument.

Would Opportunity Matter?

Wilson's emphasis on opportunity structure is supported by Richard Freeman's 1991 study of the impact of tight labor markets on disadvantaged youth. He used several different data sets and research strategies "to contrast the economic position of young men across local labor markets that differ in their rates of unemployment" (p. 103). His conclusion was that

[D]espite the social pathologies that plague disadvantaged young men, particularly the less educated black youths, and despite the 1980s twist in the American labor market that worked against those with fewer skills, tight labor markets substantially improved their economic position. (Freeman 1991, 119)

Freeman's study did not address how social conditions changed in poor neighborhoods with tight labor markets; perhaps they lagged behind. But if willingness to work is any measure, youth do respond to real changes in economic conditions.

Paul Osterman (1991) studied the effect of the superheated Boston economy of the late 1980s on poverty and social status. Boston was a particularly strong test case of the culture versus opportunity debate:

Boston's experience is also appropriate because Massachusetts is among the most generous states in the country in its welfare and other social policies. . . .

> If the neoconservatives are right, generosity should have inhibited
> the response of poor people to the economic opportunities afforded
> by long-term growth. If liberals are right, the combination of full
> employment and active social policy should have paid off in a reduc-
> tion of poverty rates. (p. 130)

Osterman's findings strongly support the notion that full employment makes significant inroads against poverty. Although a not
insignificant minority (about 10 percent) remained outside the
labor market, "poverty rates fell substantially in Boston, and it is
very clear that the poor did respond to economic opportunity when
it was offered" (p. 130). On the other hand, Osterman notes that
full employment in Boston did not solve all problems. For example,
the percentage of households headed by single women was virtually unchanged.

Freeman's and Osterman's analyses did not specifically investigate the impact of economic growth on ghetto and barrio neighborhoods. But my analysis in chapter 6 strongly supports Wilson's
policy position. If the cultural effects of ghetto and barrio poverty
persisted long after changes in economic opportunities, then levels
of neighborhood poverty would respond slowly to such changes.
Nevertheless, large increases in mean income in many southern
cities and some northern ones generated sizable declines in neighborhood poverty. And if ghettos and barrios were self-perpetuating,
then much of the variance in neighborhood poverty should be
unexplained by my models, which include only metropolitan-level
variables. My cross-sectional econometric models implicitly assume
that all changes in neighborhood poverty are instantaneous following changes in the parameters.[2] Thus, large lags in the response
of ghetto residents to changes in economic opportunity would result
in a worse fit of the model and less variance explained. Given the
R^2 values and highly significant coefficients on the models' income-
generation variables in all specifications, the lag in response to economic conditions must be relatively short.

This evidence is not definitive, of course. The R^2 statistics in my
regressions are not 1.00; as always, some residual variance remains
unexplained. Yet the evidence from 1970 to 1990 is that both rapid
increases *or decreases* in neighborhood poverty are possible in

response to changes in economic opportunities. The conclusion I draw is that neighborhood poverty is not primarily the product of "the people who live there" or a "ghetto culture" that discourages upward mobility, but the predictable result of the economic status of minority communities and the degree to which minorities are residentially segregated from whites and from each other by income. Neighborhood effects may well exist, and pathologies in the poor neighborhoods may well be destructive to people living there. But such phenomena, I would argue, are more like symptoms than root causes.

The concept of social isolation, however, does imply that in some circumstances such policies may be useful: in the context of actual increases in economic opportunity. The tangle of pathology to which Wilson alludes does affect the expectations people have about what they can hope to achieve, and it does lead people to develop harmful behavior and addictions. In the context of expanding opportunities, programs and policies that combat addictions, encourage school completion and responsible parenting, educate people about the labor market, and build self-esteem might play a useful role by reducing the influence of destructive patterns developed earlier.

But if the basic economic situation is further deteriorating, such policies may be akin to trying to sweep back the ocean. "Bad communities defeat good programs," concludes David Rusk, former Mayor of Albuquerque and policy analyst. Even if such programs help certain individuals, he points out that "successful clients of social programs typically move away. As a result, in inner cities, individual success does not translate into community success" (Rusk 1993, 121). If deterioration in the economy is impoverishing more and more people, and if employed and middle-class people keep fleeing from the path of poor neighborhoods, no "self-help" program will be able to stem the spread of urban blight.[3] As a consequence, such policies should be pursued with the understanding that they can have only a marginal impact.

Measuring Neighborhood Effects

An increasing body of evidence demonstrates that, even after controlling for personal and family characteristics, neighborhoods have independent effects on individuals that deepen and prolong their poverty. For example, other things being equal, teenagers living in poor neighborhoods are more likely to become pregnant and drop out of school (Anderson 1991; Crane 1991; Hogan and Kitagawa 1985; Mayer 1991). Males raised in welfare-dependent communities earn less later in life than similar males from other types of neighborhoods (Corcoran and others 1992). Social isolation in high-poverty neighborhoods helps to create and maintain an "oppositional culture" that makes it difficult for children to succeed in school (Anderson 1989, 1994).

On the other hand, research on neighborhood effects has been criticized for not adequately taking into account unmeasured differences between families in ghetto neighborhoods and families outside the ghetto (Tienda 1991). In other words, some effects thought to be attributable to neighborhoods may simply reflect the characteristics of families who end up living in the poorest neighborhoods—those with the greatest personal problems, the lowest employment-related skills, and the weakest motivation or concern for the environment in which their children are being raised. Several studies have suggested that the effects of neighborhoods disappear when appropriate statistical methods are used to account for this "self-selection bias" (Evans, Oates, and Schwab 1992; Plotnick and Hoffman 1993).

Studies of the Gautreaux program in Chicago by James Rosenbaum and his associates have been particularly influential. The Gautreaux program came about as part of the resolution of a lawsuit by Chicago public housing residents against the Department of Housing and Urban Development (HUD) (Rosenbaum 1995). Qualifying public housing residents are offered the opportunity to move to private housing in a variety of different neighborhoods, ranging from low-income black urban neighborhoods to white suburban neighborhoods. Since all the housing opportunities are superior to life in the housing projects, most of the residents accept the first housing opportunity they are offered (Popkin, Rosenbaum, and Meaden 1993).

Rosenbaum and his colleagues used this natural experiment to answer questions about the differences in inner-city and suburban housing locations, both in terms of adults' economic fortunes and in terms of the development outcomes of the program participants' children. Those who moved to the suburbs had higher levels of employment than those who moved to the inner city, though they did not have gains in hours worked or wages. More important, perhaps, the children of suburban movers did better in school and had higher levels of college attendance. Rosenbaum (1995) concludes that there is a "geography of opportunity," meaning that "where individuals live affects their opportunities and life outcomes" (p. 231). These findings have led to the creation of similar programs in other cities, as well as HUD's Moving Opportunity Program.

From Analysis to Policy

My research concludes that income generation had the most dramatic effect overall on ghetto and barrio poverty, and that the neighborhood sorting index plays a secondary role, except perhaps in explaining changes between 1970 and 1980 in the Northeast and Midwest. This does not mean that public policies must follow the same path. The relevant question for public policy is not how large an effect each underlying variable has, but how much public policies can affect neighborhood poverty. Both the size of the effect (based on the regression coefficients) *and* the size of the feasible policy-induced change in the underlying variable factor into the potential impact on neighborhood poverty. Some underlying variables are harder to change than others. To fully evaluate proposals for reducing ghetto poverty, one has to consider not only the magnitude of the effect per unit change in the variable, but also how many units of change are possible to achieve through available, politically feasible policy options. Policy conclusions, therefore, hinge on the power of public measures to affect income generation and neighborhood sorting.

My analyses in chapter 6 address how changes—whether arising from policy shifts or not—in income generation and neighborhood sorting are likely to affect neighborhood poverty. Table 7.1 shows the predicted level of ghetto poverty with all variables set at their mean values, except for the regional dummy variables; the Midwest is set to 1, and the other two are set to zero.[4] In a hypothetical midwestern metropolitan area with average values for its income-

Table 7.1   Changes in Predicted Ghetto Poverty for One-Standard-
Deviation Change in Income-Generation and Neighborhood
Sorting Parameters

	Mean	Standard Deviation (SD)	Predicted Neighborhood Poverty	Change Based on One SD Change
Percent in Ghettos, Black, 1990	—	—	15.9%	—
Income generation				
One increase				
MSAMEAN	42.239	6.621	9.1	−6.8
INCRATIO$_{blk}$	0.650	0.045	13.4	−2.5
One decrease				
INEQUALITY	1.025	0.121	14.5	−1.4
INEQUAL$_{blk}$	0.891	0.064	14.5	−1.4
Neighborhood sorting				
One SD decrease				
DISSIM$_{wht/blk}$	0.681	0.106	13.7	−2.2
NSI	0.424	0.054	14.1	−1.8

Notes: Based on regression model 3, table 6.2. Variable means and standard deviations are weighted and based on 116 MSAs included in the regression. Predicted
ghetto poverty levels are calculated with all variables set at mean values except for
indicated variables, set at ± one standard deviation.

generation and neighborhood sorting variables, almost 16 percent
of the the area's black residents would live in high-poverty census
tracts. Table 7.1 shows the decline in ghetto poverty that would
result from increasing or decreasing (depending on the sign of the
coefficient) each of the parameters by one standard deviation while
holding the other variables constant.

For example, a $6,621 increase in the mean household income
of the metropolitan area would lower the ghetto poverty rate by 6.8
percentage points, dropping it from 16 to 9 percent. This is obviously a substantial reduction, and the next largest impact is less
than half as big. The next largest effect was for the ratio of black
mean income to overall mean income. A one-standard-deviation
increase in that variable would result in a 2.5-percentage-point drop
in the ghetto level. The neighborhood sorting variables had the next

largest effects. A one-standard-deviation *decrease* in racial segregation as measured by the index of dissimilarity would decrease ghetto poverty by 2.2 percentage points. The impact for overall economic segregation is 1.8 percentage points.[5] A one-standard-deviation decrease in overall income inequality and inequality of black income would each result in a 1.4-standard-deviation drop in the ghetto poverty level for blacks.[6]

Policies that could potentially affect either income generation or neighborhood sorting are the subject of the following sections. In many cases the goal is clear, but the specific remedies are highly controversial. For example, one way to restore income growth is to increase the rate of productivity growth. Thus, macroeconomic policies promoting productivity will reduce ghetto poverty in the long run. But economists disagree about how to stimulate productivity. These differences include both technical issues and political concerns.

Policies That Primarily Affect Income Generation

As shown in table 7.1, an increase in overall income level has more than twice the effect on ghetto poverty than a comparable change in any other income-generation or neighborhood sorting variable. Although the effect was not as large, decreases in either overall income inequality or black inequality would also reduce ghetto poverty. Three types of policies could improve mean income, reduce inequality, or both: macroeconomic policies, human capital policies, and redistributive tax policies.

Macroeconomic Policies

Macroeconomic policies have an important impact on ghetto poverty through their effect on income distribution. Basically, policies that increase mean income while reducing (or at least not increasing) the variance of income will help to reduce ghetto poverty. Presumably, if there was consensus on how to manage macroeconomic policy to maximize noninflationary growth, we would already be pursuing such policies, regardless of their side benefits for urban ghettos. Although a review of macroeconomic policies is beyond the scope of this book, a few observations are in order.

First, there is no realistic way to increase the mean household income of metropolitan areas in the long run without increasing productivity growth.[7] Income grew rapidly from 1946 to 1973. Since then, the incomes of American workers and families have grown very little. Between 1960 and 1973, the median earnings of year-round, full-time workers increased from $23,389 to $33,250 (in 1992 inflation-adjusted dollars). Unfortunately, this was the peak; by 1992, two decades later, the figure was $30,358.[8] Household and family incomes have increased over the period, but almost entirely because spouses worked more hours. The consensus of economic opinion is that the slowdown in productivity growth is a major contributor to wage stagnation.

Productivity growth slowed for reasons about which economists differ. Nonetheless, virtually all economists agree that productivity growth is the key to increasing living standards. "Productivity growth is important," write William Baumol and Kenneth McLennan, "because it is the key determinant of a nation's future standard of living. . . . The failure of a nation's productivity to grow condemns its work force to a stationary income level and forces the society to forgo improvements in its quality of life" (1985, p. 5). The implications for income distribution are clear: real incomes can grow only as fast as productivity.

Second, unemployment has been used as the principal weapon in the war against inflation. Unemployment obviously reduces mean income, but it also increases inequality because it strikes hardest at the lower end of the income distribution (Blank and Blinder 1986). The correct balance between inflation and unemployment cannot be derived from an economic law; both inflation and unemployment generate economic inefficiencies, but the distribution of costs and benefits to various segments of society is quite different (Blinder 1987, chapter 2).

Ultimately, the relative balance between inflation and unemployment reflects a value judgment. Alan Blinder (1987) argues that "America has struck this balance between inflation and unemployment in the wrong place by exaggerating the perils of inflation and underestimating the virtues of low employment" (p. 33). This is a controversial proposal; but it is simplistic (although common) to call for full-employment policies without addressing the employment-inflation trade-off. And if we as a society continue to choose unemployment as the lesser of two evils, we should at least have a full discussion of the value judgments that decision entails, particularly in the current context of relatively low inflation.

Human Capital Strategies

One approach to raising productivity is to improve the human capital—the basic knowledge, skills, and abilities—of the labor force, particularly those who are now the least productive. Yet, in 1963, Banfield and Wilson wrote: "An . . . important feature of Negro social structure is the fairly large and growing number of young people who have more education than the job market enables them to use" (Banfield and Wilson 1963, 7). In the context of today's labor market, this is an astonishing remark. Changes over the past thirty years, many of them for the better, have reversed the situation. First, labor market discrimination on the basis of race has been reduced, although by no means eliminated. Educated blacks are far more likely to obtain employment commensurate with their education today than in 1963. Second, the returns to education, especially college, have increased sharply over the period. Such returns increased especially rapidly during the 1980s after a period of stagnation in the late 1970s (Bound and Johnson 1995; Juhn, Murphy, and Pierce 1991).

The combination of increasing returns to skill and increasing economic segregation is particularly worrisome. "In the context of locally run schools," argues economist Frank Levy (1995), "growing income stratification by place makes it harder for poor and working class children to acquire large amounts of human capital" (p. 35). This poses a fundamental dilemma and sets up a pernicious feedback mechanism whereby poverty is translated into low skill attainment through geographic variations in the quality of schools and other social and economic resources. If the neighborhood social milieu influences a student's work habits and these work habits determine coursework mastery (Farkas and others 1990), then geographical concentrations of poverty could widen the human capital gap even if ghetto schools were the equal of schools elsewhere.

The sharp wage premium for skills seems to be a permanent feature of the modern economy. In that context, if the goal is to reduce neighborhood poverty by increasing mean income and reducing inequality, one important policy goal should be to dramatically increase the quality of education and opportunities for training and retraining. Special efforts should be made to improve the education and skills of those with the least; if successful, such measures would help reduce inequality.

The growing consensus on the importance of these goals, both as anti-poverty policies and as policies to enhance U.S. competitiveness, is not, however, matched by a consensus on how to achieve them. There is considerable disagreement about how education and training can actually be improved, how much it will cost, who should do it, and how to pay for it. Some see the need for massive new investments in teacher salaries, computers, compensatory education, and longer school days or years. Others believe that current resources could be better applied if competition among schools was fostered by school choice plans, and if educational standards were enforced through more testing programs for teachers and students. Without progress in educating inner-city children, however, it is certain that many of them will fare poorly in the increasingly technological marketplace—in effect, creating the next generation of ghetto and barrio residents.

One significant area of disagreement is about which policies are more effective in reducing poverty—those that improve education and training in general or policies that target poor individuals or the residents of poor neighborhoods. Both could help, but in different ways. Policies to increase the level of human capital across the board ought to lead—other things being equal—to increases in productivity and hence real wages, higher household income, and lower neighborhood poverty. Policies that especially enhance the human capital of those who now have the least should also increase the mean—but only slightly—and, more important, reduce the variance in income, again leading to declines in neighborhood poverty. The choice hinges on the trade-off between political viability and efficiency in service delivery.[9]

Tax Policy

The traditional way for the government to affect income distribution is through the tax code. Recent reforms in the Earned Income

Tax Credit have transformed an obscure provision, meant to offset the social security payroll tax for low-income workers, into a large wage subsidy for low-income parents. In tax year 1996, a worker with up to $11,000 of *earned* income and two children could receive a credit of $3,370 from the government, increasing the effective wage rate of the worker by 31 percent (Scholz 1994, 3).

The program receives more widespread support than AFDC and other spending on the poor because it is work related. However, substantial reductions in the EITC were included in the Republican budgets, which President Clinton vetoed. The future of the credit—and, indeed, any redistributive policy—is uncertain at best, given the severe fiscal constraints facing the federal government. Even if the tax code could be made substantially more progressive, a future Congress or admininstration could easily undo the changes. Thus, in the long run, it would be far better to enable more workers to achieve incomes above the poverty level through education, training, and productivity growth.

Public Policy and Neighborhood Sorting

Although income generation was shown to be the most important factor in determining ghetto poverty, other factors related to neighborhood sorting were relevant. Racial segregation, as measured by the index of dissimilarity, and economic segregation, as measured by the neighborhood sorting index, had significant effects in cross-sectional and longitudinal analyses. Racial segregation has been declining (Farley and Frey 1994; Harrison and Weinberg 1992; Massey and Denton 1987). But economic segregation (as measured by the NSI) has been increasing, especially among minority groups (Jargowsky 1996). These changes are taking place in the context of a profound sociodemographic restructuring of metropolitan areas. Any attempt to discuss policies regarding racial and economic segregation must start with a discussion of this restructuring and its correlates.

Changing Metropolitan Structure

Metroplitan areas are undergoing important sociodemographic changes. Foremost among these is a continuing trend toward decentralization. A dramatic example is the Milwaukee metropolitan area (discussed in chapter 2), which showed a uniform pattern of population decline in the central part of the city and uniform population gains in all surrounding areas. Although Milwaukee's experience may be extreme, the general pattern of declining cores and expanding peripheries is very widespread (Kleinberg 1995, 121–23; Waddell 1995). Most large central cities had absolute declines in population. Between 1960 and 1990, central cities' share of the metropolitan population declined from 51 percent to 40 percent (Frey 1993). Without annexation, this relative decline would have been even greater.

In a recent report, *The Technological Reshaping of Urban America*, Congress's Office of Technology Assessment (OTA) describes how new technologies are transforming the nation's metropolitan areas. The OTA's report could well have included the following observation by a noted academic:

> Human geography has been profoundly modified by human invention. [New technologies], by converting the world into one vast whispering gallery, have dissolved the distances and broken through the isolation which once separated races and people . . . [resulting in] an increasingly wider division of labor. (Park 1926, 14)

Perhaps the OTA cannot be faulted for overlooking this quote, given that it is from an article by the sociologist Robert Park published in 1926. The new technologies *he* was referring to were the telephone, the telegraph, and the radio; the OTA has in mind the explosion of high-speed, high-volume networked communications and a shift from the production of tangible goods to knowledge-based goods. Its report concludes that "the new technology system is creating an ever more spatially dispersed and footloose economy, which in turn is causing metropolitan areas to be larger, more dispersed and less densely populated" (Office of Technology Assessment 1995, 1).

This economic restructuring may be positive and adaptive in an economic sense, but it has profoundly negative implications for inner-city residents. As Mark Alan Hughes (1993) notes, in six of the eight largest metropolitan areas "most if not all job growth during the 1980s was located in the suburbs" (p. 16). He also notes that "there is an extreme pattern in these metropolitan areas: poverty and joblessness are concentrated in formerly central cities while prosperity and job growth are deconcentrating toward the metropolitan periphery" (p. 17).

For every two steps forward, we seem to take at least one step back. Metropolitan areas have transformed in response to residents' demands for spatial amenities and to changing modes of production. From an economic point of view, these are positive adaptations to changes in production technology and business opportunities. But the pooling of poor individuals in urban centers—hardly a new development, since that has always been a function of cities (Hicks 1994, 815)—is no longer a viable means for poor individuals to get connected to the larger economy.

Implications for Economic Segregation

These large-scale changes in metropolitan organization have provided opportunities for people to sort themselves out in new ways. Deconcentration does not have to lead to more segregation. Indeed, racial segregation has declined slightly as resettlement to the urban periphery has progressed. But economic segregation has risen. "The natural locational forces of U.S. metropolitan areas," writes Peter Salins (1993), "in combination with the effects of their jurisdictional fragmentation, conspire to keep most poor households in the central cities" (p. 92). Whereas suburbs evolved into "fiscal and quality-of-life sanctuaries," the inner cities have been relegated to a role akin to the poorhouse of an earlier era.

As middle-class whites and blacks left inner-city neighborhoods, they were making rational adjustments to a changing economic landscape. But it was not only blacks in the ghetto who were moving. The movement of middle-income blacks out of inner-city neighborhoods is but another manifestation of deconcentration, the "dominant dynamic of advanced urban development" (Hicks 1987, 442; see also White 1987, 226). Attempts to halt or reverse the movement of middle-income blacks out of the inner city would probably be futile and, of course, it would be profoundly unfair to deny blacks the same life-improvement paths that earlier generations of middle-class whites took. Such considerations led the 1990 Committee on National Urban Policy to conclude:

Federal policies and programs should seek to eliminate barriers to residential mobility through full enforcement of fair housing, equal access and other anti-discrimination laws and regulations, enabling people to leave ghettos if they choose, for example through programs of housing vouchers. (Lynn and McGeary 1990, 264)

As Paul Peterson (1985) put it, "the best urban policy . . . would be directed toward dispersing racial concentrations by increasing the choices available to racial minorities" (p. 26). In essence, the argument is that if we cannot bring jobs to the people, we should bring people to the jobs.

A significant weakness of the ghetto dispersal strategy is its assumption that blacks' low economic status is a function of where they live. The committee recognized this weakness:

[But] the emptying out of ghettos through residential mobility would not in itself have much impact on the fortunes of the people who had lived there. They would continue to have problems no matter where they lived, because they typically face the liabilities of low levels of education, skills, and work experience; poor health and disabilities; teenage and single parenthood; and racial discrimination. (Lynn and McGeary 1990, 264)

In criticizing ghetto dispersal strategies, Hughes has argued that spatial assimilation follows from economic assimilation, not the other way around (Hughes 1987). This led him to support an economic mobility strategy that would actively assist inner-city minorities to find out about, obtain, and commute to jobs (Hughes 1991). "The whole point," Hughes states, "is to increase the size of the black middle class in order to facilitate the eventual dispersal of the ghetto" (1987, p. 516). But even mobility strategies will not help much if ghetto residents cannot find jobs that pay better than public assistance.[10]

Public policies can help the inner-city poor take advantage of employment opportunities beyond the confines of the ghetto, and even in other cities and regions. The following initiatives could be part of an "economic mobility strategy" (Hughes 1987, 514–17; see also the President's Commission for a National Agenda for the Eighties 1980, 57):

Employment information systems that overcome the information barriers to suburban employment;

Restructuring of public transit to promote reverse commuting;

Relocation assistance for workers moving to new jobs;

Subsidies (direct or tax) for commuting costs.

As noted above, measures that connect the poor to employment opportunities can help remove the penalty associated with inner-city location.

If mobility or ghetto dispersion strategies work, however, the more motivated and skilled persons from inner cities will benefit the most. As Wilson argues in *The Truly Disadvantaged*: "As their economic and educational resources improve they will very likely follow the path worn by many other former ghetto residents and move to safer or more desirable neighborhoods" (p. 158). This will further destabilize inner-city communities and *worsen* conditions for those who remain behind.

Neighborhood Revitalization

A quite different approach is to bring jobs back to poor central-city neighborhoods and to neighborhoods now in the path of urban blight. The key policy in this area has been the enterprise zone. Enterprise zones take many different forms, but the basic premise is that government policies—zoning, property taxes, pollution regulations, and other forms of "red tape"—have kept the free market from exploiting the economic opportunities of urban neighborhoods, such as proximity to markets and cheap labor (Butler 1981).

Some of the criticisms of enterprise zones are that most direct public subsidies and initial benefits (such as increased property values) may go to firms and nonresident landlords; new jobs may not go to ghetto residents; public subsidies may divert public funds from expenditures that more directly benefit ghetto residents, such as education or police protection; and firms willing to relocate because of public inducements may be the most marginal and provide the weakest base for long-term development (Wilder and Rubin 1988, 2–3; see also Levitan and Miller 1992). "Urban enterprise zones may resuscitate individual neighborhoods," observed Peterson (1985), "but these kinds of policies only shift problems from one neighborhood to another or from one city to the next" (p. 24). A review of enterprise zones in Great Britain has confirmed that they "have major effects in influencing the location of enterprises and very minor effects in stimulating new economic activities" (Gunther and Leathers 1987, 889). A sample of 140 enterprise zones from across the United States found that only 5 percent of the firms in them were minority owned, and that a disproportionate share of the jobs (relative to the metropolitan economy) were minimum-wage jobs (Glover 1993).

Altering the Metropolitan System

Ghetto dispersal, mobility strategies, and enterprise zones have a common flaw: they have little effect on the economic and social systems that give rise to geographic fragmentation of metropolitan areas. Government policies at all levels have contributed to this fragmentation:

> The decentralization of metropolitan regions was made possible by advances in transport and telecommunications technology, but federal and state polices going back to the 1950s have been instrumental in accelerating and expanding the process. Federal highway construction programs have paid for the network of expressways that brought the farflung reaches of suburbia within commuting range of metropolitan job sites, permitting the urbanization of a metropolitan frontier far from the edge of the central city. Federal income tax rules and federal home mortgage programs brought home ownership within the financial reach of millions of middle-income city residents, creating a market for new housing subdivisions at the metropolitan frontier. Federal water and sewer construction subsidies underwrote the infrastructure of newly created (or at least newly populated) suburban jurisdictions, and federal grants paid for the preparation of their land use and infrastructure plans. And not insignificantly, federal corporate tax rules have made it more profitable for manufacturing firms to build new plants in the suburbs than to rebuild their old ones in the central city. (Salins 1993, 97)

State governments also have contributed to decentralization and economic segregation by tolerating exclusionary zoning and "not in my back yard" attitudes on the part of local governments. Federal and state government policies did not create the desire of people to live in neighborhoods segregated by race and income, nor were they the driving forces behind metropolitan decentralization. But these policies have enabled and accelerated these underlying processes; in effect, throwing gasoline on the fire. In contrast, government policy worked against the tendency of people to segregate themselves by race and ethnicity. No one could seriously claim that housing market discrimination has ended, but federal policies since the Fair Housing Act of 1965 have counterbalanced discriminatory attitudes and institutions, resulting in small declines in racial segregation. The situation would be quite different today if the laws passed in 1965 had endorsed, encouraged, and provided financial incentives for segregationary actions.

The worst aspect of current state and federal policies is the way that they encourage spatial tensions while providing ineffective forms of relief to the ghetto and barrio neighborhoods that result. Rather than address this general framework of policies, both explicit urban policies and nonurban policies with urban effects, that exacerbates tensions between the central city and metropolitan periphery, current policies seek to identify neighborhoods that have failed and provide a separate solution for economic development in those areas. Enterprise zones, for example, can never incorporate such areas into the mainstream economy but will only sustain them at a minimal level with a patchwork of subsidies and handouts.

A better approach would be to pressure both state and local government and private developers to move toward more socioeconomically mixed development patterns. Government policy, especially the pervasive practice of exclusionary zoning and other forms of political fragmentation, in many cases *increases* the pressure toward economic fragmentation of metroplitan areas. Rather than funding enterprise zones to clean up after the damage is done, the federal government ought to get strongly behind efforts to strengthen the regional government's capacity (Orfield 1996; Rusk 1993) to break down exclusionary zoning and control the placement of public amenities so as to influence the actions of private developers. The federal government cannot force states and local governments to undertake these actions, but it can work to get local governments to understand that all residents of metropolitan areas ultimately share a common destiny. Less ambitiously, the federal government could structure fiscal incentives so that state and local governments would have to forgo large sums of federal money if they do not at least act as if they believe in sustainable metropolitan development patterns.

Housing Policy

Fixed-structure public housing tends to artificially segregate the poor. Through subsidies, such housing anchors the poor to specific neighborhoods. Through density and family selection, an ungovernable and volatile mix of social problems creates a climate of havoc, fear, drug abuse, and violence. For these reasons, in recent years high-rise public housing projects are more likely to be blown up than built. Federal housing policy has evolved into a constellation of programs such as Section 236, Section 202, and Section 8 New Construction and Rehabilitation, which are decentralized or provide "portable" benefits. As a result, public housing was already less concentrated in 1980 than in 1970, as measured by the index of dissimilarity (Warren 1986).

Our single most important housing policy, however, is the home-mortgage interest deduction. The deduction, which reduces taxable income and hence lowers taxes in proportion to a taxpayer's marginal tax rate, is worth substantially more to higher-income individuals. The deduction amounts to a $55 billion dollar subsidy for upscale housing, stimulating demand, raising market prices, and creating higher profit margins for builders. Because housing markets of different levels of quality are intricately related on both the supply and demand sides, the deduction also affects the availability and prices of lower-quality housing. At least partly as a result of the deduction, there is a shortage of affordable housing for low-income renters, and three out of five low-income renters pay more than 50 percent of their income in rent (Lazere 1995, 1–2).[11] For those simply priced out of the market, the last resort is public housing, trailer parks, or—if they can get one—a Section 8 voucher.

Thus, I would argue that housing projects and the mortgage interest deduction are intricately connected. By stimulating the high end of the housing market and providing virtually no support for the lower end of the housing market, conditions of demand and supply result in high prices and constricted supply of low- and moderate-income housing. When, inevitably, the most economically disadvantaged segment of the population is forced out of the private housing market, the federal government becomes the last-resort housing provider, with all its attendant resegregation and poverty-concentrating effects. To change this backward dynamic, it is not *public* housing policy that needs to be revised or expanded but the general framework within which housing markets operate.

A serious effort to improve housing conditions for the poor must include some attempt to level the playing field by adjusting how subsidies are allocated in the nation's largest housing "program." The program is usually considered politically untouchable, and perhaps it is. Nevertheless, in 1996, several presidential candidates and the House of Representatives majority leader have offered flat-tax proposals that change or even totally eliminate the deduction, so the question is at least on the table. Any change would have to be undertaken with extreme caution to avoid wreaking havoc on property values and the loan portfolios based on them. It might be possible to restructure the deduction so that it does not change the amount of the subsidy for most current beneficiaries, improving the proposal's political viability. For example, the current 100 percent *deduction* of mortgage interest could be changed to a 28 percent tax *credit*. The credit could be made refundable, similar to the Earned Income Tax Credit. To the average taxpayer, paying a 28 percent marginal rate, there would be no change in tax liability. Those in higher tax brackets would, of course, pay more taxes, and those in lower brackets who held mortgages would pay substantially less or even receive a refund.

Continuing Progress on Racial Segregation

Racial segregation contributes to ghetto poverty in several ways. First, the historical pattern of segregation combined with inferior service delivery (particularly schools) has impeded the development of human capital in the black community (Kain 1992; Massey and Denton 1993).[12] The powerful effects in my econometric models of the variable for the ratio of black mean income to the overall metropolitan mean are, therefore, partly an indirect effect of past racial segregation. Current racial segregation contributes directly to ghetto poverty (see chapter 6, as well as Massey and Eggers 1990).

Racial segregation has been declining, despite inconsistent and lackluster enforcement of the Fair Housing Act. Although consensus exists on the importance of combating overt racial discrimination, the same cannot be said for the goal of proactively encouraging racial integration. The Department of Housing and Urban Development (HUD) has shied away from policies that go beyond preventing overt racial discrimination in housing to actually promote integration (DeMarco and Galster 1993, 145). Policies that seek to stabilize integrated or partially integrated neighborhoods or that encourage individuals to make prointegrative moves are likely to be attacked as social engineering. Such policies may also be attacked as paternalistic by some within the black community, who do not necessarily see integrated neighborhoods as a goal (Leigh and McGhee 1986). Moreover, the goal of creating stable integrated communities may run into explicit conflict with the goal of ending racial discrimination in housing. For example, given the tendency of whites to leave neighborhoods that have reached a certain percentage of blacks (the so-called tipping phenomenon), prointegrative policies often require "occupancy quotas that are designed to limit black population to a specified proportion of the community" (Smith 1993, 117; see also Clark 1993, 170).

Despite these complexities, abundant opportunities to continue breaking down racial segregation exist. HUD should aggressively monitor local public housing authorities to ensure that federally funded public housing does not worsen racial segregation, as it has done in the past (Bickford and Massey 1991). Additional resources could be devoted to investigating and prosecuting overt racial discrimination by private housing providers, real estate agents, and mortgage lenders. Moreover, the federal government should provide incentives for local communities to pursue prointegration policies and should nurture and support communities that have achieved some degree of stable integration.

Chaos or Community?

Neighborhood poverty is the predictable result of two metropolitan processes: income generation and neighborhood sorting. Although a "tangle of pathology" may emerge in such neighborhoods, the pathologies are a symptom of the problem, not its cause. The root causes of the increases in ghettos and barrios in many northern cities are the changing opportunity structure faced by the minority community and, to a lesser degree, the changing spatial organization of the metropolis.

Given the responsiveness of neighborhood poverty to changes in economic opportunity, the potential exists for macroeconomic policies to have a large impact on the problem. To the extent that incomes continue to stagnate or even decline and inequality continues to increase, neighborhood poverty will rise. In this sense, the fortunes of the ghetto and barrio residents are closely allied to the fortunes of the average citizen. The expansion of high-poverty areas is driven by the same economic realities that make it hard for many young families to get by without two incomes and slowly erode their standard of living.

The second most important set of policies for dealing with neighborhood poverty has to do with human capital. With such policies, one could imagine focusing on ghetto and barrio residents alone. To some degree, this can be achieved through programs that are geographically targeted, following the Head Start model. On the other hand, the argument can be made that the failure of the U.S. education and training systems to serve poor neighborhoods is part of a much broader failure of these systems. Moreover, broader reforms may be more likely to win widespread political support and to be sustainable in the long run than intensive remedial efforts in ghettos and barrios.

The endemic social problems of poor neighborhoods have left many residents unprepared to take advantage of new economic opportunities. Thus, programs that emphasize culture, values, and self-esteem are important but only in the context of increasing economic opportunities for the poor. But they must not be stand-alone efforts, because the behavior of the poor is not the cause of neighborhood poverty.

The continuing trend toward metropolitan deconcentration also contributes to neighborhood poverty. Public efforts to reverse fundamental metropolitan transformations would surely be ineffective, inefficient in an economic sense, and ultimately futile. The movement of middle-class blacks out of inner-city neighborhoods is actually positive (for individuals) in the sense that it is part of the overall process of adjustment to changing economic realities. The policy implications of the changing spatial organization of cities are complex. But first and foremost, public policies ought not to make matters worse by exacerbating the natural tendency toward economic segregation. Political fragmentation, restrictive zoning, a skewed housing subsidy, and other federal policies have done just that, and need to be reviewed and fundamentally reoriented. Strategies of economic mobility, such as job-information banks and support for reverse commuting, may help the poor link up to jobs in the metropolitan periphery.

Finally, even though most inner-city neighborhoods will never return to their historical levels of population and economic activity, the public has a responsibility not to abandon such areas. The residents of such neighborhoods need protection from violent crime and appropriate levels of city services. The federal government can play a role in helping financially strained central cities meet these obligations, especially in view of suburb–central city fiscal imbalances. Many inner-city neighborhoods do have very valuable—in some cases, irreplaceable—physical infrastructures and cultural or historical significance, as well as potential for economic renewal. Although it is impossible to generalize about such prospects, because cities and neighborhoods are so different, some inner-city economic development projects that capitalize on existing neighborhood strengths should be pursued. It is important, however, that such projects be carefully considered in light of the economic realities of the city and the neighborhood. They cannot work miracles or reverse fundamental economic changes. To the extent that they can help to anchor economically viable neighborhoods, these public interventions serve important public purposes.

Neighborhood poverty is a complex problem. The hopelessness and despair in many poor neighborhoods is a symptom of broader metropolitan processes. It is quite possible to dramatically reduce levels of neighborhood poverty, as the experience of smaller southern cities in the 1970s has shown. People do react to real changes in the level of economic opportunity, as indicated by the work of Freeman and Osterman. If the nation pursues policies that raise incomes, reduce inequality, and unite rather than divide our society, neighborhood poverty can be significantly reduced and its effects ameliorated. The alternative is to continue blundering down the futile path of letting our cities become hollow shells and allowing our society to divide into two distinct groups—one with access to good neighborhoods and schools and the other warehoused in vast urban wastelands.

History and current events suggest that a strong nation, even one with no significant external threat, may find itself in decline because of internal racial and ethnic conflicts. Such conflicts are especially acute when there are large economic disparities among groups, and when the groups are geographically and socially isolated from one another. Although the ethnic conflicts in places like Somalia, Rwanda, and Bosnia may seem beyond anything that could happen in the United States, we should learn the lessons of these tragedies. And a persistent, low-level political conflict, on the order of the Quebec separatist movement, is not an impossibility in the United States. This is exactly the fear embodied in the Kerner Commission's warning that we are becoming "two societies . . . separate and unequal." In the post–Cold War era, this prospect poses the greatest threat to the United States' long-term economic and political stability—a controversial claim, perhaps, but one that needs to be considered and debated.

Without ignoring the important improvements in the status of black Americans, such as the beginnings of integration in many professions and the emergence of a black middle class, the expansion of ghettos over the past two decades suggests that the Kerner Commission was at least partly correct. We must adapt the programs and policies of the commission to take account of what we have learned about program design and to reflect new fiscal and political realities. And we must find the political will and the means to ensure that millions of our fellow citizens need not live in economically devastated and socially isolated neighborhoods. Finally, we must find a new and viable structure for metropolitan areas in the twenty-first century, a larger urban *community* rather than an agglomeration of separate and antagonistic *places*. Martin Buber, the Jewish theologian, argued that the form of community needs to be continuously re-created: "Realization of the idea of community, like the realization of any idea, does not exist once for all and generally valid but always only as a moment's answer to a moment's question" (Buber 1967, 97). The task is difficult and the results of even our best efforts are uncertain, but to continue along our current path is to give the wrong answer to Martin Luther King's question: "Where do we go from here—chaos or community?"

Data Comparability

This appendix discusses several technical issues that arise when comparing estimates of neighborhood poverty from 1990 to those from previous years. In addition, it describes the tract-level and SMSA-level data for 1970 and 1980. The 1990 data were described in chapter 3.

Exclusion of New Metropolitan Areas

To improve the validity of comparisons between 1970 and later years, the analysis in chapter 2 was limited to metropolitan areas that had been in continuous existence since 1970. Yet, nearly one hundred metropolitan areas have grown large enough in the past two decades to meet official standards for metropolitan classification. To explore the effect of excluding these newer areas, table A-1 compares the full set of 1990 metropolitan areas to those used in chapter 2. The exclusions have little effect, either in the number of people living in poor tracts or in the racial composition of their residents.

Changes in Metropolitan Boundaries

Boundary changes of census tracts and metropolitan areas complicate the comparison of neighborhood poverty data over time. Some boundary adjustments correspond to real changes in the population and organization of metropolitan areas. In addition to normal

Table A.1   Comparison of Population Figures for All Metropolitan Areas
and the 1970–90 Subset, 1990

	All Neighborhoods			High-Poverty Neighborhoods		
	All MSAs	239 MSAs	%	All MSAs	239 MSAs	%
Persons (thousands)						
All Incomes	194,273	177,913	91.6	8,446	7,973	94.4
White	152,424	138,091	90.6	2,816	2,559	90.9
Black	25,141	23,927	95.2	4,312	4,152	96.3
Hispanic	19,842	18,888	95.2	2,052	1,978	96.4
Below Poverty	22,833	20,915	91.6	3,938	3,745	95.1
White	12,612	11,238	89.1	1,066	977	91.7
Black	6,660	6,320	94.9	2,196	2,120	96.5
Hispanic	4,756	4,511	94.8	1,030	995	96.6
Racial Composition (%)						
All Incomes	100.0	100.0		100.0	100.0	
White	78.5	77.6		33.3	32.1	
Black	12.9	13.4		51.1	52.1	
Hispanic	10.2	10.6		24.3	24.8	
Below Poverty	100.0	100.0		100.0	100.0	
White	55.2	53.7		27.1	26.1	
Black	29.2	30.2		55.8	56.6	
Hispanic	20.8	21.6		26.2	26.6	

Source: Census tract data for 1970–90, tabulations by author.

growth, the U.S. population is quite mobile; in 1991, more than 17 percent of Americans moved (U.S. Bureau of the Census 1992, vii). Some areas grow and others decline.

Boundary changes also arise because of the Census Bureau's revisions of and improvements in geographic concepts and categories—at the expense of data comparability over time. In 1983, the Census Bureau made wholesale changes in the way that urban areas are divided into metropolitan areas, significantly tightening the criteria for peripheral counties to be included in metropolitan areas. As a result, about sixty counties were dropped from the 1980 inventory of metropolitan counties. I have added these counties back to their (former) metropolitan areas in 1990 to facilitate comparisons over time.

In addition, some counties were switched from one metropolitan area to another. Bergen County, New Jersey, for example, was placed in three different metropolitan areas in the 1970, 1980, and 1990 censuses. To the extent possible, I adjusted the 1970 and 1990 data to reflect 1980 boundaries. The adjustments consisted of moving counties from one metropolitan area to another; in New England, it means moving "minor civil divisions."[1]

No correction was made for the addition of peripheral, formerly nonmetropolitan counties to metropolitan areas. In the simplest case, the development of empty farmland in 1980 into suburban housing is accompanied by an influx of people, both from downtown and from outside the area. Since my goal was to compare changes in the whole metropolitan area over time, I chose to view the additional county as real growth and not be concerned with the change in the geographic area per se.

These peripheral counties were inhabited to some degree before they were added to a metropolitan area in the 1980 or 1990 census. Technically, their populations should be consistently included or excluded, but such an adjustment is not possible. Most of these peripheral areas were not divided into tracts in the years before they were added to their metropolitan area. Even if they were, the census is not longitudinal and does not indicate which individuals were long-time residents. It *would* be possible to exclude all of the newer counties, but the movement of higher-income groups to the periphery of the metropolitan area is an important part of the story. Excluding these counties would discard a decidedly nonrandom subset of the data. Such a procedure would wreak havoc with the denominator for calculating the percentage of persons living in ghettos.

The most sensible solution, I believe, is to treat the peripheral counties as real growth, especially since the criteria for including them were considerably tightened over the period, as mentioned above. A county that did not qualify in 1980 but did in 1990 experienced a considerable increase in its size and economic integration with the central portion of its metropolitan area. Although this strategy introduces a small degree of measurement error in the comparisons over time, I concluded that including them generated less error than omitting them.

Tract-Level Data for 1980

Data for 1980 came from several sources. Tract-level data were from Summary Tape File 4A.[2] These tapes contain selected tract-level cross-tabulations of social and economic characteristics. The data for individuals are not provided, so that the data cannot be retabulated if the Census Bureau did not include the desired cross-tabulation. Each census tract has a summary record; additional records are provided for up to six different race/ethnicity groups (white, black, Hispanic, Indian, Asian, and other). Although simple counts of non-Hispanic whites, non-Hispanic blacks, and Hispanics by tract are available, it is impossible to get unduplicated counts or figures for the detailed cross-tabulations. For example, one cannot obtain figures for non-Hispanic black income at the tract level.

The data contain two types of suppression to protect confidentiality. The first is primary suppression. Data based on counts of persons are suppressed for a given race group if there are fewer than thirty persons of that group. In other words, if there are fewer than thirty blacks, the black person–based tables are suppressed. Data based on counts of households or families are suppressed if there are fewer than ten households of a racial group. The criteria are applied separately. Thus, for a given tract/race, it is possible to have household information but not person information, or the other way around.

The second type of suppression is complementary suppression. The object of complementary suppression is to prevent researchers from breaching the primary suppression. For example, suppose all persons in a census tract are either white or black. Suppose the tract has a total of 1,000 persons—980 whites and 20 blacks. The black record is suppressed for person-based tables because of primary suppression. One could, however, subtract the white information from the totals to reconstruct most of the black record. (Some information, such as medians, cannot be reconstructed this way.) To prevent this, in the tract described above, data on the 980 whites would also be suppressed. If there are more than two groups involved, the next smallest group to the groups that are subject to primary suppression is selected if complementary suppression is needed. (The same principle is independently applied to household-based data.)

Complementary suppression can have a rather large effect on the data for separate racial groups, especially when the group is small relative to the total population. If only a handful of blacks live in each of the census tracts concerned, that could result in the suppression of all blacks in these tracts. Not only could this be a large proportion of blacks, the suppression could also systematically exclude blacks and bias the results. Thus, I needed to devise a method to overcome the effect of complementary suppression.

My basic procedure was as follows. First, I analyzed each tract to determine which groups, if any, in that tract were subject to complementary suppression. Second, I would try to reconstruct data for the suppressed group by the methods described below. If at least 90 percent of the reconstructed group were members of the suppressed group, I would use the data for the reconstructed group. Otherwise, the suppression was allowed to stand.

Reconstructing data was done as follows. If the group subject to complementary suppression was the largest group, then the tract summary data (all races) was the reconstructed group. If the group subject to complementary suppression was not the largest group, then all nonsuppressed groups were subtracted from the totals to get the reconstructed group. Unlike the first method, data in the form of medians cannot be reconstructed in this way.

What are the effects of this methodology? It is less than ideal to use the data for a group which is, say, 91 percent black and 9 percent Asian as if the entire group were black. But the alternative is to discard the 91 percent entirely. For example, suppose that one is interested in mean income and the percentage of households headed by females. The table below shows how the data might be affected by this technique:

	Black (Comp. Suppres.)	Asian (Primary Suppres.)	Reconstructed Group If blacks are: 90%	99%
Mean Income	$12,000	$15,000	$12,300	$12,030
Female-Headed	.45	.15	.42	.45

It seems preferable to make errors of the magnitude shown in the table than simply to discard the data on thousands of persons or households. Moreover, the larger the size of the group that is being complementarily suppressed, the smaller the error, since the primary suppression group cannot exceed thirty persons (or ten households).

Tract-Level Data for 1970

For 1970, tract-level data are taken from the Fourth Count Population Summary Tape, which has no complementary suppression. There is primary suppression, though the rules by which it was applied are unclear. Working with census tract data from 1970 presents many challenges. Calculating the correct poverty rate, for example, requires selecting ten data items from three tables. The most important complication is that the household concept was not well developed in 1970. Data were presented for families and unrelated individuals, with no household-level aggregations. Even in the published data, some "totals" presented in tables merely add counts of families to counts of unrelated individuals—a clearly invalid procedure.

The biggest problem for my analysis was that I needed a variable comparable to mean household income at the tract level. Getting a good count of households was not too difficult; I added families to "primary individuals" (the head of a household of unrelated individuals). Total household income turned out to be harder. The reported income of unrelated individuals includes income from persons who do not live in households, such as prisoners and residents of nursing homes—in other words, people living in group quarters. Adding family income and unrelated income therefore overestimates household income, and dividing by the count of households gives an overestimate of mean household income. Adding people in group quarters to the count of households would probably correct too much, leading to an underestimate, assuming that persons in group quarters tend to earn less than the average household. In most cases, the actual difference is small because the number of persons in group quarters is small relative to the number of households. Still, I took the average of the known overestimate and the supposed underestimate of mean household income to get a final estimate. As the number of persons in group quarters approaches zero, the three estimates converge.

There is no way to know for certain whether this method biases the 1970 data on mean income for any given census tract up or down, but I feel more comfortable than if there were a definite upward bias for all tracts. An alternative approach would have been to look solely at family income. As argued above, however, the correct unit for studying geographic concepts is the household. Moreover, given changes over time in family composition, especially in the black community, looking only at families could clearly understate total neighborhood income in 1980 relative to 1970.

SMSA-Level Data for 1970 and 1980

Despite all the techniques for fixing complementary suppression in 1980, data for some tracts for some racial groups remain suppressed, both by primary and "unfixable" complementary suppression. Thus, metropolitan totals based on aggregating tracts do not match published data exactly. For this reason, I also use data from Summary Tape File 4C, which contains totals at the SMSA level for the same data items as the tract tapes. I also make use of an SMSA-level tabulation of the Fourth Count to get SMSA totals that match published data.

Appendix B

Neighborhood Poverty Data

Table B.1: High-poverty Census Tracts and Residents, 1970–1990

	High-Poverty Census Tracts			Change in Number of Tracts			Population			Change in Population		
	1970	1980	1990	70–80	80–90	70–90	1970	1980	1990	70–80	80–90	70–90
New England												
BOSTON	10	12	15	2	3	5	40,539	23,281	31,757	−17,258	8,476	−8,782
BRIDGEPORT	1	7	4	6	−3	3	3,795	18,291	6,086	14,496	−12,205	2,291
BRISTOL	0	0	0	0	0	0	0	0	0	0	0	0
BROCKTON	1	0	0	−1	0	−1	1,523	0	0	−1,523	0	−1,523
DANBURY	0	0	0	0	0	0	0	0	0	0	0	0
FALL RIVER	0	0	1	0	1	1	0	0	19	0	19	19
FITCHBURG	1	0	0	−1	0	−1	574	0	0	−574	0	−574
HARTFORD	4	12	10	8	−2	6	14,850	27,961	26,802	13,111	−1,159	11,952
LAWRENCE MA	0	1	5	1	4	5	0	3,321	12,656	3,321	9,335	12,656
LEWISTON ME	0	0	1	0	1	1	0	0	1,613	0	1,613	1,613
LOWELL MA	0	1	5	1	4	5	0	1,180	12,768	1,180	11,588	12,768
MANCHESTER	1	0	0	−1	0	−1	894	0	0	−894	0	−894
MERIDEN	0	1	1	1	0	1	0	278	290	278	12	290
NASHUA NH	0	0	0	0	0	0	0	0	0	0	0	0
NEW BEDFORD	0	0	0	0	0	0	0	0	0	0	0	0
NEW BRITAIN	0	1	0	1	−1	0	0	1,328	0	1,328	−1,328	0
NEW HAVEN	0	3	2	3	−1	2	0	7,484	4,760	7,484	−2,724	4,760
NEW LONDON	2	1	2	−1	1	0	3,345	538	328	−2,807	−210	−3,017
NORWALK	0	0	0	0	0	0	0	0	0	0	0	0
PITTSFIELD	0	0	1	0	1	1	0	0	32	0	32	32

PORTLAND ME	1	0	2	−1	2	1	388	0	2,366	−388	2,366	1,978
PROVIDENCE	1	3	4	2	1	3	197	7,590	9,406	7,393	1,816	9,209
SPRINGFD MA	1	6	11	5	5	10	143	19,455	43,814	19,312	24,359	43,671
STAMFORD CT	0	0	0	0	0	0	0	0	0	0	0	0
WATERBURY	0	0	1	1	0	1	0	3,443	253	3,443	−3,190	253
WORCESTER	0	1	4	1	3	4	0	3,820	8,413	3,820	4,593	8,413
Middle Atlantic												
ALBANY NY	0	3	2	3	−1	2	0	2,713	8,654	2,713	5,941	8,654
ALLENTOWN	0	0	2	0	2	2	0	0	9,641	0	9,641	9,641
ALTOONA PA	0	0	1	0	1	1	0	0	1,702	0	1,702	1,702
ATLANTIC CY	1	4	4	3	0	3	1,323	5,287	9,282	3,964	3,995	7,959
BINGHAMTON	0	0	2	0	2	2	0	0	4,366	0	4,366	4,366
BUFFALO NY	3	15	26	12	11	23	5,463	32,790	72,230	27,327	39,440	66,767
ERIE PA	0	3	5	3	2	5	0	4,789	13,082	4,789	8,293	13,082
HARRISBURG	0	2	1	2	−1	1	0	6,656	5,658	6,656	−998	5,658
JERSEY CITY	0	3	2	3	−1	2	0	7,708	8,445	7,708	737	8,445
JOHNSTOWN	0	0	2	0	2	2	0	0	3,948	0	3,948	3,948
LANCASTR PA	0	1	2	1	1	2	0	3,354	5,424	3,354	2,070	5,424
NASSAU-SUFF	0	2	2	2	0	2	0	3,167	8,814	3,167	5,647	8,814
NEW YORK	74	314	279	240	−35	205	300,527	1,002,015	960,292	701,488	−41,723	659,765
NEWARK NJ	9	39	21	30	−18	12	34,045	112,635	49,189	78,590	−63,446	15,144
N.EAST PENN	2	0	2	−2	2	0	2,528	0	3,483	−2,528	3,483	955
PATERSON NJ	1	11	3	10	−8	2	2,220	29,089	5,483	26,869	−23,606	3,263
PHILADELPHIA	28	69	70	41	1	42	111,827	266,511	241,863	154,684	−24,648	130,036
PITTSBURGH	14	19	42	5	23	28	30,702	38,371	74,898	7,669	36,527	44,196

(continued)

Table B.1: High-poverty Census Tracts and Residents, 1970–1990 (continued)

	High-Poverty Census Tracts			Change in Number of Tracts			Population			Change in Population		
	1970	1980	1990	70–80	80–90	70–90	1970	1980	1990	70–80	80–90	70–90
READING PA	0	2	2	2	0	2	0	4,055	7,076	4,055	3,021	7,076
ROCHESTR NY	4	8	20	4	12	16	8,072	13,794	33,510	5,722	19,716	25,438
SYRACUSE NY	2	7	14	5	7	12	11,311	24,254	38,150	12,943	13,896	26,839
TRENTON NJ	0	1	1	1	0	1	0	3,190	5,110	3,190	1,920	5,110
UTICA NY	1	2	4	1	2	3	1,256	1,562	3,094	306	1,532	1,838
VINELAND NJ	1	0	0	−1	0	−1	675	0	0	−675	0	−675
YORK PA	1	0	0	−1	0	−1	2,111	0	0	−2,111	0	−2,111
East North Central												
AKRON OH	3	6	19	3	13	16	5,604	8,488	48,632	2,884	40,144	43,028
ANDERSON IN	0	0	1	0	1	1	0	0	2,734	0	2,734	2,734
ANN ARBOR	2	4	8	2	4	6	14,877	17,894	36,182	3,017	18,288	21,305
APPLETON WI	0	0	2	0	2	2	0	0	7,348	0	7,348	7,348
BAY CITY MI	0	0	1	0	1	1	0	0	1,139	0	1,139	1,139
BLOOMING.IL	0	1	3	1	2	3	0	7,999	11,689	7,999	3,690	11,689
CANTON	0	2	5	2	3	5	0	2,961	9,873	2,961	6,912	9,873
CHAMPAIGN	3	4	4	1	0	1	14,681	21,568	24,536	6,887	2,968	9,855
CHICAGO	48	136	184	88	48	136	156,270	369,970	396,200	213,700	26,230	239,930
CINCINNATI	17	23	31	6	8	14	54,720	56,930	74,387	2,210	17,457	19,667
CLEVELAND	20	42	69	22	27	49	62,268	72,141	100,432	9,873	28,291	38,164
COLUMBUS OH	6	22	24	16	2	18	26,994	63,671	86,657	36,677	22,986	59,663
DAVENPORT	0	1	7	1	6	7	0	564	10,790	564	10,226	10,790

224

DAYTON OH	4	13	17	9	4	13	5,479	29,381	50,887	23,902	21,506	45,408
DECATUR	1	1	2	0	1	1	3,689	3,317	2,324	-372	-993	-1,365
DETROIT	24	51	149	27	98	125	55,913	120,469	418,947	64,556	298,478	363,034
EVANSVILLE	1	1	1	0	0	0	798	1,559	1,318	761	-241	520
FLINT	0	2	15	2	13	15	0	3,495	51,714	3,495	48,219	51,714
FORT WAYNE	0	1	4	1	3	4	0	4,109	5,080	4,109	971	5,080
GARY	1	6	11	5	5	10	1,334	12,729	21,408	11,395	8,679	20,074
GRAND RAPID	0	3	4	3	1	4	0	4,989	7,042	4,989	2,053	7,042
GREEN BAY	0	0	0	0	0	0	0	0	0	0	0	0
HAMILTON	0	3	4	3	1	4	0	11,345	20,704	11,345	9,359	20,704
INDIANAPOLIS	4	5	9	1	4	5	11,991	14,818	21,650	2,827	6,832	9,659
JACKSON MI	1	0	4	-1	4	3	4,643	0	8,438	-4,643	8,438	3,795
KALAMAZOO	1	5	8	4	3	7	7,694	8,365	27,951	671	19,586	20,257
KENOSHA WI	0	0	0	0	0	0	0	0	0	0	0	0
LA CROSSE	0	0	2	0	2	2	0	0	10,305	0	10,305	10,305
LAFAYETT.IN	1	2	6	1	4	5	5,520	8,485	26,354	2,965	17,869	20,834
LANSING MI	2	3	8	1	5	6	17,893	19,818	19,368	1,925	-450	1,475
LIMA OH	0	2	4	2	2	4	0	4,698	6,771	4,698	2,073	6,771
LORAIN OH	1	0	2	-1	2	1	1,199	0	2,062	-1,199	2,062	863
MADISON	3	3	4	0	1	1	19,316	19,608	27,744	292	8,136	8,428
MANSFIELD	0	2	3	2	1	3	0	1,191	3,474	1,191	2,283	3,474
MILWAUKEE	11	19	59	8	40	48	17,319	31,982	140,825	14,663	108,843	123,506
MUNCIE IND	0	0	4	0	4	4	0	0	11,175	0	11,175	11,175
MUSKEGON MI	0	0	5	0	5	5	0	0	12,239	0	12,239	12,239
PEORIA IL	0	4	6	4	2	6	0	8,724	10,779	8,724	2,055	10,779
RACINE WI	0	0	2	0	2	2	0	0	4,602	0	4,602	4,602

(continued)

Table B.1: High-poverty Census Tracts and Residents, 1970–1990 (continued)

	High-Poverty Census Tracts			Change in Number of Tracts			Population			Change in Population		
	1970	1980	1990	70–80	80–90	70–90	1970	1980	1990	70–80	80–90	70–90
ROCKFORD IL	0	1	3	1	2	3	0	4,452	9,676	4,452	5,224	9,676
SAGINAW	1	3	9	2	6	8	3,427	8,022	24,353	4,595	16,331	20,926
SOUTH BEND	2	2	1	0	−1	−1	10,463	4,105	1,525	−6,358	−2,580	−8,938
SPRINGFD IL	1	0	2	−1	2	1	2,417	0	4,000	−2,417	4,000	1,583
SPRINGFD OH	0	1	1	1	0	1	0	3,225	948	3,225	−2,277	948
STEUBENVILL	0	2	4	2	2	4	0	3,258	5,756	3,258	2,498	5,756
TERRE HAUTE	2	0	2	−2	2	0	5,764	0	3,006	−5,764	3,006	−2,758
TOLEDO	4	12	21	8	9	17	7,826	22,465	55,184	14,639	32,719	47,358
YOUNGSTOWN	2	5	17	3	12	15	3,213	6,745	33,478	3,532	26,733	30,265
West North Central												
CEDAR RAPID	0	0	1	0	1	1	0	0	2,067	0	2,067	2,067
COLUMBIA MO	2	3	6	1	3	4	5,074	8,199	21,049	3,125	12,850	15,975
DES MOINES	2	1	2	−1	1	0	701	580	7,773	−121	7,193	7,072
DUBUQUE	1	0	0	−1	0	−1	853	0	0	−853	0	−853
DULUTH	1	1	6	0	5	5	1,514	63	9,090	−1,451	9,027	7,576
FARGO	0	0	2	0	2	2	0	0	9,237	0	9,237	9,237
KANSAS CITY	9	12	24	3	12	15	15,894	17,746	31,896	1,852	14,150	16,002
LINCOLN NE	1	2	3	1	1	2	5,583	7,993	3,674	2,410	−4,319	−1,909
MINNEAPOLIS	7	11	33	4	22	26	11,438	24,374	79,048	12,936	54,674	67,610
OMAHA	3	7	8	4	1	5	4,063	8,752	16,825	4,689	8,073	12,762
ROCHESTR MN	2	1	1	−1	0	−1	1,670	499	850	−1,171	351	−820

ST JOSEPH	1	0	2	−1	2	1	1,042	4,132	0	−1,042	4,132	3,090
ST LOUIS	18	26	39	8	13	21	85,696	109,516	87,490	1,794	22,026	23,820
SIOUX CITY	0	0	2	1	1	2	0	4,517	1,802	1,802	2,715	4,517
SIOUX FALLS	0	1	1	0	1	1	0	1,252	0	0	1,252	1,252
SPRINGFD MO	1	1	4	0	3	3	1,805	13,163	3,967	2,162	9,196	11,358
TOPEKA	0	0	0	0	0	0	0	0	0	0	0	0
WATERLOO IA	0	0	2	0	2	2	0	3,461	0	0	3,461	3,461
WICHITA KA	1	1	6	0	5	5	3,977	15,104	1,756	−2,221	13,348	11,127
South Atlantic												
ALBANY GA	3	5	9	2	4	6	18,040	23,725	16,413	−1,627	7,312	5,685
ASHEVILLE	1	1	3	0	2	2	3,091	3,127	2,151	−940	976	36
ATLANTA GA	19	36	36	17	0	17	58,312	92,053	94,123	35,811	−2,070	33,741
AUGUSTA GA	6	5	7	−1	2	1	26,016	22,132	14,270	−11,746	7,862	−3,884
BALTIMORE	24	37	38	13	1	14	95,581	106,648	121,696	26,115	−15,048	11,067
CHARLEST.NC	19	8	13	−11	5	−6	67,743	27,609	26,658	−41,085	951	−40,134
CHARLEST.WV	3	2	2	−1	0	−1	7,611	3,847	2,083	−5,528	1,764	−3,764
CHARLOTTE	7	8	9	1	1	2	19,584	25,045	22,968	3,384	2,077	5,461
COLUMBIA SC	10	4	11	−6	7	1	30,550	24,702	13,635	−16,915	11,067	−5,848
COLUMBUS GA	17	10	13	−7	3	−4	54,459	28,294	27,169	−27,290	1,125	−26,165
FAYETTEV.NC	6	4	5	−2	1	−1	18,027	8,952	10,492	−7,535	−1,540	−9,075
FORT LAUDER	1	4	4	3	0	3	2,642	13,473	22,759	20,117	−9,286	10,831
GAINESVILLE	2	4	7	2	3	5	10,769	45,583	26,054	15,285	19,529	34,814
GREENSBORO	5	5	6	0	1	1	17,012	18,026	8,749	−8,263	9,277	1,014
GREENVILLE	1	5	8	4	3	7	3,578	18,422	9,806	6,228	8,616	14,844
HUNTINGTON	6	1	5	−5	4	−1	13,990	12,063	3,905	−10,085	8,158	−1,927

(continued)

Table B.1: High-poverty Census Tracts and Residents, 1970–1990 *(continued)*

	High-Poverty Census Tracts			Change in Number of Tracts			Population			Change in Population		
	1970	1980	1990	70–80	80–90	70–90	1970	1980	1990	70–80	80–90	70–90
JACKSONV.FL	7	12	12	5	0	5	32,567	39,318	27,005	6,751	−12,313	−5,562
LYNCHBURG	0	1	3	1	2	3	0	1,128	5,133	1,128	4,005	5,133
MACON GA	8	8	11	0	3	3	26,474	21,003	22,380	−5,471	1,377	−4,094
MIAMI	7	14	33	7	19	26	41,888	67,330	148,083	25,442	80,753	106,195
NEWPORT VA	2	2	4	0	2	2	7,222	7,635	8,158	413	523	936
NORFOLK	21	17	20	−4	3	−1	93,819	63,054	53,116	−30,765	−9,938	−40,703
ORLANDO FL	5	5	5	0	0	0	16,849	16,047	16,773	−802	726	−76
PENSACOLA	5	5	7	0	2	2	21,546	11,629	14,132	−9,917	2,503	−7,414
PETERSBURG	0	1	1	1	0	1	0	450	461	450	11	461
RALEIGH-DUR	8	3	8	−5	5	0	23,753	3,314	23,369	−20,439	20,055	−384
RICHMOND VA	7	6	9	−1	3	2	20,185	16,586	23,954	−3,599	7,368	3,769
ROANOKE VA	0	0	2	0	2	2	0	0	4,929	0	4,929	4,929
SAVANNAH GA	12	13	11	1	−2	−1	27,781	25,857	15,060	−1,924	−10,797	−12,721
TALLAHASSEE	5	6	10	1	4	5	15,005	24,975	36,036	9,970	11,061	21,031
TAMPA	16	15	16	−1	1	0	51,688	44,711	40,956	−6,977	−3,755	−10,732
WASHINGTON	10	10	10	0	0	0	36,054	35,928	20,609	−126	−15,319	−15,445
W.PALM BCH	4	4	6	0	2	2	18,415	12,925	16,018	−5,490	3,093	−2,397
WHEELING WV	0	0	0	0	0	0	0	0	0	0	0	0
WILMINGT.DE	4	8	3	4	−5	−1	10,750	13,618	4,470	2,868	−9,148	−6,280
WILMINGT.NC	3	3	5	0	2	2	9,907	6,734	9,120	−3,173	2,386	−787

East South Central

BILOXI MISS	2	1	4	−1	3	2	6,508	3,599	9,305	−2,909	5,706	2,797
BIRMINGHAM	18	16	14	−2	−2	−4	59,690	44,727	54,871	−14,963	10,144	−4,819
CHATTANOOGA	7	6	7	−1	1	0	20,947	17,611	13,963	−3,336	−3,648	−6,984
GADSDEN ALA	0	0	1	0	1	1	0	0	1,482	0	1,482	1,482
HUNTSVIL.AL	4	3	4	−1	1	0	13,912	7,790	10,572	−6,122	2,782	−3,340
JACKSON MS	16	8	17	−8	9	1	61,856	25,280	51,965	−36,576	26,685	−9,891
KNOXVILLE	10	9	8	−1	−1	−2	36,172	29,324	24,959	−6,848	−4,365	−11,213
LEXINGTON	1	2	3	1	1	2	5,355	7,214	10,836	1,859	3,622	5,481
LOUISVILLE	15	17	11	2	−6	−4	33,812	33,909	35,277	97	1,368	1,465
MEMPHIS	38	37	50	−1	13	12	148,451	108,247	141,094	−40,204	32,847	−7,357
MOBILE AL	19	16	26	−3	10	7	61,180	43,689	59,438	−17,491	15,749	−1,742
MONTGOMERY	10	6	10	−4	4	0	46,236	29,403	33,347	−16,833	3,944	−12,889
NASHVILLE	5	11	11	6	0	6	20,498	40,709	32,834	20,211	−7,875	12,336
TUSCALOOSA	3	4	6	1	2	3	15,814	12,715	26,988	−3,099	14,273	11,174

West South Central

ABILENE TX	0	0	2	0	2	2	0	0	1,536	0	1,536	1,536
AMARILLO TX	0	1	7	1	6	7	0	2,128	8,093	2,128	5,965	8,093
AUSTIN TX	2	9	11	7	2	9	19,163	39,477	42,097	20,314	2,620	22,934
BATON ROUGE	6	7	16	1	9	10	38,596	21,327	60,375	−17,269	39,048	21,779
BEAUMONT TX	4	5	15	10	10	11	6,973	8,448	23,311	1,475	14,863	16,338
BROWNSVILLE	24	16	30	−8	14	6	96,741	62,016	136,312	−34,725	74,296	39,571
BRYAN TX	4	2	6	−2	4	2	16,745	7,941	39,934	−8,804	31,993	23,189
CORPUS CHRS	14	6	10	−8	4	−4	58,219	23,217	41,066	−35,002	17,849	−17,153
DALLAS	20	24	48	4	24	28	69,849	53,812	126,471	−16,037	72,659	56,622
EL PASO	11	8	20	−3	12	9	54,132	30,282	110,735	−23,850	80,453	56,603

(continued)

229

Table B.1: High-poverty Census Tracts and Residents, 1970–1990 (continued)

	High-Poverty Census Tracts			Change in Number of Tracts			Population			Change in Population		
	1970	1980	1990	70–80	80–90	70–90	1970	1980	1990	70–80	80–90	70–90
FORT SMITH	2	0	2	−2	2	0	6,292	0	1,853	−6,292	1,853	−4,439
GALVESTON	3	3	4	0	1	1	8,307	5,806	6,890	−2,501	1,084	−1,417
HOUSTON	12	13	51	1	38	39	43,242	47,364	162,487	4,122	115,123	119,245
LAFAYETT.LA	3	0	8	−3	8	5	14,787	0	27,433	−14,787	27,433	12,646
LAKE CHRLES	4	1	5	−3	4	1	17,015	1,826	11,988	−15,189	10,162	−5,027
LAREDO TX	12	8	13	−4	5	1	49,270	34,258	66,005	−15,012	31,747	16,735
LAWTON OK	1	1	1	0	0	0	3,716	848	2,410	−2,868	1,562	−1,306
LITTLE ROCK	6	1	4	−5	3	−2	23,735	4,277	13,167	−19,458	8,890	−10,568
LUBBOCK TX	5	1	8	−4	7	3	18,683	2,166	19,428	−16,517	17,262	745
MCALLEN TX	31	21	37	−10	16	6	136,873	123,963	234,467	−12,910	110,504	97,594
MIDLAND TX	0	0	3	0	3	3	0	0	10,804	0	10,804	10,804
MONROE LA	7	9	12	2	3	5	24,711	28,810	34,782	4,099	5,972	10,071
NEW ORLEANS	30	30	67	0	37	37	125,768	96,417	165,751	−29,351	69,334	39,983
ODESSA TX	0	0	4	0	4	4	0	0	11,516	0	11,516	11,516
OKLAHOMA CY	11	10	24	−1	14	13	19,091	17,679	39,420	−1,412	21,741	20,329
PINE BLUFF	7	5	5	−2	0	−2	33,028	12,372	13,513	−20,656	1,141	−19,515
SAN ANGELO	2	0	2	−2	2	0	4,956	0	2,778	−4,956	2,778	−2,178
SAN ANTONIO	19	18	31	−1	13	12	117,936	80,248	152,936	−37,688	72,688	35,000
SHERMAN TX	0	0	1	0	1	1	0	0	325	0	325	325
SHREVEPORT	16	8	18	−8	10	2	69,401	18,816	59,130	−50,585	40,314	−10,271
TEXARKANA	1	2	2	1	0	1	707	6,393	4,587	5,686	−1,806	3,880

TULSA	6	1	11	-5	10	5	16,069	2,759	29,066	-13,310	26,307	12,997
TYLER TX	0	0	4	0	4	4	0	0	10,105	0	10,105	10,105
WACO TX	4	5	9	1	4	5	16,112	19,112	33,038	3,000	13,926	16,926
WICHITA TX	3	2	6	-1	4	3	7,163	4,284	8,398	-2,879	4,114	1,235
Mountain												
ALBUQUERQUE	8	3	5	-5	2	-3	19,479	8,509	12,523	-10,970	4,014	-6,956
BILLINGS	0	0	2	0	2	2	0	0	4,088	0	4,088	4,088
BOISE ID	0	0	0	0	0	0	0	0	0	0	0	0
COLORADO SP	0	1	2	1	1	2	0	841	1,640	841	799	1,640
DENVER	10	8	12	-2	4	2	24,098	17,926	29,632	-6,172	11,706	5,534
GREAT FALLS	0	0	2	0	2	2	0	0	2,540	0	2,540	2,540
LAS VEGAS	1	0	2	-1	2	1	2,623	0	8,258	-2,623	8,258	5,635
PHOENIX	13	14	23	1	9	10	41,119	43,719	78,620	2,600	34,901	37,501
PROVO-OREM	1	3	3	2	0	2	8,097	25,488	28,148	17,391	2,660	20,051
PUEBLO CO	1	1	5	0	4	4	1,996	1,046	8,051	-950	7,005	6,055
RENO	0	0	0	0	0	0	0	0	0	0	0	0
SALT LAKE	4	4	6	0	2	2	4,827	3,192	7,456	-1,635	4,264	2,629
TUCSON	4	3	13	-1	10	9	11,208	17,077	52,879	5,869	35,802	41,671
Pacific												
ANAHEIM CA	0	1	1	1	0	1	0	3,000	95	3,000	-2,905	95
BAKERSFIELD	3	2	4	-1	2	1	10,484	5,694	22,333	-4,790	16,639	11,849
EUGENE OR	1	1	3	0	2	2	5,699	5,937	11,900	238	5,963	6,201
FRESNO	8	3	14	-5	11	6	25,411	8,310	82,023	-17,101	73,713	56,612
HONOLULU	3	3	5	0	2	2	5,282	7,379	6,911	2,097	-468	1,629
LOS ANGELES	33	40	56	7	16	23	96,837	119,855	267,666	23,018	147,811	170,829

(continued)

Table B.1: High-poverty Census Tracts and Residents, 1970–1990 (continued)

	High-Poverty Census Tracts			Change in Number of Tracts			Population			Change in Population		
	1970	1980	1990	70–80	80–90	70–90	1970	1980	1990	70–80	80–90	70–90
MODESTO CA	0	0	3	0	3	3	0	0	3,327	0	3,327	3,327
OXNARD CA	0	0	0	0	0	0	0	0	0	0	0	0
PORTLAND OR	3	3	10	0	7	7	3,677	4,912	15,304	1,235	10,392	11,627
RIVERSIDE	1	1	6	0	5	5	3,166	1,521	22,523	−1,645	21,002	19,357
SACRAMENTO	1	3	6	2	3	5	998	6,435	24,624	5,437	18,189	23,626
SALEM OREG	0	1	0	1	−1	0	0	2,291	0	2,291	−2,291	0
SALINAS CA	0	0	0	0	0	0	0	0	0	0	0	0
SAN DIEGO	4	2	8	−2	6	4	18,603	4,553	38,644	−14,050	34,091	20,041
SAN FRANCIS	13	12	13	−1	1	0	31,721	30,489	41,737	−1,232	11,248	10,016
SAN JOSE CA	1	1	0	0	−1	−1	5,353	700	0	−4,653	−700	−5,353
SANTA BARBA	3	2	4	−1	2	1	14,203	11,466	19,857	−2,737	8,391	5,654
SANTA ROSA	0	0	0	0	0	0	0	0	0	0	0	0
SEATTLE	3	4	9	1	5	6	10,024	5,360	24,775	−4,664	19,415	14,751
SPOKANE WA	4	4	6	0	2	2	3,759	3,219	6,766	−540	3,547	3,007
STOCKTON CA	2	4	5	2	1	3	9,575	7,193	25,858	−2,382	18,665	16,283
TACOMA WA	1	3	5	2	2	4	3,041	6,106	12,688	3,065	6,582	9,647
VALLEJO CA	0	0	1	0	1	1	0	0	96	0	96	96

Source: See Chapter 2 and Appendix A.

232

Table B.2: Residents of High-Poverty Areas by Race and Ethnicity, 1970–1990

	Non-Hispanic White (est.)			Black			Hispanic		
	1970	1980	1990	1970	1980	1990	1970	1980	1990
New England									
BOSTON	24,674	9,037	11,379	13,133	10,170	13,244	2,732	4,074	7,134
BRIDGEPORT	581	2,804	634	2,162	7,027	3,044	1,052	8,460	2,408
BRISTOL	0	0	0	0	0	0	0	0	0
BROCKTON	1,414	0	0	109	0	0	0	0	0
DANBURY	0	0	0	0	0	0	0	0	0
FALL RIVER	0	0	19	0	0	0	0	0	0
FITCHBURG	574	0	0	0	0	0	0	0	0
HARTFORD	2,150	3,558	358	10,060	12,616	10,813	2,640	11,787	15,631
LAWRENCE MA	0	1,912	2,055	0	0	1,301	0	1,409	9,300
LEWISTON ME	0	0	1,565	0	0	20	0	0	28
LOWELL MA	0	940	9,866	0	0	306	0	240	2,596
MANCHESTER	894	0	0	0	0	0	0	0	0
MERIDEN	0	176	108	0	0	0	0	102	182
NASHUA NH	0	0	0	0	0	0	0	0	0
NEW BEDFORD	0	0	0	0	0	0	0	0	0
NEW BRITAIN	0	772	0	0	120	0	0	436	0
NEW HAVEN	0	1,912	690	0	4,234	2,396	0	1,338	1,674
NEW LONDON	3,274	490	180	30	48	74	41	0	74
NORWALK	0	0	0	0	0	0	0	0	0
PITTSFIELD	0	0	32	0	0	0	0	0	0
PORTLAND ME	388	0	2,262	0	0	40	0	0	64

(continued)

233

Table B.2: Residents of High-Poverty Areas by Race and Ethnicity, 1970–1990 (continued)

	Non-Hispanic White (est.)			Black			Hispanic		
	1970	1980	1990	1970	1980	1990	1970	1980	1990
PROVIDENCE	197	2,701	2,916	0	3,827	4,202	0	1,062	2,288
SPRINGFD MA	143	7,314	11,975	0	1,444	9,109	0	10,697	22,730
STAMFORD CT	0	0	0	0	0	0	0	0	0
WATERBURY	0	1,427	151	0	66	44	0	1,950	58
WORCESTER	0	1,105	3,559	0	538	1,143	0	2,177	3,711
Middle Atlantic									
ALBANY NY	0	1,925	2,545	0	752	5,765	0	36	344
ALLENTOWN	0	0	6,100	0	0	631	0	0	2,910
ALTOONA PA	0	0	1,638	0	0	64	0	0	0
ATLANTIC CY	1,022	2,551	590	164	1,407	7,762	137	1,329	930
BINGHAMTON	0	0	3,919	0	0	410	0	0	37
BUFFALO NY	3,418	7,224	17,273	1,841	23,108	49,121	204	2,458	5,836
ERIE PA	0	3,104	6,870	0	1,618	5,511	0	67	701
HARRISBURG	0	1,940	1,316	0	4,341	3,616	0	375	726
JERSEY CITY	0	959	156	0	4,918	7,105	0	1,831	1,184
JOHNSTOWN	0	0	3,035	0	0	820	0	0	93
LANCASTR PA	0	512	1,503	0	1,458	1,677	0	1,384	2,244
NASSAU-SUFF	0	2,967	6,994	0	63	1,380	0	137	440
NEW YORK	39,782	68,983	18,032	140,892	511,480	482,735	119,853	421,552	459,525
NEWARK NJ	611	6,103	1,862	32,143	85,926	39,083	1,291	20,606	8,244
N.EAST PENN	2,160	0	3,153	368	0	323	0	0	7
PATERSON NJ	247	2,520	82	1,797	15,913	4,722	176	10,656	679

PHILADELPHIA	13,735	43,232	36,030	93,565	184,375	146,127	4,527	38,904	59,706
PITTSBURGH	7,779	10,776	24,995	22,923	27,276	49,431	0	319	472
READING PA	0	1,975	3,362	0	615	857	0	1,465	2,857
ROCHESTR NY	7,986	6,879	7,090	86	5,524	19,908	0	1,391	6,512
SYRACUSE NY	10,516	15,931	20,920	795	7,543	15,586	0	780	1,644
TRENTON NJ	0	675	736	0	1,809	2,288	0	706	2,086
UTICA NY	194	741	1,853	1,062	821	1,130	0	0	111
VINELAND NJ	444	0	0	55	0	0	176	0	0
YORK PA	530	0	0	1,524	0	0	57	0	0
East North Central									
AKRON OH	1,992	3,281	35,271	3,612	5,114	13,004	0	93	357
ANDERSON IN	0	0	1,570	0	0	1,091	0	0	73
ANN ARBOR	14,040	15,437	32,073	746	2,092	3,005	91	365	1,104
APPLETON WI	0	0	7,187	0	0	41	0	0	120
BAY CITY MI	0	0	780	0	0	203	0	0	156
BLOOMING.IL	0	6,928	10,772	0	968	780	0	103	137
CANTON	0	980	5,104	0	1,981	4,715	0	0	54
CHAMPAIGN	13,850	20,260	20,261	691	966	3,328	140	342	947
CHICAGO	8,105	21,702	24,245	144,423	323,160	328,223	3,742	25,108	43,732
CINCINNATI	18,654	13,353	23,421	35,837	43,010	50,574	229	567	392
CLEVELAND	7,321	7,937	19,356	54,009	63,347	74,861	938	857	6,215
COLUMBUS OH	21,707	42,969	48,394	4,996	20,080	37,341	291	622	922
DAVENPORT	0	516	5,283	0	48	4,790	0	0	717
DAYTON OH	4,030	8,206	15,264	1,449	20,984	35,363	0	191	260
DECATUR	1,684	977	592	1,867	2,340	1,724	138	0	8
DETROIT	16,286	22,515	73,731	39,127	96,255	333,014	500	1,699	12,202

(continued)

Table B.2: Residents of High-Poverty Areas by Race and Ethnicity, 1970–1990 (continued)

	Non-Hispanic White (est.)			Black			Hispanic		
	1970	1980	1990	1970	1980	1990	1970	1980	1990
EVANSVILLE	762	322	434	36	1,237	876	0	0	8
FLINT	0	205	15,922	0	3,119	34,049	0	171	1,743
FORT WAYNE	0	433	1,250	0	3,557	3,730	0	119	100
GARY	112	938	2,176	1,222	11,486	16,574	0	305	2,658
GRAND RAPID	0	1,208	1,540	0	3,501	5,277	0	280	225
GREEN BAY	0	0	0	0	0	0	0	0	0
HAMILTON	0	7,321	16,458	0	3,963	4,052	0	61	194
INDIANAPOLIS	4,405	3,716	3,767	7,431	10,990	17,750	155	112	133
JACKSON MI	2,513	0	5,009	2,130	0	3,116	0	0	313
KALAMAZOO	7,492	5,997	19,339	202	2,224	7,909	0	144	703
KENOSHA WI	0	0	0	0	0	0	0	0	0
LA CROSSE	0	0	10,154	0	0	68	0	0	83
LAFAYETT.IN	5,389	8,254	24,612	83	150	1,044	48	81	698
LANSING MI	16,775	18,744	14,855	1,018	824	3,489	100	250	1,024
LIMA OH	0	1,434	3,294	0	3,166	3,470	0	98	7
LORAIN OH	636	0	1,492	454	0	484	109	0	86
MADISON	18,785	18,805	26,182	457	569	914	74	234	648
MANSFIELD	0	1,110	1,741	0	81	1,733	0	0	0
MILWAUKEE	8,113	8,448	32,641	8,923	22,445	92,116	283	1,089	16,068
MUNCIE IND	0	0	10,560	0	0	464	0	0	151
MUSKEGON MI	0	0	3,902	0	0	8,050	0	0	287
PEORIA IL	0	3,264	4,267	0	5,200	6,253	0	260	259

RACINE WI	0	0	950	0	0	3,037	0	0	615
ROCKFORD IL	0	1,621	3,983	0	2,501	5,217	0	330	476
SAGINAW	23	1,085	2,578	3,189	5,765	18,617	215	1,172	3,158
SOUTH BEND	8,423	904	442	1,821	3,201	982	219	0	101
SPRINGFD IL	828	0	1,729	1,589	0	2,192	0	0	79
SPRINGFD OH	0	2,702	743	0	523	205	0	0	0
STEUBENVILL	0	1,396	3,486	0	1,862	2,201	0	0	69
TERRE HAUTE	5,457	0	2,523	307	0	464	0	0	19
TOLEDO	1,517	13,037	33,090	6,309	8,933	19,228	0	495	2,866
YOUNGSTOWN	1,344	1,084	10,145	1,797	5,502	21,105	72	159	2,228
West North Central									
CEDAR RAPID	0	0	1,805	0	0	229	0	0	33
COLUMBIA MO	4,602	7,773	17,861	412	351	2,802	60	75	386
DES MOINES	576	436	5,291	125	144	2,295	0	0	187
DUBUQUE	853	0	0	0	0	0	0	0	0
DULUTH	1,514	63	8,796	0	0	256	0	0	38
FARGO	0	0	9,002	0	0	64	0	0	171
KANSAS CITY	3,652	3,205	8,890	12,152	13,029	19,920	90	1,512	3,086
LINCOLN NE	5,445	7,314	3,138	105	464	442	33	215	94
MINNEAPOLIS	9,069	18,360	57,100	2,176	5,449	19,269	193	565	2,679
OMAHA	363	1,588	5,996	3,700	7,127	10,059	0	37	770
ROCHESTR MN	1,670	499	521	0	0	181	0	0	148
ST JOSEPH	786	0	3,311	190	0	747	66	0	74
ST LOUIS	11,372	7,812	11,924	74,002	78,996	96,786	322	682	806
SIOUX CITY	0	1,654	3,521	0	104	490	0	44	506
SIOUX FALLS	0	0	1,217	0	0	11	0	0	24

(continued)

Table B.2: Residents of High-Poverty Areas by Race and Ethnicity, 1970–1990 *(continued)*

	Non-Hispanic White (est.)			Black			Hispanic		
	1970	1980	1990	1970	1980	1990	1970	1980	1990
SPRINGFD MO	1,805	3,967	12,232	0	0	838	0	0	93
TOPEKA	0	0	0	0	0	0	0	0	0
WATERLOO IA	0	0	1,906	0	0	1,484	0	0	71
WICHITA KA	107	78	4,874	3,870	1,634	9,623	0	44	607
South Atlantic									
ALBANY GA	2,927	2,034	1,839	15,113	14,141	21,766	0	238	120
ASHEVILLE	992	601	1,945	2,099	1,550	1,153	0	0	29
ATLANTA GA	7,320	8,120	8,976	50,949	85,169	81,560	43	834	1,517
AUGUSTA GA	4,237	871	4,197	21,745	13,241	17,829	34	158	106
BALTIMORE	8,661	14,652	11,978	86,649	105,796	94,091	271	1,248	579
CHARLEST.NC	14,359	2,859	7,382	53,238	23,434	19,992	146	365	235
CHARLEST.WV	5,224	1,049	2,588	2,387	1,034	1,221	0	0	38
CHARLOTTE	1,850	1,949	1,933	17,734	20,651	22,907	0	368	205
COLUMBIA SC	5,961	1,796	6,854	24,589	11,712	17,591	0	127	257
COLUMBUS GA	16,375	7,656	6,575	37,781	19,277	21,527	303	236	192
FAYETTEV.NC	5,014	1,567	1,071	13,013	8,925	7,729	0	0	152
FORT LAUDER	220	373	943	2,362	22,035	12,401	60	351	129
GAINESVILLE	7,422	20,981	32,761	2,855	3,550	10,256	492	1,523	2,566
GREENSBORO	1,939	2,360	1,322	15,073	6,284	16,640	0	105	64
GREENVILLE	446	899	8,236	3,132	8,786	10,172	0	121	14
HUNTINGTON	13,679	3,905	11,713	311	0	315	0	0	35
JACKSONV.FL	6,001	11,257	5,406	26,384	27,308	21,292	182	753	307

LYNCHBURG	0	1,055	1,548	0	38	3,561	0	35	24
MACON GA	5,475	4,399	4,970	20,999	16,561	17,324	0	43	86
MIAMI	3,584	11,016	9,356	35,741	48,404	92,443	2,563	7,910	46,284
NEWPORT VA	964	0	1,309	6,225	7,577	6,808	33	109	41
NORFOLK	35,841	23,487	4,999	57,016	38,136	47,657	962	1,431	460
ORLANDO FL	2,643	1,815	2,393	14,074	14,078	14,002	132	154	378
PENSACOLA	3,789	2,791	3,459	17,405	8,779	10,548	352	59	125
PETERSBURG	0	119	71	0	331	390	0	0	0
RALEIGH-DUR	6,338	24	10,307	17,373	3,153	12,755	42	137	307
RICHMOND VA	2,268	923	4,277	17,861	15,393	19,513	56	270	164
ROANOKE VA	0	0	832	0	0	4,020	0	0	77
SAVANNAH GA	1,881	1,343	1,468	25,900	24,295	13,538	0	219	54
TALLAHASSEE	7,981	14,080	17,358	6,796	10,330	17,414	228	565	1,264
TAMPA	8,710	6,872	8,028	38,245	34,402	28,768	4,733	3,437	4,160
WASHINGTON	12,128	8,269	1,243	23,806	27,421	18,861	120	238	505
W.PALM BCH	4,238	1,159	324	12,831	10,420	14,486	1,346	1,346	1,208
WHEELING WV	0	0	0	0	0	0	0	0	0
WILMINGT.DE	1,490	1,355	555	9,038	11,831	3,821	222	432	94
WILMINGT.NC	1,865	1,016	1,544	8,042	5,668	7,540	0	50	36
East South Central									
BILOXI MISS	1,788	402	3,966	4,656	3,197	5,265	64	0	74
BIRMINGHAM	14,002	3,852	4,027	45,612	40,395	50,720	76	480	124
CHATTANOOGA	3,950	1,104	1,564	16,997	16,238	12,376	0	269	23
GADSDEN ALA	0	0	1,149	0	0	333	0	0	0
HUNTSVIL.AL	4,921	1,849	4,400	8,991	5,806	6,099	0	135	73
JACKSON MS	8,454	668	3,701	53,331	24,428	48,062	71	184	202

(continued)

239

Table B.2: Residents of High-Poverty Areas by Race and Ethnicity, 1970–1990 (continued)

	Non-Hispanic White (est.)			Black			Hispanic		
	1970	1980	1990	1970	1980	1990	1970	1980	1990
KNOXVILLE	24,193	19,727	16,446	11,893	9,198	8,367	86	399	146
LEXINGTON	1,899	3,011	6,614	3,456	4,087	4,170	0	116	52
LOUISVILLE	9,848	11,453	15,172	23,919	22,327	19,951	45	129	154
MEMPHIS	20,872	11,025	10,856	127,135	96,196	129,681	444	1,026	557
MOBILE AL	9,255	4,107	4,792	51,669	39,009	54,495	256	573	151
MONTGOMERY	9,673	3,715	5,373	36,414	25,456	27,771	149	232	203
NASHVILLE	4,914	12,640	6,108	15,584	27,571	26,548	0	498	178
TUSCALOOSA	4,100	6,531	14,806	11,714	6,184	11,975	0	0	207
West South Central									
ABILENE TX	0	0	719	0	0	287	0	0	530
AMARILLO TX	0	635	3,116	0	1,380	1,920	0	113	3,057
AUSTIN TX	13,953	23,939	19,649	185	10,175	8,400	5,025	5,363	14,048
BATON ROUGE	11,967	4,486	18,499	25,988	16,247	40,786	641	594	1,090
BEAUMONT TX	290	1,248	2,311	6,634	6,826	20,270	49	374	730
BROWNSVILLE	14,203	5,217	10,658	420	128	301	82,118	56,671	125,353
BRYAN TX	6,993	7,208	31,720	6,933	252	3,500	2,819	481	4,714
CORPUS CHRS	7,910	2,070	3,934	7,355	2,705	3,410	42,954	18,442	33,722
DALLAS	5,238	5,265	24,512	60,736	45,507	71,090	3,875	3,040	30,869
EL PASO	4,318	852	7,139	867	606	1,645	48,947	28,824	101,951
FORT SMITH	4,943	0	1,220	1,349	0	629	0	0	4
GALVESTON	668	76	918	6,941	5,230	5,236	698	500	736
HOUSTON	2,643	3,375	12,049	38,131	37,822	93,591	2,468	6,167	56,847

LAFAYETT.LA	4,060	0	8,867	10,727	0	18,236	0	0	330
LAKE CHRLES	2,774	69	1,031	14,166	1,757	10,851	75	0	106
LAREDO TX	3,695	1,229	1,954	0	0	51	45,575	33,029	64,000
LAWTON OK	579	714	506	3,080	134	1,805	57	0	99
LITTLE ROCK	6,005	0	1,566	17,684	4,230	11,561	46	51	40
LUBBOCK TX	6,921	786	5,285	7,612	201	5,820	4,150	1,179	8,323
MCALLEN TX	14,460	9,112	17,816	159	35	420	122,254	114,816	216,231
MIDLAND TX	0	0	1,405	0	0	3,021	0	0	6,378
MONROE LA	1,577	2,310	4,981	22,971	26,301	29,717	163	199	84
NEW ORLEANS	10,555	4,349	17,511	113,151	90,708	145,314	2,062	1,360	2,926
ODESSA TX	0	0	1,454	0	6,997	2,209	0	0	7,853
OKLAHOMA CY	3,890	9,988	23,203	14,368	9,460	12,240	833	694	3,977
PINE BLUFF	8,762	2,748	1,223	24,187	0	12,220	79	164	70
SAN ANGELO	156	0	792	1,667	9,434	947	3,133	0	1,039
SAN ANTONIO	4,336	5,115	9,681	11,629	0	13,899	101,971	65,699	129,356
SHERMAN TX	0	0	245	0	18,403	54	0	0	26
SHREVEPORT	8,368	27	7,070	60,836	5,411	51,749	197	386	311
TEXARKANA	666	892	530	41	1,489	4,057	0	90	0
TULSA	2,144	1,231	13,609	13,925	0	14,732	0	39	725
TYLER TX	0	0	1,650	0	6,627	7,091	0	0	1,364
WACO TX	7,405	10,023	14,778	6,428	3,576	13,929	2,279	2,462	4,331
WICHITA TX	662	177	2,440	5,723		4,646	778	531	1,312
Mountain									
ALBUQUERQUE	2,602	6,018	6,259	1,674	0	127	15,203	2,491	6,137
BILLINGS	0	0	3,286	0	0	118	0	0	684
BOISE ID	0	0	0	0	0	0	0	0	0

(continued)

241

Table B.2: Residents of High-Poverty Areas by Race and Ethnicity, 1970–1990 (continued)

	Non-Hispanic White (est.)			Black			Hispanic		
	1970	1980	1990	1970	1980	1990	1970	1980	1990
COLORADO SP	0	587	1,103	0	98	224	0	156	313
DENVER	6,116	4,644	11,311	5,760	3,367	7,564	12,222	9,915	10,757
GREAT FALLS	0	0	2,399	0	0	75	0	0	66
LAS VEGAS	100	0	562	2,523	0	7,529	0	0	167
PHOENIX	13,957	13,819	27,884	8,438	6,140	9,140	18,724	23,760	41,596
PROVO-OREM	7,946	24,536	26,879	0	50	83	151	902	1,186
PUEBLO CO	1,559	698	3,477	111	98	176	326	250	4,398
RENO	0	0	0	0	0	0	0	0	0
SALT LAKE	3,047	1,747	4,259	1,281	930	966	499	515	2,231
TUCSON	2,478	14,467	29,302	592	321	2,621	8,138	2,289	20,956
Pacific									
ANAHEIM CA	0	2,343	38	0	270	0	0	387	57
BAKERSFIELD	906	908	2,654	5,294	3,420	6,916	4,284	1,366	12,763
EUGENE OR	5,501	5,728	11,014	86	78	251	112	131	635
FRESNO	4,082	219	35,313	12,426	6,156	9,674	8,903	1,935	37,036
HONOLULU	4,864	6,710	6,179	179	0	124	239	669	608
LOS ANGELES	17,019	19,018	38,860	58,906	62,728	79,696	20,912	38,109	149,110
MODESTO CA	0	0	1,887	0	0	248	0	0	1,192
OXNARD CA	0	0	0	0	0	0	0	0	0
PORTLAND OR	2,733	2,479	7,451	768	2,246	6,877	176	187	976
RIVERSIDE	1,567	662	7,039	879	383	3,665	720	476	11,819
SACRAMENTO	447	4,799	16,136	88	408	3,791	463	1,228	4,697

SALEM OREG	0	2,028	0	0	153	0	0	110	0
SALINAS CA	0	0	0	0	0	0	0	0	0
SAN DIEGO	13,528	963	3,656	2,758	992	10,782	2,317	2,598	24,206
SAN FRANCIS	14,713	11,757	12,509	14,097	16,715	22,555	2,911	2,017	6,673
SAN JOSE CA	4,605	550	0	275	62	0	473	88	0
SANTA BARBA	13,231	9,989	16,482	305	274	517	667	1,203	2,858
SANTA ROSA	0	0	0	0	0	0	0	0	0
SEATTLE	8,091	4,344	20,124	1,327	836	3,213	606	180	1,438
SPOKANE WA	3,713	3,118	6,144	46	0	364	0	101	258
STOCKTON CA	2,410	4,515	11,707	3,957	776	3,949	3,208	1,902	10,202
TACOMA WA	2,512	4,390	8,640	489	1,453	3,420	40	263	628
VALLEJO CA	0	0	41	0	0	0	0	0	55

Source: See Chapter 2 and Appendix A.

Table B.3: Neighborhood Poverty and Concentration of the Poor

| | Non-Hispanic White (est.) | | | | | | Black | | | | | | Hispanic | | | | | |
| | Neighborhood Poverty Rate | | | Concentration of the Poor | | | Neighborhood Poverty Rate | | | Concentration of the Poor | | | Neighborhood Poverty Rate | | | Concentration of the Poor | | |
	70	80	90	70	80	90	70	80	90	70	80	90	70	80	90	70	80	90
New England																		
BOSTON	1	0	0	3	1	2	10	7	6	20	10	13	8	6	6	26	11	11
BRIDGEPORT	0	1	0	1	3	2	8	20	7	22	39	20	6	28	6	23	47	15
BRISTOL	0	0	0	0	0	0	0	0	0	0	0	0	0	0	0	.	0	0
BROCKTON	1	0	0	2	0	0	4	0	0	7	0	0	0	0	0	0	0	0
DANBURY	0	0	0	0	0	0	0	0	0	0	0	0	0	0	0	0	0	0
FALL RIVER	0	0	0	0	0	0	0	0	0	0	0	0	0	0	0	.	0	0
FITCHBURG	1	0	0	1	0	0	0	0	0	0	0	0	0	0	0	0	0	0
HARTFORD	0	1	0	3	3	0	20	21	13	36	44	35	18	35	28	29	52	47
LAWRENCE MA	0	1	1	0	2	3	0	0	19	0	0	25	0	11	26	0	17	32
LEWISTON ME	0	0	2	0	0	7	0	0	4	.	.	17	0	0	7	0	0	25
LOWELL MA	0	0	4	0	2	21	0	0	9	0	0	22	0	5	22	0	11	29
MANCHESTER	1	0	0	3	0	0	0	0	0	0	0	0	0	0	0	0	0	0
MERIDEN	0	0	0	0	1	3	0	0	0	0	0	0	0	2	2	0	9	10
NASHUA NH	0	0	0	0	0	0	0	0	0	0	0	0	0	0	0	0	0	0
NEW BEDFORD	0	0	0	0	0	0	0	0	0	0	0	0	0	0	0	0	0	0
NEW BRITAIN	0	1	0	0	4	0	0	3	0	0	9	0	0	6	0	0	0	0
NEW HAVEN	0	1	0	0	2	1	0	9	4	0	15	9	0	10	8	0	15	12
NEW LONDON	2	0	0	1	1	0	0	1	1	0	1	2	2	0	1	0	0	4
NORWALK	0	0	0	0	0	0	0	0	0	0	0	0	0	0	0	0	0	0

PITTSFIELD	0	0	0	0	0	0	0	0	0	0	0	0	0	0	0	0	0
PORTLAND ME	3	0	.	4	0	0	3	0	0	3	0	0	6	0	1	1	0
PROVIDENCE	8	10	0	5	6	0	20	22	0	12	17	0	1	1	0	0	0
SPRINGFD MA	60	55	0	49	45	0	42	11	0	25	5	0	8	6	0	3	2
STAMFORD CT	0	0	0	0	0	0	0	0	0	0	0	0	0	0	0	0	0
WATERBURY	1	37	0	0	25	0	1	1	0	0	1	0	0	2	0	0	1
WORCESTER	32	48	0	19	32	0	23	46	0	12	11	0	4	2	0	1	0
Middle Atlantic																	
ALBANY NY	5	1	0	2	1	0	24	5	0	14	3	0	2	1	0	0	0
ALLENTOWN	19	0	0	10	0	0	9	0	0	5	0	0	4	0	0	1	0
ALTOONA PA	0	0	.	0	0	.	13	0	0	6	0	0	4	0	0	1	0
ATLANTIC CY	15	30	10	5	18	6	33	8	1	18	4	1	2	9	3	0	2
BINGHAMTON	5	0	0	1	0	0	17	0	3	10	0	0	5	0	0	1	0
BUFFALO NY	38	33	8	25	17	4	54	31	0	40	21	2	6	2	2	2	1
ERIE PA	35	8	0	23	4	0	50	22	0	38	14	0	9	4	0	3	1
HARRISBURG	15	23	0	8	10	0	20	26	0	9	13	0	1	2	0	0	0
JERSEY CITY	2	3	0	1	1	0	16	13	0	9	7	0	0	0	0	0	0
JOHNSTOWN	19	0	.	9	0	.	31	0	0	22	0	0	4	0	0	1	0
LANCASTR PA	24	25	0	15	16	0	31	39	0	18	23	0	1	0	0	0	0
NASSAU-SUFF	0	0	0	0	0	0	0	0	0	1	0	0	1	0	0	0	0
NEW YORK	41	43	22	24	28	14	40	43	13	21	27	7	0	5	2	0	1
NEWARK NJ	12	33	4	4	16	4	21	38	18	9	21	9	0	2	0	0	0
N.EAST PENN	0	0	.	0	0	.	13	0	11	5	0	11	2	0	1	0	0
PATERSON NJ	1	26	0	1	17	1	15	37	8	7	27	4	0	4	0	1	1
PHILADELPHIA	62	55	14	36	35	12	31	37	21	16	21	11	4	4	2	1	1
PITTSBURGH	13	10	0	4	4	0	45	31	24	28	16	14	4	2	1	1	1

(continued)

Table B.3: Neighborhood Poverty and Concentration of the Poor (continued)

	Non-Hispanic White (est.)						Black						Hispanic					
	Neighborhood Poverty Rate			Concentration of the Poor			Neighborhood Poverty Rate			Concentration of the Poor			Neighborhood Poverty Rate			Concentration of the Poor		
	70	80	90	70	80	90	70	80	90	70	80	90	70	80	90	70	80	90
READING PA	0	1	1	0	2	3	0	8	9	0	18	20	0	17	18	0	26	34
ROCHESTR NY	1	1	1	2	1	3	0	7	21	0	14	33	0	8	22	0	10	39
SYRACUSE NY	2	3	3	4	7	13	4	25	40	4	40	59	0	17	21	0	22	50
TRENTON NJ	0	0	0	0	2	0	0	3	4	0	6	8	0	7	11	0	13	25
UTICA NY	0	0	1	0	1	2	14	12	8	28	27	20	0	0	2	0	0	6
VINELAND NJ	0	0	0	2	0	0	0	0	0	1	0	0	3	0	0	9	0	0
YORK PA	0	0	0	1	0	0	20	0	0	30	0	0	30	0	0	6	0	0
East North Central																		
AKRON OH	0	1	6	2	3	21	7	9	20	11	13	30	0	5	9	0	0	32
ANDERSON IN	0	0	1	0	0	0	0	0	11	0	0	1	0	0	9	0	0	0
ANN ARBOR	7	7	13	24	25	42	4	8	10	6	16	10	4	11	20	8	25	29
APPLETON WI	0	0	2	0	0	8	0	0	5	0	0	9	0	0	5	0	0	7
BAY CITY MI	0	0	1	0	0	2	0	0	17	0	0	17	0	0	4	0	0	5
BLOOMING.IL	0	6	9	0	3	15	0	21	14	0	1	6	0	14	11	0	0	18
CANTON	0	0	1	0	2	7	0	8	19	0	15	30	0	0	2	0	0	2
CHAMPAIGN	9	13	13	21	38	39	7	7	20	8	11	29	7	14	29	3	32	40
CHICAGO	0	0	0	1	3	3	12	23	23	24	42	45	1	4	5	3	11	12
CINCINNATI	2	1	2	8	6	10	24	25	27	43	50	52	4	10	5	25	28	18
CLEVELAND	0	1	1	3	3	8	16	19	21	33	37	41	5	4	19	15	7	35
COLUMBUS OH	3	4	4	4	16	20	5	15	23	8	26	43	7	10	10	13	19	24

(continued)

DAVENPORT	0	0	0	1	7	0	0	25	0	0	32	0	0	6	0	0	10
DAYTON OH	1	1	3	6	10	2	20	31	5	38	52	0	5	4	0	12	24
DECATUR	1	1	6	5	2	19	17	12	39	31	19	18	0	1	68	0	0
DETROIT	0	1	2	4	13	5	11	35	11	21	54	1	3	16	3	8	36
EVANSVILLE	0	0	1	0	0	0	8	5	0	15	9	0	0	1	.	0	0
FLINT	0	0	0	0	13	0	4	40	0	8	56	0	2	19	0	7	34
FORT WAYNE	0	4	0	0	2	0	14	12	0	26	26	0	2	1	0	0	2
GARY	0	0	0	2	4	1	9	14	3	16	25	0	1	6	0	2	17
GRAND RAPID	0	0	0	2	2	0	11	13	0	16	22	0	2	1	0	5	2
GREEN BAY	0	0	0	0	0	0	0	0	.	.	0	0	0	0	0	0	0
HAMILTON	0	3	6	15	22	0	33	31	0	41	44	2	5	13	0	12	29
INDIANAPOLIS	0	0	0	2	1	5	7	10	13	14	20	2	2	1	18	7	1
JACKSON MI	2	0	4	0	17	25	0	26	0	0	59	0	0	15	0	0	22
KALAMAZOO	4	2	7	9	23	2	11	32	2	16	45	0	4	12	0	14	20
KENOSHA WI	0	0	0	0	0	0	0	0	0	0	0	0	0	0	0	0	0
LA CROSSE	0	0	0	0	30	0	0	14	0	.	18	0	0	12	0	0	13
LAFAYETT.IN	5	7	19	19	45	9	9	42	4	7	34	5	7	40	0	17	51
LANSING MI	5	4	3	10	17	7	3	10	0	3	22	1	2	6	1	1	15
LIMA OH	0	1	2	4	8	0	29	28	0	42	45	0	5	0	0	5	0
LORAIN OH	0	0	1	0	3	3	0	2	6	0	3	1	0	1	6	0	1
MADISON	7	6	7	22	32	17	11	9	13	15	9	4	8	12	11	13	20
MANSFIELD	0	1	2	5	7	0	1	18	0	2	23	0	0	0	0	0	0
MILWAUKEE	1	1	3	4	16	8	15	47	15	24	65	1	3	33	1	7	55
MUNCIE IND	0	0	9	0	30	0	0	7	0	0	14	0	0	17	0	0	22
MUSKEGON MI	0	0	3	0	8	0	0	37	0	0	49	0	0	6	0	0	7
PEORIA IL	0	1	1	6	5	0	24	25	0	44	44	0	9	7	0	25	27

Table B.3: Neighborhood Poverty and Concentration of the Poor *(continued)*

	Non-Hispanic White (est.)						Black						Hispanic					
	Neighborhood Poverty Rate			Concentration of the Poor			Neighborhood Poverty Rate			Concentration of the Poor			Neighborhood Poverty Rate			Concentration of the Poor		
	70	80	90	70	80	90	70	80	90	70	80	90	70	80	90	70	80	90
RACINE WI	0	0	1	0	0	6	0	0	18	0	0	22	0	0	7	0	0	13
ROCKFORD IL	0	1	2	0	3	8	0	12	22	0	26	41	0	5	5	0	6	8
SAGINAW	0	1	1	0	2	4	12	16	50	21	29	65	2	10	24	1	20	36
SOUTH BEND	3	0	0	9	1	1	10	15	4	19	29	7	10	0	2	31	0	3
SPRINGFD IL	1	0	1	2	0	3	21	0	15	34	0	28	0	0	7	0	0	0
SPRINGFD OH	0	2	0	0	6	2	0	4	1	0	7	2	0	0	0	0	0	0
STEUBENVILL	0	1	3	0	4	8	0	31	39	0	47	58	0	0	11	0	0	8
TERRE HAUTE	3	0	2	2	2	5	6	0	8	2	0	10	0	0	2	0	0	8
TOLEDO	0	2	5	1	5	16	11	13	27	20	25	37	0	3	13	0	6	26
YOUNGSTOWN	0	0	2	2	1	8	4	10	39	6	17	52	1	3	33	1	5	53
West North Central																		
CEDAR RAPID	0	0	1	0	0	5	0	0	7	0	0	11	0	0	2	0	0	9
COLUMBIA MO	6	8	17	12	22	35	10	6	34	11	13	48	15	7	31	20	5	47
DES MOINES	0	0	1	1	1	7	1	1	16	2	3	23	0	0	3	0	0	9
DUBUQUE	1	0	0	2	0	0	0	0	0	.	0	0	0	0	0	.	0	0
DULUTH	1	0	4	2	0	12	0	0	19	0	0	33	0	0	3	.	0	9
FARGO	0	0	6	0	0	9	0	0	15	0	0	6	0	0	10	0	0	12
KANSAS CITY	0	0	1	2	2	4	8	8	10	15	15	19	0	5	7	0	10	20
LINCOLN NE	3	4	2	1	4	8	5	16	9	0	24	13	2	9	3	11	17	7
MINNEAPOLIS	1	1	2	4	5	15	7	12	22	21	22	33	1	3	8	6	10	18

	1	2	3	4	5	6	7	8	9	10	11	12	13	14	15	16	17	18
OMAHA	0	0	1	0	2	4	10	16	20	19	32	35	0	0	5	0	1	11
ROCHESTR MN	2	1	0	6	0	0	0	0	23	0	0	0	0	0	18	0	0	0
ST JOSEPH	1	0	4	4	0	11	8	0	27	12	0	39	7	0	4	72	0	3
ST LOUIS	1	0	1	3	2	2	20	19	23	32	33	39	2	3	3	4	15	13
SIOUX CITY	0	1	3	0	5	11	0	20	23	0	41	28	0	3	14	0	0	25
SIOUX FALLS	0	0	1	0	0	6	0	·	1	0	·	5	0	0	4	0	0	0
SPRINGFD MO	1	2	5	3	2	12	0	0	23	0	0	32	0	0	5	0	0	11
TOPEKA	0	0	0	0	0	0	0	0	0	0	0	0	0	0	0	0	0	0
WATERLOO IA	0	0	1	0	0	5	0	0	17	0	0	25	0	0	8	0	0	18
WICHITA KA	0	0	1	0	0	6	14	5	26	18	9	36	0	0	3	0	1	11
South Atlantic																		
ALBANY GA	5	3	3	17	14	13	49	31	42	57	44	58	0	19	12	0	24	56
ASHEVILLE	1	0	1	2	1	4	16	11	8	25	16	15	0	0	2	·	0	0
ATLANTA GA	1	1	0	5	3	1	16	17	11	31	33	27	0	4	3	0	14	7
AUGUSTA GA	2	0	2	8	2	5	31	13	14	41	23	27	2	4	2	0	16	13
BALTIMORE	1	1	1	3	5	5	18	19	15	35	38	35	2	7	2	9	23	10
CHARLEST.NC	7	1	2	13	1	7	56	18	13	66	27	24	7	6	3	0	20	3
CHARLEST.WV	2	0	1	7	1	3	19	8	9	38	18	17	0	0	4	0	0	14
CHARLOTTE	1	0	0	3	1	1	19	15	13	30	28	29	0	8	3	0	28	8
COLUMBIA SC	3	1	2	8	0	7	29	10	13	39	16	26	0	3	4	0	10	19
COLUMBUS GA	10	5	5	26	18	17	56	23	24	71	41	45	8	4	3	11	21	9
FAYETTEV.NC	3	1	1	10	3	2	26	12	9	42	24	21	0	0	1	0	0	5
FORT LAUDER	0	0	0	0	0	0	3	20	6	4	29	11	1	1	0	5	4	0
GAINESVILLE	9	18	21	25	40	45	13	13	26	16	16	31	20	30	37	34	47	58
GREENSBORO	0	0	0	1	1	0	13	4	9	22	8	19	0	3	1	0	16	3
GREENVILLE	0	0	2	1	1	7	7	9	9	10	16	18	4	4	0	0	8	2

(continued)

Table B.3: Neighborhood Poverty and Concentration of the Poor (continued)

	Non-Hispanic White (est.)						Black						Hispanic					
	Neighborhood Poverty Rate			Concentration of the Poor			Neighborhood Poverty Rate			Concentration of the Poor			Neighborhood Poverty Rate			Concentration of the Poor		
	70	80	90	70	80	90	70	80	90	70	80	90	70	80	90	70	80	90
HUNTINGTON	6	1	4	14	4	8	5	0	5	3	0	5	0	0	3	0	0	13
JACKSONV.FL	1	2	1	6	7	3	22	17	12	30	27	21	3	5	1	11	16	7
LYNCHBURG	0	1	1	0	1	2	0	0	11	0	0	18	0	5	3	.	0	0
MACON GA	4	3	3	14	10	10	35	20	17	40	30	25	0	2	4	0	6	4
MIAMI	0	1	2	1	3	5	19	17	23	28	29	41	1	1	5	2	3	11
NEWPORT VA	0	0	0	1	0	2	8	7	5	15	16	16	1	2	0	0	12	3
NORFOLK	7	4	1	2	2	6	34	17	17	49	28	37	13	12	2	10	11	7
ORLANDO FL	1	0	0	2	1	1	23	16	11	28	24	21	2	1	0	10	1	1
PENSACOLA	2	1	1	6	2	3	41	18	19	43	24	27	10	1	2	17	3	2
PETERSBURG	0	0	0	0	0	1	0	1	1	0	1	2	0	0	0	0	0	0
RALEIGH-DUR	2	0	2	3	0	3	16	2	7	22	6	14	2	4	4	0	14	4
RICHMOND VA	1	0	1	2	0	4	14	9	10	24	22	28	2	7	2	0	36	5
ROANOKE VA	0	0	0	0	0	1	0	0	15	0	0	24	0	0	6	.	0	22
SAVANNAH GA	2	1	1	8	3	4	40	29	15	53	47	29	0	10	2	0	14	4
TALLAHASSEE	11	12	10	20	28	33	26	27	24	30	34	32	15	25	22	47	48	38
TAMPA	1	1	0	3	1	1	35	24	16	45	41	29	8	4	3	16	10	7
WASHINGTON	1	0	0	1	0	0	3	3	2	9	9	7	0	0	0	0	1	1
W.PALM BCH	2	0	0	1	0	0	21	13	14	27	24	22	10	5	2	22	12	3
WHEELING WV	0	0	0	0	0	0	0	0	0	0	0	0	0	0	0	0	0	0
WILMINGT.DE	0	0	0	1	1	0	15	16	4	28	32	11	5	6	1	11	12	1
WILMINGT.NC	2	1	1	9	3	3	31	19	23	38	28	37	0	6	3	.	16	7

East South Central

BILOXI MISS	2	0	2	4	0	8	21	9	14	26	12	18	3	0	2	0	0	0
BIRMINGHAM	3	1	1	9	2	2	21	17	21	27	27	34	3	10	3	0	28	12
CHATTANOOGA	2	0	0	6	1	2	35	27	21	50	49	42	0	12	1	0	23	5
GADSDEN ALA	0	0	1	0	0	4	0	0	2	0	0	6	0	0	0	0	0	0
HUNTSVIL.AL	3	1	1	7	2	5	26	13	11	36	27	29	16	6	2	0	20	8
JACKSON MS	5	0	2	12	1	4	55	19	29	65	26	41	13	9	10	0	17	25
KNOXVILLE	7	4	3	14	11	7	43	29	23	59	42	36	0	19	4	0	30	8
LEXINGTON	1	1	2	4	4	7	16	12	11	24	24	21	1	7	2	0	26	4
LOUISVILLE	1	1	2	7	7	8	24	19	16	40	40	35	12	4	3	28	8	8
MEMPHIS	4	2	2	17	6	6	44	26	32	56	39	50	13	14	8	53	33	24
MOBILE AL	4	1	1	9	6	4	46	31	42	51	41	55	22	15	3	26	34	6
MONTGOMERY	7	2	3	19	5	9	52	27	26	54	37	43	0	10	10	82	28	19
NASHVILLE	1	2	1	5	4	3	16	20	17	27	35	35	0	11	2	0	28	17
TUSCALOOSA	5	7	13	9	10	32	42	17	31	44	21	37	0	0	22	.	0	49
ABILENE TX	0	0	1	0	0	1	0	0	4	0	0	7	0	0	3	0	0	6
AMARILLO TX	0	0	2	0	3	8	0	17	20	0	21	28	0	1	12	0	2	17
AUSTIN TX	6	6	4	12	13	13	1	20	12	1	33	20	11	6	9	18	8	16
BATON ROUGE	6	1	5	18	5	17	32	12	26	35	18	35	16	7	15	38	16	34
BEAUMONT TX	0	0	1	0	1	2	10	8	24	12	13	33	0	3	5	1	10	12
BROWNSVILLE	43	11	23	53	23	40	86	18	33	98	9	60	77	35	59	87	43	69
BRYAN TX	16	10	34	14	23	52	75	2	26	82	3	28	45	5	29	58	12	35
CORPUS CHRS	5	1	3	8	5	6	63	21	25	72	36	43	34	12	19	51	20	32
DALLAS	0	0	1	1	1	4	17	11	13	29	24	26	3	1	6	7	3	12
EL PASO	3	1	5	4	3	13	9	3	7	20	4	17	24	10	25	44	19	39
FORT SMITH	3	0	1	6	0	1	20	0	8	20	0	11	0	0	0	.	0	0

(continued)

Table B.3: Neighborhood Poverty and Concentration of the Poor *(continued)*

	Non-Hispanic White (est.)						Black						Hispanic					
	Neighborhood Poverty Rate			Concentration of the Poor			Neighborhood Poverty Rate			Concentration of the Poor			Neighborhood Poverty Rate			Concentration of the Poor		
	70	80	90	70	80	90	70	80	90	70	80	90	70	80	90	70	80	90
GALVESTON	1	0	1	2	0	1	21	14	14	34	30	25	3	2	2	11	6	7
HOUSTON	0	0	1	0	1	3	10	7	15	15	15	28	1	1	8	4	4	13
LAFAYETT.LA	5	0	6	10	0	11	45	0	36	43	0	40	0	0	11	0	0	5
LAKE CHRLES	2	0	1	5	0	1	45	5	28	50	9	38	6	0	5	0	0	17
LAREDO TX	36	15	24	34	28	50	0	.	52	0	.	44	73	36	51	84	49	65
LAWTON OK	1	1	1	2	4	3	28	1	9	47	1	24	1	0	1	0	0	4
LITTLE ROCK	2	0	0	5	0	1	30	5	11	40	8	18	2	2	1	0	5	4
LUBBOCK TX	5	1	3	2	0	11	58	1	35	65	2	40	13	3	16	17	6	26
MCALLEN TX	38	17	32	64	31	42	74	12	41	39	25	71	85	50	66	92	60	76
MIDLAND TX	0	0	2	0	0	9	0	0	36	0	0	46	0	0	28	0	0	44
MONROE LA	2	2	5	5	3	12	73	65	67	75	71	77	23	20	8	30	60	17
NEW ORLEANS	2	1	2	5	2	7	35	23	34	50	41	49	5	3	6	11	9	11
ODESSA TX	0	0	2	0	0	5	0	0	39	0	0	43	0	0	21	0	0	27
OKLAHOMA CY	1	1	3	3	4	10	27	10	12	37	16	22	8	4	12	10	7	19
PINE BLUFF	17	5	3	25	7	6	70	26	33	71	31	38	25	20	20	100	30	46
SAN ANGELO	0	1	1	2	0	4	55	0	24	63	0	43	24	0	4	39	0	8
SAN ANTONIO	1	1	2	4	4	6	20	13	16	28	25	29	26	14	21	43	24	36
SHERMAN TX	0	0	0	0	0	1	0	0	1	0	0	3	0	0	1	0	0	4
SHREVEPORT	4	0	3	11	0	7	64	15	40	66	22	47	6	7	7	0	20	15
TEXARKANA	1	1	1	3	2	1	0	19	14	0	24	22	0	9	0	0	13	0

City																		
TULSA	0	0	2	2	0	6	36	3	25	40	8	35	0	0	5	0	0	12
TYLER TX	0	0	1	0	0	3	0	0	23	0	0	29	0	0	15	0	0	30
WACO TX	7	8	11	16	27	36	27	24	47	31	31	57	21	17	19	35	30	28
WICHITA TX	1	0	2	1	1	7	62	33	42	73	50	59	11	7	12	18	10	27
Mountain																		
ALBUQUERQUE	1	2	2	5	9	10	25	0	1	40	0	2	12	2	3	24	3	6
BILLINGS	0	0	3	0	0	10	0	0	31	0	0	57	0	0	22	0	0	27
BOISE ID	0	0	0	0	0	0	0	0	0	0	0	0	0	0	0	0	0	0
COLORADO SP	0	0	0	0	1	1	0	1	0	0	0	3	0	1	1	0	1	2
DENVER	1	0	1	3	1	4	12	4	8	27	14	18	9	6	5	22	15	12
GREAT FALLS	0	0	3	0	0	10	0	0	7	0	0	15	0	0	5	0	0	11
LAS VEGAS	0	0	0	0	0	1	10	0	11	21	0	20	0	0	0	0	0	1
PHOENIX	2	1	2	7	5	7	26	13	12	42	28	25	13	12	12	24	25	22
PROVO-OREM	6	12	11	6	32	30	.	100	33	.	100	38	6	17	15	0	33	28
PUEBLO CO	2	1	5	0	0	12	6	4	8	0	0	17	1	1	10	0	0	16
RENO	0	0	0	0	0	0	0	0	0	0	0	0	0	0	0	0	0	0
SALT LAKE	0	0	0	2	1	2	19	11	9	39	35	23	1	1	3	4	5	9
TUCSON	1	4	6	6	11	20	6	2	13	15	6	22	10	2	13	24	5	23
Pacific																		
ANAHEIM CA	0	0	0	0	0	0	0	1	0	0	0	0	0	0	0	0	0	0
BAKERSFIELD	0	0	1	2	1	3	29	16	23	38	26	30	8	2	8	12	3	15
EUGENE OR	3	2	4	8	6	13	16	8	12	23	10	17	5	2	9	10	2	19
FRESNO	1	0	9	3	0	28	62	24	29	72	36	37	9	1	16	14	3	24
HONOLULU	1	1	1	4	5	6	3	0	0	1	0	2	1	1	1	2	4	6
LOS ANGELES	0	0	1	1	1	4	8	7	8	16	14	17	2	2	5	5	4	9

(continued)

Table B.3: Neighborhood Poverty and Concentration of the Poor (continued)

	Non-Hispanic White (est.)						Black						Hispanic					
	Neighborhood Poverty Rate			Concentration of the Poor			Neighborhood Poverty Rate			Concentration of the Poor			Neighborhood Poverty Rate			Concentration of the Poor		
	70	80	90	70	80	90	70	80	90	70	80	90	70	80	90	70	80	90
MODESTO CA	0	0	1	0	0	3	0	0	4	0	0	5	0	0	1	0	0	3
OXNARD CA	0	0	0	0	0	0	0	0	0	0	0	0	0	0	0	0	0	0
PORTLAND OR	0	0	1	2	1	3	3	7	17	5	11	23	1	1	2	5	1	5
RIVERSIDE	0	0	0	0	0	2	2	0	2	0	0	6	0	0	2	0	0	4
SACRAMENTO	0	1	1	0	1	5	0	1	4	0	1	8	1	1	3	2	3	6
SALEM OREG	0	1	0	0	0	0	0	11	0	0	0	0	0	1	0	0	0	0
SALINAS CA	0	0	0	0	0	0	0	0	0	0	0	0	0	0	0	0	0	0
SAN DIEGO	1	0	0	0	0	1	5	1	7	8	1	15	1	1	5	1	2	10
SAN FRANCIS	1	0	0	2	2	2	4	4	5	9	9	12	1	1	1	2	2	4
SAN JOSE CA	1	0	0	3	0	0	2	0	0	4	0	0	0	0	0	0	0	0
SANTA BARBA	6	4	6	23	20	31	5	3	5	11	7	12	1	2	3	3	5	5
SANTA ROSA	0	0	0	0	0	0	0	0	0	0	0	0	0	0	0	0	0	0
SEATTLE	1	0	1	4	2	5	3	2	4	9	4	7	3	1	3	19	2	8
SPOKANE WA	1	1	2	6	4	6	2	0	7	8	0	6	0	2	4	0	11	5
STOCKTON CA	1	2	3	3	5	12	25	4	15	39	9	22	6	3	9	12	6	18
TACOMA WA	1	1	2	4	6	9	3	5	8	7	14	17	0	2	3	5	7	7
VALLEJO CA	0	0	0	0	0	0	0	0	0	0	0	0	0	0	0	0	0	1

Source: See Chapter 2 and Appendix A.

254

Notes

1. Studying Neighborhood Poverty

1. An excellent introduction to this literature is Jencks and Mayer (1990a). More recent papers supporting neighborhood effects are Brooks-Gunn and others (1993), Case and Katz (1991), and Crane (1991). However, other researchers find that when methods to control for the selection of families are employed, neighborhood effects diminish or disappear (Evans and others 1992; Plotnick and Hoffman 1993).

2. For an interesting introduction to this literature, see "Urban Poverty: A State of the Art Review of the Literature," which is the appendix to William Julius Wilson's *The Truly Disadvantaged*, co-authored with Robert Aponte.

3. However, BNAs are much larger because their population density is lower.

4. The federal poverty standard suffers from a number of well-known deficiencies (Ruggles 1990), a full discussion of which is beyond the scope of this book.

5. The total of poor and nonpoor persons may be slightly less than the total population of the neighborhood, because poverty status is not calculated for some persons. For example, persons living in army barracks or other group quarters are not classified as either poor or nonpoor.

6. Given that Chicago's community areas are much larger than census tracts, they should encompass more income heterogeneity. Thus, the lower rate employed by Wilson (30 percent) is probably not that

different in effect from the 40 percent rate applied by subsequent researchers at the tract level.

7. The fieldwork was conducted from 1987 to 1989 and involved visits to the poor neighborhoods of many cities, among them Baltimore, Chicago, Detroit, Jackson, Mississippi, Little Rock, Memphis, Philadelphia, and San Antonio.

8. Unless otherwise noted, the figures in this chapter are tabulated by the author from the 1990 census, Summary Tape File 3A, multiple volumes by state released on CD-ROM at various times in 1992 and 1993.

9. These nonmetropolitan neighborhoods with high poverty levels are discussed later in this chapter.

10. The average sample size for tracts in 1990 was 630 persons. Assuming a true poverty rate of 40 percent, the margin of error for an estimate of the poverty rate in an average size tract is $\pm$ 3.8 percentage points at a 95 percent confidence interval.

11. George Farkas and a number of anonymous reviewers have raised similar points.

12. However, in the foreword to Wirth's book (1928), Robert Park took a broader view: "'Ghetto,' as it is conceived here, is no longer a term that is limited in its application to the Jewish people. It has come into use in recent times as a common noun—a term which applies to any segregated racial or cultural group" (pp. vii–viii).

13. Of these, eighty-nine are 100 percent black, twenty-nine are 100 percent non-Hispanic white and seven are 100 percent Hispanic.

14. These specific figures depend on classifying neighborhoods by whether a two-thirds majority exists. However, the point remains that not all members of a group live in neighborhoods dominated by that group.

15. Dependents of such persons are also included. See also Van Haitsma (1989), whom Mincy cites. The underclass is distinguished from the lower class, which includes persons whose primary means of support are low-status, low-reward occupations, also called "the working poor."

16. Unpublished research by David Rodda of Abt Associates indicates that New York is among the most expensive and Tulsa among the least expensive metropolitan areas in the United States.

17. An equivalence scale takes into account economies of scale within a household. To maintain an equal standard of living, two people do not need twice the income of one person. One advantage of using

the poverty line is that it does build in an equivalence scale, albeit a crude one.

18. Massey and Eggers elaborate, "Wilson (1987, pp. 49–55) measures the concentration of poverty by defining poverty areas. . . . He then counts the number of areas that meet this criterion and shows that the proportion of poor in them has increased. Subsequent researchers have quibbled about the definitions of a poverty area . . . but all have adopted virtually the same approach: define 'poverty' or 'underclass' areas, count them, and then count the number of people they contain" (p. 1159).

19. Despite the difference in conceptual underpinnings, the correlation between the black poor's exposure to poverty (Massey and Eggers's measure) and the concentration of the black poor (Jargowsky and Bane's measure) is high. In 1980, the unweighted correlation between the two measures was 0.789; the weighted correlation was 0.881. Both correlations include 306 metropolitan areas. I recomputed the Massey and Eggers's measure, since they report it for only a limited number of cities. My calculation of the exposure measure and theirs may differ slightly, since they perform an interpolation to remove the double-counting of black Hispanics.

20. "A member of the underclass," they argue, "would be someone in an underclass area who engages in various socially costly behaviors" (p. 321). For my purposes, however, I am interested only in their geographic identification scheme.

2. Neighborhood Poverty Between 1970 and 1990

1. A metropolitan area usually contains a central city of at least 50,000 persons and additional outlying counties that are economically integrated with the central city, although other configurations are possible. For more details, see U.S. Bureau of the Census (1991), appendix 1. (See also Frey and Speare 1988, chapter 2 and appendix F.)

2. The smallest unit in untracted areas are usually "minor civil divisions," defined through legislation and history rather than socioeconomic homogeneity. They vary greatly in size and structure.

3. Details of the adjustments are discussed in appendix A.

4. See table A-1 in appendix A for a comparison of the full set of 1990 metropolitan statistical areas and the subset I analyze.

5. An additional 437,000 persons lived in high-poverty neighborhoods in the newer metropolitan areas, bringing the 1990 total for all metropolitan areas to 8.4 million.

6. A small amount of this increase can probably be attributed to a change in the 1990 census's suppression procedures. In previous years, data for tracts with very small populations were suppressed (see appendix A). But fewer than thirty of the 1990 ghetto tracts had populations small enough to guarantee that their data would have been suppressed in earlier years. Also note that high-poverty tracts in newer metropolitan areas bring the 1990 total to 2,866.

7. In practice, decisions on splitting, joining, and creating tracts are handled by local Census Bureau committees together with local planning departments. In addition to splitting and joining tracts to keep the population in the appropriate range, tract boundaries are changed to reflect new highways or new land-use patterns (White 1987, appendix B).

8. This process will be explored in more detail, in the section on Milwaukee's ghetto.

9. As noted earlier, however, comparisons of 1970 census data to later data are possibly compromised by the changes in the Census Bureau's methodology for counting Hispanics.

10. Divisions are smaller units than regions. The Northeast is divided into New England and the Mid-Atlantic divisions. The South is divided into the South Atlantic, East South Central, and West South Central. (The West South Central is usually referred to as the Southwest.) The Midwest is divided into the East North Central and West North Central. The West comprises the Mountain and Pacific divisions. Metropolitan areas that overlap regions have been assigned to one region based on population.

11. The large nonghetto tract that appears to cut through the ghetto is actually a nearly uninhabited tract adjacent to Interstate Highway 94 and the Menomonee River.

12. This discussion ignores births and deaths for simplicity. Births and deaths could matter in two ways. The net population gain could occur differentially among income groups. Perhaps more important, any change in the number of persons in a household affects the poverty threshold used to determine whether or not a household is poor.

13. The Panel Study of Income Dynamics (PSID) provides such data for a limited number of individuals, linking them to data on the neighborhoods (census tracts) in which they live (Gramlich, Laren, and Sealand 1992).

14. Boundary changes were negated by combining tracts until the combined areas could be identified in all three censuses. Tracts that did not

exist in 1970 or 1980 were excluded from the analysis, so the totals shown may not match published totals for the metropolitan area.

3. Neighborhood Poverty in 1990

1. The tract data do not separate poor Hispanics by ethnic subgroup.

2. In the 1990 census, 52 percent of Hispanics identified themselves as white, 3 percent as black, and 45 percent as "other."

3. The actual figure is probably somewhere between 18 and 27 percent, because at least some Hispanics specify their race as black.

4. He makes the same argument with regard to high-poverty neighborhoods.

5. Outside metropolitan areas, residents of high-poverty areas were 41 percent white—a figure roughly similar to the smaller metropolitan areas.

6. The national average for all high-poverty census tracts is 24 percent with at least some college. See chapter 4.

7. Nor are certain institutionalized persons and military personnel in barracks.

8. Of the 8.4 million persons living in high-poverty areas in 1990, about four hundred thousand resided in college dormitories. Ideally, I would simply exclude persons in college dorms from the analysis altogether, but the aggregated nature of the census tract data precludes this possibility. The data are provided as a series of cross-tabulations at the census tract level rather than as data on individuals. While the number of persons in college dorms is given for each tract, those individuals cannot be identified and removed from other tables on race, income, or any other characteristic.

9. Specifically, non-Hispanic whites decline from 1.9 million to 1.3 million; non-Hispanic blacks decline from 4.2 million to 4.1 million; and Hispanics decline from 2.1 million to 2.0 million. The count of dorm residents drops 98 percent—from 398,308 to 9,862. Of 2,866 high-poverty tracts, 176 exceed 10 percent living in college dorms.

10. All averages are weighted by the appropriate base population.

11. Moreover, this is the average for the region; many metropolitan areas in the Midwest have even higher levels (see table 3.9 and appendix B).

12. Outside metropolitan areas, block numbering areas are used as proxies for neighborhoods. See chapter 1 for a discussion of the similarities and differences between BNAs and census tracts.

13. As noted in chapter 1, however, the sense of neighborhood implied by BNAs is not comparable to census tracts because of the vast differences in land area and population density.

14. To exclude metropolitan areas with no significant numbers of blacks or Hispanics, only those metropolitan areas with at least fifty thousand residents of the indicated group are included.

15. Chapter 1 discusses this measure in conceptual terms.

16. Note that 1980 means and standard deviations, based on areas classified as census tracts in that year, are used to identify underclass tracts in 1990.

17. See Kasarda (1993, p. 257) for the reasons he omits this component; see also chapter 1 of this volume and Tobin (1993, p. 15–17).

18. Like Mincy and Wiener, he uses the 1980 means and standard deviations but includes only tracts in the one hundred largest central cities, so the exact cutoffs are different than in Mincy and Wiener's study. On the poverty dimension, the cutoff level is 33.2 percent.

19. The exact figure is 49 percent, compared with only 14 percent when the overall poverty rate rather than the black poverty rate is used. These data are not shown in table 3.12.

4. Characteristics of High-Poverty Neighborhoods

1. Because such persons are hidden in a sense, they are also less likely to be interviewed by reporters writing about life in a poor neighborhood.

2. Although it is equally applicable to research on the underclass, Snow and his colleagues' comment was made in reference to research on the homeless. They noted that researchers have an easier time identifying homeless persons who are mentally ill or frequently intoxicated, compared with persons who are homeless but work and carry on other normal activities during daylight hours.

3. The Public Use Microdata Sample (PUMS) provides data on individuals but not by census tract because of concerns about confidentiality.

4. An actual median cannot be computed for all units within the neighborhood types, since the values for individual housing units are not reported. Instead, the figures reported are the mean of the neighborhood medians, weighted by the number of housing units.

5. See note 4 above. The value figure is weighted by the number of owner-occupied units in the tract, and the rent figure is weighted by rental units.

6. These figures are computed by looking at the percentage owner-occupied of all occupied housing units, disaggregating by the race/ethnicity of the household head.

7. It may seem confusing that some of the figures refer to 1989 and others to 1990. The reason has to do with the wording of questions on the census form. Questions about employment and labor force participation ask respondents to report their status on the day of the census. In contrast, the question on which table 4.4 is based asks respondents how many weeks they were employed last year. Respondents do not know for certain how many weeks they will work in the census year because the forms are filled out before the year is over.

8. Public assistance includes Aid to Families with Dependent Children (AFDC), Supplemental Security Income (SSI), and state general assistance benefits. In the data I am using, AFDC figures are not reported separately.

9. It could be argued, however, that AFDC cases in high-poverty areas are more likely to be long-term cases requiring more intensive intervention.

10. The proportion of families headed by a single man is relatively small—3 to 8 percent for all the cells in table 4.10. In other words, most of the rest of the families with children are married-couple families.

11. This is one of the few items in the tract-level data for which it is possible to conduct a crude multivariate analysis.

12. However, it should be noted that part of this reduction could reflect the indirect effect of neighborhood poverty on female-headship.

5. Theory and Evidence on Inner-City Poverty

1. Hughes defines the North as "Middle Atlantic or East North Central census divisions plus the Baltimore MSA." See Hughes (1989).

2. All figures in the paragraph are calculated from Mills and Hamilton (1984, table 4, p. 64). The table is based on a sample of eighteen metropolitan areas.

3. Wilson argues that "what needs to be considered is a youth's lack of access to the job network," not merely physical distance (1987, p. 60). To the extent that such access to the job network is something other than physical distance, however, the explanation is not spatial.

4. The index of dissimilarity treats each areal unit as independent and does not consider the units' location. A checkerboard pattern of all-white and all-black neighborhoods would have an index of dissimilarity of 1

(the measure's maximum). Yet such a pattern has far different implications for spatial mismatch than does a centralized location of the black
neighborhoods where job growth is decentralized (Galster 1987, 23).

5. In other words, R^2 increased by 0.21 when deconcentration variables
    are added, compared to 0.05 when deindustrialization variables are
    added. The size of his sample and the collinearity between the vari-
    ables limited the usefulness of a regression with both measures.

6. For black males, the pattern of changes was similar, despite big dif-
    ferences in the underlying levels. As a proportion of black male
    employment, white-collar jobs increased; blue-collar held steady; ser-
    vice workers grew. Again, the big loser was the farm sector, declining
    from 26 percent in 1950 to 4 percent in 1980.

7. The contrast between whites and blacks is particularly striking if zero
    earners are included. The variance of log earnings is the inequality
    measure most sensitive to the lower end of the distribution. For
    blacks, it increased from 1.67 in 1940 to 4.00 in 1980 (including zero
    earners). The comparable figures for whites were 2.25 and 2.65.
    Danziger and Gottschalk note that the question of whether to include
    zero earners depends on what assumption is made about the actual
    earnings opportunities of the zero earners.

8. Specifically, their dependent variable (see chapter 1) is the exposure
    of the black poor to poverty.

9. Wilson also argued that this outmigration left inner-city neighborhoods
    without "social buffers" to ameliorate the effects of economic downturns.

10. For the metropolitan areas with at least one million residents, the
    overall range was 10 to 41 percent.

11. The income brackets in 1970 and 1980 do not line up after adjusting
    for inflation. To approximate constant income groupings, Massey and
    Eggers shift families between income brackets using a linear interpo-
    lation with a Pareto adjustment in the upper tail. This method may
    introduce some bias into their measure, because one would not
    expect the density to be constant within brackets even if the distrib-
    ution were smooth. In addition, they create unduplicated counts of
    blacks, whites, and Hispanics by assuming that, within tracts, the pro-
    portion of white and black Hispanics is the same in every income
    bracket. Again, this may introduce a bias in SMSAs with significant
    Hispanic populations, since the proportion of white and black His-
    panics could be expected to vary by income level.

12. This measure is not independent of the mean and variance of house-
    hold income (Jargowsky 1996). However, it is probably a better mea-

sure of economic segregation than a simple index of dissimilarity of the poor from the nonpoor (Abramson and Tobin 1994) because it incorporates a much greater degree of information about income distribution.

13. Poverty concentration is defined as the exposure of poor families of a given race group to poverty, that is, the percentage of poor in the neighborhood of the average poor family. This measure is defined and justified by Massey and Eggers (1990). See also chapter 1.

14. Geocodes allow researchers to link data on individuals to data about the neighborhoods in which they live.

15. Because of lost addresses, neighborhood rates cannot be determined for the interim years.

16. This somewhat overstates Wilson's view, since he does not assign middle-class flight priority over structural economic transformations.

17. These figures represent the index of dissimilarity between non-Hispanic whites and blacks, calculated from census tract data. Census tracts with more than 40 percent of residents in institutions are excluded, as suggested by Massey and Denton (1988).

18. Coefficients (and *t* ratios) are as follows: group poverty rate, 3.5 (1.9); racial segregation, 1.0 (6.5); economic segregation, 0.679 (4.1).

6. An Analysis of Neighborhood Poverty

1. In chapters 1–4, neighborhoods were classified by their poverty rates. Although the relationship between neighborhood poverty rate and mean income is not exact, the two are closely related. Neighborhoods with the highest poverty rates will be those with the lowest mean incomes. Any errors in classification at the margin are not important in the context of the general conceptual argument being made here.

2. Census tract data do not provide information on individuals. But the mean of the household distribution may be calculated by dividing the aggregate income by the total number of households. The mean of the neighborhood distribution is computed by taking the mean of the tract mean household income, weighted by the number of households in each tract.

3. Chapter 5 and Jargowsky (1996) discuss the NSI's properties and empirical trends in economic segregation based on this measure.

4. I use blacks rather than the overall figures for two reasons. First, neighborhood poverty levels for this group are the highest and, hence, of more interest in terms of public policy. Second, overall neighborhood

poverty levels are so low that the "noise" in the data (random fluctuations, measurement error) overwhelms the signal, and the model performs poorly.

5. The level may seem high, but as many as 59.9 percent of ghetto residents may be above the federal poverty line.

6. This figure is calculated by generating a predicted 1990 level of ghetto poverty from the 1990 mean household income, while leaving income inequality and neighborhood sorting at their 1980 levels. The "mean only" set of predictions contains no information about any changes over the decade in inequality or neighborhood sorting. The "variance explained" figure is then calculated as in a regression, by comparing the sum of the squared errors (actual minus predicted) to the total variation. The methodology is discussed in detail in Jargowsky (1991, chapter 4).

7. It should be noted that in auxiliary regressions, the percentage of jobs in professional and managerial occupations is a strong predictor of MSA mean income, whereas the percentage of jobs in manufacturing industries is not. See also Danziger (1976) and Massey and Eggers (1991, 1992) for a discussion of the determinants of metropolitan economic status.

8. The first job-share variables are omitted because they do not strengthen the model's explanatory power and are redundant according to the conceptual framework laid out above. Their effect (if any) is felt through the income-generation and neighborhood sorting processes.

9. A bivariate regression, not shown, has a large and statistically significant positive coefficient on percent black. So even though cities with larger black populations do have higher ghetto poverty, this heightened propensity toward ghettoization is accounted for by the differences in the income generation and neighborhood sorting among metropolitan areas.

10. Moreover, the standard error on NSI_{blk} increases only slightly when the NSI is added (from 0.548 to 0.543) and the variance inflation factor (a multicollinearity diagnostic) is less than two—well below the level that indicates a multicollinearity problem.

11. This is analogous to left-out variable bias, in which the left-out variable is constrained to have a coefficient of zero.

12. As in the cross-sectional analyses, the dependent variable is expressed in log-odds form.

13. For the null hypothesis that this coefficient equal 1, the t score is -12.3. This finding suggests "regression to the mean."

14. The condition of a high R^2 and few significant coefficients is often an indication of multicollinearity. Here, however, few of the coefficients have high bivariate correlations and the variance inflation factors (a common multicollinearity diagnostic) are not particularly high.

7. *Chaos or Community? Directions for Public Policy*

1. Although it is universally known as the Moynihan Report the actual title was "The Negro Family: The Case for National Action" and appeared as a chapter in Rainwater and Yancey (1967).

2. This is a general feature of any cross-sectional regression model that does not explicitly build in lagged variables. The "change" models, however, compare the change in ghetto poverty over ten years to the change over ten years in the independent variables. Again, no explicit lag is built in.

3. These policies include programs whose primary goal is to influence their clients' values, beliefs, self-esteem, and behavior. Self-help programs are different from human capital programs, whose primary goal is to build knowledge and skills. In practice, some programs have elements of both.

4. Because of the transformation of the dependent variables to log-odds form, the effect of the independent variable on ghetto poverty is not linear and depends on the values of the other variable. To assess the impact of one variable, one must first stipulate the values of all other variables in the model.

5. Economic segregation within the black community is not shown because the coefficient was not statistically significant in the regression table 7.1 is based on; in the changes regression, however, black economic segregation was significant whereas overall economic segregation was not.

6. The *PCTBLACK* variable is not relevant for policy, hence it is not shown in the table. It is included in the calculations, however, set at its mean value.

7. Of the sharp decreases in ghetto poverty in 1970–90, many can be traced to increases in mean income as a metropolitan area recovered from an economic downturn. Once "full employment" is reached, however, any further improvements will depend on productivity growth rather than business-cycle fluctuations.

8. For blacks, the median earnings of full-year, full-time workers was $23,423 in 1973 and $22,369 in 1992. For Hispanics, the figure was $24,019 in 1974 (the first available year) and $20,049 in 1992. (All

figures from Current Population Reports, Series P60-184, Table B-17 [1993 census, B36].)

9. For an interesting discussion of the trade-offs between universal and targeted policies, see the trio of articles by Greenstein, Wilson, and Skocpol in Jencks and Peterson (1991).

10. Escape from ghetto and barrio neighborhoods, even if it does not bring economic success, at least removes people from an environment where fear of crime is pervasive. Fear of crime deters people from working, since they must commute back and forth to a job, sometimes returning home after dark (Rosenbaum and Popkin 1991). Jencks and Edin report that half of the welfare mothers in a sample they interviewed would not live in Chicago's ghettos, even though they had to cheat the welfare system to afford the rents in better neighborhoods (1990, p. 35).

11. Metropolitan areas vary greatly, however, in housing market conditions. Some metropolitan areas do have neighborhoods with affordable low-income housing.

12. Despite the drag imposed by racial segregation, the gap between blacks and whites on test scores and educational attainment has been closing. This progress toward equalization could have been even faster in an integrated society.

Appendix A: Data Compatability

1. Technically, I changed the MSA code of tracts in the affected county. In New England, I worked with tract parts, because metropolitan areas in New England are composed of towns and places, not counties. Tracts are not necessarily contiguous with towns and places, so part of a tract may be recoded whereas another part is not. After recoding the tracts and tract parts, I reaggregated tract parts to whole tracts when possible, that is, when they were not in separate metropolitan areas.

2. The data for whole tracts only were purchased from National Planning Data Corporation. Data for split tracts and other levels of aggregation were removed (retaining the whole tract records).

References

Anderson, Elijah. 1989. "Sex Codes and Family Life Among Inner-City Youth." *Annals of the American Academy of Political and Social Sciences* 501: 59–78.
———. 1990. *Street Wise: Race, Class, and Change in an Urban Community.* Chicago: University of Chicago Press.
———. 1991. "Neighborhood Influences on Inner-City Teenage Pregnancy." In *The Urban Underclass*, edited by Christopher Jencks and Paul E. Peterson. Washington: The Brookings Institution.
———. 1994. "The Code of the Streets." *Atlantic Monthly*, May, pp. 81–94.
Auletta, Ken. 1982. *The Underclass.* New York: Random House.
Bane, Mary Jo, and David T. Ellwood. 1989. "One Fifth of the Nation's Children: Why Are They Poor?" *Science* 245: 1047–53.
Bane, Mary Jo, and Paul A. Jargowsky. 1988. "The Links Between Government Policy and Family Structure: What Matters and What Doesn't." In *The Changing American Family and Public Policy*, edited by Andrew J. Cherlin. Washington: The Urban Institute Press.
Banfield, Edward C., and James Q. Wilson. 1963. *City Politics.* Cambridge, Mass.: Harvard University Press.
Baumol, William J., and Kenneth McLennan. 1985. "U.S. Productivity Growth and Its Implications." In *Productivity Growth and U.S. Competitiveness*, edited by William J. Baumol and Kenneth McLennan. New York: Oxford University Press.
Bean, Frank D., and Marta Tienda. 1987. *The Hispanic Population of the United States.* New York: Russell Sage Foundation.
Bickford, Adam, and Douglas S. Massey. 1991. "Segregation in the Second Ghetto: Racial and Ethnic Segregation in American Public Housing, 1977." *Social Forces* 69: 1011–36.
Blank, Rebecca M., and Alan S. Blinder. 1986. "Macroeconomics, Income Distribution, and Poverty." In *Fighting Poverty: What Works and What*

Doesn't, edited by Sheldon H. Danziger and Daniel H. Weinberg. Cambridge, Mass.: Harvard University Press.

Blinder, Alan S. 1987. *Hard Heads, Soft Hearts: Tough-Minded Economics for a Just Society*. Reading, Mass.: Addison-Wesley.

Bound, John, and Harry J. Holzer. 1993. "Industrial Shifts, Skills Levels, and the Labor Market for White and Black Males." *Review of Economics and Statistics* 75: 387–96.

Bound, John, and George Johnson. 1992. "Changes in the Structure of Wages in the 1980s: An Evaluation of Alternative Explanations." *American Economic Review* 82: 371–92.

———. 1995. "What Are the Causes of Rising Wage Inequality in the United States?" *Economic Policy Review*, vol. 1. New York: Federal Reserve Bank of New York.

Brooks-Gunn, Jeanne, Greg J. Duncan, Pamela Kato Klebanov, and Naomi Sealand. 1993. "Do Neighborhoods Influence Child and Adolescent Development?" *American Journal of Sociology* 99: 353–95.

Buber, Martin. 1967 [1992]. "Comments on the Idea of Community." Reprinted in *On Intersubjectivity and Cultural Creativity*, edited by S. N. Eisenstadt. Chicago: University of Chicago Press.

Butler, Stuart M. 1981. *Enterprise Zones: Greenlining the Inner Cities*. New York: Universe Books.

Case, Anne C., and Lawrence F. Katz. 1991. "The Company You Keep: The Effects of Family and Neighborhood on Disadvantaged Youths." Working paper no,3705. Cambridge, MA: National Bureau of Economic Research.

Clark, Kenneth B. 1965. *Dark Ghetto: Dilemmas of Social Power*. New York: Harper & Row.

Clark, William A. V. 1993. "Neighborhood Transitions in Multiethnic/Racial Contexts." *Journal of Urban Affairs* 15: 161–72.

Corcoran, Mary, Roger Gordon, Deborah Laren, and Gary Solon. 1992. "The Association Between Men's Economic Status and Their Family and Community Origins." *Journal of Human Resources* 27: 575–601.

Crane, Jon. 1991. "Effects of Neighborhood on Dropping Out of School and Teenage Childbearing." In *The Urban Underclass*, edited by Christopher Jencks and Paul E. Peterson. Washington: The Brookings Institution.

Danziger, Sheldon H., and Peter Gottschalk. 1987. "Earnings Inequality, the Spatial Concentration of Poverty, and the Underclass." *American Economic Review* 77: 211–15.

DeMarco, Donald L., and George C. Galster. 1993. "Prointegrative Policy: Theory and Practice." *Journal of Urban Affairs* 15: 141–60.

Dent, David J. 1992. "The New Black Suburbs." *New York Times Magazine*, June 14.

Duncan, Otis Dudley, and Beverly Duncan. 1955. "A Methodological Analysis of Segregation Indexes." *American Sociological Review* 20: 210–17.

Edsall, Thomas Byrne, and Mary D. Edsall. 1991. "Race." *Atlantic Monthly*, May, pp. 53–86.

Eggers, Mitchell L., and Douglas S. Massey. 1991. "The Structural Determinants of Urban Poverty: A Comparison of Whites, Blacks, and Hispanics." *Social Science Research* 20: 217–55.

———. 1992. "A Longitudinal Analysis of Urban Poverty: Blacks in U.S. Metropolitan Areas Between 1970 and 1980." *Social Science Research* 21: 175–203.

Eig, Jonathan. 1992. "On the Edge of Nowhere: Pam Lovejoy and Her Children Live Precariously as Modern Day Nomads." *Dallas Life Magazine*, May 10, pp. 8–25.

Ellwood, David T. 1986. "The Spatial Mismatch Hypothesis: Are There Jobs Missing in the Ghetto?" In *The Black Youth Employment Crisis*, edited by Richard B. Freeman and Harry J. Holzer. Chicago: University of Chicago Press.

———. 1988. *Poor Support: Poverty in the American Family*. New York: Basic Books.

Erickson, Eugene, Joseph B. Kadane, and John W. Tukey. 1987. "Adjusting the 1980 Census of Housing and Population." In *Census Undercount and Feasibility of Adjusting Census Figures*, vol. 100-23. Hearing before the Subcommittee on Census and Population, Committee on Post Office and Civil Service, U.S. House of Representatives (100th Congress). Washington: U.S. Government Printing Office.

Evans, William N., Wallace E. Oates, and Robert M. Schwab. 1992. "Measuring Peer Group Effects: A Study of Teenage Behavior." *Journal of Political Economy* 100: 966–91.

Farkas, George. 1974. "Specification, Residuals, and Contextual Effects." *Sociological Methods and Research* 2: 333–63.

Farkas, George, Robert P. Grobe, Daniel Sheehan, and Yuan Shuan. 1990. "Cultural Resources and School Success: Gender, Ethnicity, and Poverty Groups Within an Urban School District." *American Sociological Review* 55: 127–42.

Farley, Reynolds, and William H. Frey. 1994. "Changes in the Segregation of Whites and Blacks During the 1980s: Small Steps Toward a More Integrated Society." *American Sociological Review* 59: 23–45.

Forman, Robert E. 1971. *Black Ghettos, White Ghettos, and Slums*. Englewood Cliffs, N.J.: Prentice-Hall.

Freeman, Richard B. 1991. "Employment and Earnings of Disadvantaged Young Men in a Labor Shortage Economy." In *The Urban Underclass*, edited by Christopher Jencks and Paul E. Peterson. Washington: The Brookings Institution.

Frey, William H. 1993. "People in Places: Demographic Trends in Urban America." In *Rediscovering Urban America: Perspectives on the 1980s*, edited by Jack Sommer and Donald A. Hicks. Washington: Office of Housing Policy Research, U.S. Department of Housing and Urban Development.

Frey, William H., and Alden Speare, Jr. 1988. "Regional and Metropolitan Growth and Decline in the United States." In *The Population of the United States in the 1980s,* edited by National Committee for Research on the 1980 Census. New York: Russell Sage Foundation.

Galster, George C., and W. Mark Keeney. 1988. "Race, Residence, Discrimination, and Economic Opportunity." *Urban Affairs Quarterly* 24: 87–117.

Galster, George C., and Ronald B. Mincy. 1993. "Understanding the Changing Fortunes of Metropolitan Neighborhoods, 1980–1990." In *Fannie Mae Annual Housing Conference 1993.* Washington: Fannie Mae Office of Housing Policy Research.

Glasgow, Douglas C. 1980. *The Black Underclass: Poverty, Unemployment, and Entrapment of Ghetto Youth.* New York: Vintage Books.

Glover, Glenda. 1993. "Enterprise Zones: Incentives Are Not Attracting Minority Firms." *Review of Black Political Economy* 22: 73–99.

Gramlich, Edward, Deborah Laren, and Naomi Sealand. 1992. "Moving Into and Out of Poor Urban Areas." *Journal of Policy Analysis and Management* 11: 273–87.

Gunther, William D., and Charles G. Leathers. 1987. "British Enterprise Zones: Implications for U.S. Urban Policy." *Journal of Economic Issues* 21: 885–93.

Hannerz, Ulf. 1969. *Soulside: Inquiries Into Ghetto Culture and Community.* New York: Columbia University Press.

Hanushek, Eric A. 1986. "The Economics of Schooling: Production and Efficiency in Public Schools." *Journal of Economic Literature* 24: 1141–77.

Harrison, Bennett, and Barry Bluestone. 1988. *The Great U-turn: Corporate Restructuring and the Polarizing of America.* New York: Basic Books.

Harrison, Roderick J., and Daniel H. Weinberg. 1992. "Changes in Racial and Ethnic Residential Segregation, 1980–1990." Paper prepared for the American Statistical Association Meetings, Boston (July 29).

Herrnstein, Richard J., and Charles Murray. 1994. *The Bell Curve: Intelligence and Class Structure in American Life.* New York: Free Press.

Hicks, Donald A. 1987. "Urban Policy in the U.S.: Introduction." *Urban Studies* 24: 439–46.

———. 1994. "Revitalizing Our Cities or Restoring Ties to Them: Redirecting the Debate." *Journal of Law Reform* 27: 813–75.

Hogan, Dennis P., and Evelyn M. Kitagawa. 1985. "The Impact of Social Status, Family Structure, and Neighborhood on the Fertility of Black Adolescents." *American Journal of Sociology* 90: 825–55.

Holzer, Harry J. 1991. "The Spatial Mismatch Hypothesis: What Has the Evidence Shown?" *Urban Studies* 28: 105–22.

Hughes, Mark Alan. 1987. "Moving up and Moving Out: Confusing Ends and Means About Ghetto Dispersal." *Urban Studies* 24: 503–17.

———. 1989. "Misspeaking Truth to Power: A Geographical Perspective on the 'Underclass' Fallacy." *Economic Geography* 65: 187–207.

————. 1991. "Employment Decentralization and Accessibility: A Strategy for Stimulating Regional Mobility." *Journal of the American Planning Association* (Summer): 288–98.

————. 1993. *Over the Horizon: Jobs in the Suburbs of Major Metropolitan Areas.* Philadelphia: Public/Private Ventures.

Ihlanfeldt, Keith R., and David L. Sjoquist. 1989. "The Impact of Job Decentralization on the Economic Welfare of Central City Blacks." *Journal of Urban Economics* 26: 110–30.

Jackson, Thomas F. 1993. "The State, the Movement, and the Urban Poor: The War on Poverty and Political Mobilization in the 1960s." In *The Underclass Debate: Views from History*, edited by Michael B. Katz. Princeton: Princeton University Press.

Jargowsky, Paul A. 1991. *Dissertation Series.* Vol. D-91-4. *Ghetto Poverty: The Neighborhood Distribution Framework.* Cambridge, Mass.: Malcolm Weiner Center for Social Policy, John F. Kennedy School of Government.

————. 1994. "Ghetto Poverty Among Blacks in the 1980s." *Journal of Policy Analysis and Management* 13: 288–310.

————. 1996. "Take the Money and Run: Economic Segregation in U.S. Metropolitan Areas." *American Sociological Review* 61: 984–98.

Jargowsky, Paul A., and Mary Jo Bane. 1990. "Ghetto Poverty: Basic Questions." In *Inner-City Poverty in the United States*, edited by Laurence E. Lynn, Jr., and Michael G. H. McGeary. Washington: National Academy Press.

————. 1991. "Ghetto Poverty in the United States: 1970 to 1980." In *The Urban Underclass*, edited by Christopher Jencks and Paul E. Peterson. Washington: The Brookings Institution.

Jaynes, Gerald David, and Robin M. Williams, Jr. 1989. *A Common Destiny: Blacks and American Society.* Washington, DC: National Academy Press.

Jencks, Christopher. 1988. "Deadly Neighborhoods." *The New Republic*, June 13, pp. 23–32.

————. 1991. "Is the American Underclass Growing?" In *The Urban Underclass*, edited by Christopher Jencks and Paul E. Peterson. Washington: The Brookings Institution.

Jencks, Christopher, and Susan E. Mayer. 1990a. "The Social Consequences of Growing up in a Poor Neighborhood." In *Inner-City Poverty in America*, edited by Laurence E. Lynn, Jr., and Michael G. H. McGeary. Washington: National Academy Press.

————. 1990b. "Residential Segregation, Job Proximity, and Black Job Opportunities." In *Inner-City Poverty in America*, edited by Laurence E. Lynn, Jr., and Michael G. H. McGeary. Washington: National Academy Press.

Juhn, Chinhui, Kevin Murphy, and Brooks Pierce. 1991. "Accounting for the Slowdown in Black-White Wage Convergence." In *Workers and Their Wages: Changing Patterns in the United States*, edited by Marvin Kosters. Washington: American Enterprise Institute.

Kain, J. F. 1968. "Housing Segregation, Negro Employment, and Metropolitan Decentralization." *Quarterly Journal of Economics* 82: 175–97.

———. 1992. "The Spatial Mismatch Hypothesis: Three Decades Later." Housing Policy Debate 3: 371–460.

Karoly, Lynn A. 1992. "The Trend in Inequality Among Families, Individuals, and Workers in the United States: A Twenty-Five Year Perspective." Santa Monica, CA: Rand Corporation.

Kasarda, John. 1988. "Jobs, Migration, and Emerging Urban Mismatches." In *Urban Change and Poverty*, edited by Laurence E. Lynn, Jr., and Michael G. H. McGeary. Washington: National Academy Press.

———. 1989. "Urban Industrial Transition and the Urban Underclass." *Annals of the American Academy of Political and Social Sciences* 501: 26–47.

———. 1993. "Inner-City Poverty and Economic Access." In *Rediscovering Urban America: Perspectives on the 1980s*, edited by Jack Sommer and Donald A. Hicks. Washington: Office of Housing Policy Research, U.S. Department of Housing and Urban Development.

Kaus, Mickey. 1994. "The Cure." *New Republic*, September 12, p. 6.

Klein, Joe. 1994. "A Tale of Two Cities: The Problem Isn't the Absence of Jobs, But the Culture of Poverty." *Newsweek*, August 15, p. 57.

Kleinberg, Benjamin. 1995. *Urban America in Transformation: Perspectives on Urban Policy and Development*. Thousand Oaks, Calif.: Sage Publications.

Korenman, Sanders, John E. Sjaastad, and Paul A. Jargowsky. 1995. "Explaining the Rise of Ghetto Poverty in the 1980s." Revised version of a paper presented at the 1995 meeting of the Population Association of America, San Francisco (April).

Kotlowitz, Alex. 1991. *There Are No Children Here: The Story of Two Boys Growing up in the Other America*. New York: Doubleday.

Kozol, Jonathan. 1995. *Amazing Grace: The Lives of Children and the Conscience of a Nation*. New York: Crown Publishers.

Lazere, Edward B. 1995. *In Short Supply: The Growing Affordable Housing Gap*. Washington: Center for Budget and Policy Priorities.

Leigh, W. A., and J. D. McGhee. 1986. "A Minority Perspective on Residential Racial Integration." In *Housing Desegregation and Federal Policy*, edited by J. M. Goering. Chapel Hill NC: University of North Carolina Press.

Lemann, Nicholas. 1991. *The Promised Land: The Great Black Migration and How It Changed America*. New York: Alfred A. Knopf.

Levitan, Sar A., and Elizabeth I. Miller. 1992. "Enterprise Zones Are No Solution for Our Blighted Areas." *Challenge*, May-June, pp. 4–8.

Levy, Frank. 1987. *Dollars and Dreams: The Changing American Income Distribution*. New York: W. W. Norton.

———. 1995. "The Future Path and Consequences of the U.S. Earnings/Education Gap." *Economic Policy Review*, vol. 1. New York: Federal Reserve Bank of New York.

Lewis, Oscar. 1966. *La Vida: A Puerto Rican Family in the Culture of Poverty—San Juan and New York*. New York: Random House.

————. 1968. "The Culture of Poverty." In *On Understanding Poverty: Perspectives from the Social Sciences*, edited by Daniel P. Moynihan. New York: Basic Books.

Liebow, Elliot. 1967. *Talley's Corner: A Study of Negro Streetcorner Men*. Boston: Little, Brown.

Lynn, Laurence E., Jr., and Michael G. H. McGeary. 1990. "Conclusions." In *Inner-City Poverty in the United States*, edited by Laurence E. Lynn, Jr., and Michael G. H. McGeary. Washington: National Academy Press.

MacLeod Jay. 1987. *Ain't No Makin' It: Leveled Aspirations in a Low-Income Neighborhood*. Boulder, Colo.: Westview Press.

Maddala, G. S. 1977. *Econometrics*. New York: McGraw-Hill.

Massey, Douglas S., and Nancy A. Denton. 1988. "The Dimensions of Racial Segregation." *Social Forces* 67: 281–315.

————. 1989. "Hypersegregation in U.S. Metropolitan Areas: Black and Hispanic Segregation Along Five Dimensions." *Demography* 26: 373–91.

————. 1993. *American Apartheid: Segregation and the Making of the Underclass*. Cambridge, Mass.: Harvard University Press.

Massey, Douglas S., and Mitchell L. Eggers. 1990. "The Ecology of Inequality: Minorities and the Concentration of Poverty, 1970–1980." *American Journal of Sociology* 95: 1153–88.

————. 1993. "The Spatial Concentration of Affluence and Poverty During the 1970s." *Urban Affairs Quarterly* 29: 299–315.

Massey, Douglas S., Andrew B. Gross, and Kumiko Shibuya. 1994. "Migration, Segregation, and the Geographic Concentration of Poverty." *American Sociological Review* 59: 425–45.

Mayer, Susan E. 1991. "How Much Does a High School's Racial and Socioeconomic Mix Affect Graduation and Teenage Fertility Rates?" In *The Urban Underclass*, edited by Christopher Jencks and Paul E. Peterson. Washington: The Brookings Institution.

Mead, Lawrence M. 1986. *Beyond Entitlement: The Social Obligations of Citizenship*. New York: The Free Press.

Meislin, Richard J. 1980. "Citicorp Insists It Will Move Card Unit to South Dakota." *The New York Times*, November 21, 1980, p. 1.

Mills, Edwin S., and Bruce W. Hamilton. 1984. *Urban Economics*. 3rd ed. Glenview, Ill.: Scott Foresman.

Mincy, Ronald B. 1991. "Underclass Variations by Race and Place: Have Large Cities Darkened Our Picture of the Underclass?" Underclass Research Project. Washington: The Urban Institute.

Mincy, Ronald B., Isabell V. Sawhill, and Douglas A. Wolf. 1990. "The Underclass: Definition and Measurement." *Science* 248: 450–53.

Mincy, Ronald B., and Susan J. Wiener. 1993. *The Under Class in the 1980s: Changing Concepts, Constant Reality*. Washington: The Urban Institute.

Murray, Charles. 1984. *Losing Ground: American Social Policy, 1950–1980*. New York: Basic Books.

————. 1993. "The Coming White Underclass." *Wall Street Journal*, October 29, p. A-14.

Ogbu, John U. 1986. "The Consequences of the American Caste System." In *The School Achievement of Minority Children: New Perspectives*, edited by Ulric Neisser. Hillsdale, NJ: Lawrence Erlbaum Associates.

Orfield, Myron. 1995. "Metropolitics: A Regional Agenda for Community and Stability." Unpublished paper.

Osterman, Paul. 1991. "Gains from Growth? The Impact of Full Employment on Poverty in Boston." In *The Urban Underclass*, edited by Christopher Jencks and Paul E. Peterson. Washington: The Brookings Institution.

Park, Robert E. 1926. "The Urban Community as a Spatial Pattern and a Moral Order." In *The Urban Community*, edited by E. W. Burgess. Chicago: University of Chicago Press.

Peterson, Paul E. 1985. "Introduction: Technology, Race and Urban Policy." In *The New Urban Reality*, edited by Paul E. Peterson. Washington: The Brookings Institution.

————. 1991. "The Urban Underclass and the Poverty Paradox." In *The Urban Underclass*, edited by Christopher Jencks and Paul E. Peterson. Washington: The Brookings Institution.

Plotnick, Robert, and Saul Hoffman. 1993. "Using Sister Pairs to Estimate How Neighborhoods Affect Young Adult Outcomes." Working Papers in Public Policy Analysis and Management, No. 93-8. Graduate School of Public Affairs, University of Washington.

Popkin, Susan J., James E. Rosenbaum, and Patricia M. Meaden. 1993. "Labor Market Experiences of Low-Income Black Women in Middle-Class Suburbs: Evidence from a Survey of Gautreaux Program Participants." *Journal of Policy Analysis and Management* 12: 556–73.

Price, Richard, and Edwin S. Mills. 1985. "Race and Residence in Earnings Determination." *Journal of Urban Economics* 17: 1–18.

Ricketts, Erol R., and Isabel V. Sawhill. 1988. "Defining and Measuring the Underclass." *Journal of Policy Analysis and Management* 7: 316–25.

Rosenbaum, James E. 1995. "Changing the Geography of Opportunity by Expanding Residential Choice: Lessons from the Gautreaux Program." *Housing Policy Debate* 6: 231–69.

Rosenbaum, James E., and Susan Popkin. 1991. "Employment and Earnings of Low-Income Blacks Who Move to Middle-Class Suburbs." In *The Urban Underclass*, edited by Christopher Jencks and Paul E. Peterson. Washington: The Brookings Institution.

Ruggles, Patricia. 1990. *Drawing the Line: Alternative Poverty Measures and Their Implications for Public Policy*. Washington, DC: Urban Institute Press.

Rusk, David. 1993. *Cities Without Suburbs*. Washington: Woodrow Wilson Center Press.

Salins, Peter D. 1993. "Cities, Suburbs, and the Urban Crisis." *The Public Interest* 113 (Fall): 91–104.

Scholz, John Karl. 1994. "Tax Policy and the Working Poor: The Earned Income Tax Credit." *Focus* 15: 3.

Smith, Richard A. 1993. "Creating Stable Racially Integrated Communities: A Review." *Journal of Urban Affairs* 15: 115–40.

Smith, James P., and Finis R. Welch. 1989. "Black Economic Progress After Myrdal." *Journal of Economic Literature* 27: 464–519.

Snow, David A., Leon Anderson, and Paul Koegel. 1994. "Distorting Tendencies in Research on the Homeless." *American Behavioral Scientist* 37: 461–75.

Stanback, T. M., and T. Noyelle. 1983. *The Economic Transformation of American Cities*. Totowa, N.J.: Allanheld and Rowman.

Sullivan, Mercer. 1989. *"Getting Paid": Youth Crime and Work in the Inner City*. Ithaca, NY: Cornell University Press.

Tienda, Marta. 1991. "Poor People and Poor Places: Deciphering Neighborhood Effects on Poverty Outcomes." In *Macro-Micro Linkages in Sociology*, edited by Joan Huber. Newberry, Calif.: Sage Publications.

Tobin, Mitchell S. 1993. "Sensitivity Analyses of the Growth and Composition of the Under Class and Concentrated Poverty." Working paper. Washington: The Urban Institute.

U.S. Congress and Office of Technology Assessment. 1995. *The Technological Reshaping of Metropolitan America*. Washington: U.S. Government Printing Office.

Van Haitsma, Martha. 1989. "A Contextual Definition of the Underclass." *Focus* 12(1): 27–31.

Voith, Richard. 1994. "Do Suburbs Need Cities?" Working paper no. 93-27. Philadelphia: Federal Reserve Bank of Philadelphia.

Wacquant, Loic J. D., and William Julius Wilson. 1989. "The Cost of Racial and Class Exclusion in the Inner City." *Annals of the American Academy of Political and Social Sciences* 501: 8–25.

Waddell, Paul. 1995. "The Paradox of Poverty Concentration: Neighborhood Change in Dallas–Fort Worth from 1970 to 1990." Unpublished paper.

Warren, Elizabeth C. 1986. "Measuring the Dispersal of Subsidized Housing in Three Cities." *Journal of Urban Affairs* 8: 19–34.

White, Michael J. 1987. "American Neighborhoods and Residential Differentiation." In *The Population of the United States in the 1980s*, edited by the National Committee for Research on the 1980 Census. New York: Russell Sage Foundation.

Wilder, Margaret G., and Barry M. Rubin. 1988. "Targeted Redevelopment Through Enterprise Zones." *Journal of Urban Affairs* 10: 1–17.

Wilson, William Julius. 1987. *The Truly Disadvantaged: The Inner-City, the Underclass and Public Policy*. Chicago: University of Chicago Press.

———. 1988. "The American Underclass: Inner City Ghettos and the Norms of Citizenship." The Godkin Lecture, delivered at the John F. Kennedy School of Government, Harvard University (April 26).

———. 1995. *The American Economist* 39: 3–14.

Wirth, Louis. 1928 [1956]. *The Ghetto*. Chicago: University of Chicago Press.

Index

life in ghettos, portrayals of. *See* inner city poverty; *The Truly Disadvantaged: The Inner-City, the Underclass and Public Policy* (Wilson)
Little Rock, Arkansas: ghetto housing, 92
Los Angeles: ghettos, 1990, 78–79; Hispanic barrios, 1990, 80; households, location of, 150; income distribution, **149**, **151**, **155**; riots following King, Rodney, verdict, 2, 59
Lynn, Laurence E., Jr., 204

M
MacLeod, Jay, 90
Maddala, G. S., 167
manufacturing industry: black ghetto poverty and, **120**; percentage of jobs in, 168; proportion of jobs in, 264*n*7; shift to service-sector jobs, 158
Massey, Douglas S.: *American Apartheid,* 117, 133–136, 140, 183; black income distribution, 130, 262*n*11; concentration of poverty, measures of, 257*n*18, 263*n*13; deindustrialization, 121; economic segregation, 154; exposure measure of poverty, 22, 257*n*19; institutionalized residents, 263*n*17; interclass conflict, 23; middle class blacks, 133–134, 133–138; migration from ghettos, 147; neighborhood poverty versus underclass, 18; racial segregation, 139–143, 181–183, 201, 209–210; residential segregation, 124, 164
Mayer, Susan E., 123–124, 255*n*1
McAllen, Texas: ghettos, 1990, 79; Hispanic barrios, 1990, 81
McGeary, Michael G. H., 204
McGhee, J. D., 210
McLennan, Kenneth, 198
Mead, Lawrence M., 116, 188
Meaden, Patricia M., 125, 194–195
mean income, 156–157, 264*n*7; data comparability, suppression of data, 218; ghetto formation, model of, 160, 162; mean household income, 196; metropolitan mean household income, 168

Meislin, Richard J., 73
Memphis: concentrated urban poverty, analysis of, 84; ghetto housing, 92
metropolitan areas: boundaries, changes in, 214–216; defined, 257*n*1; employment, growth of, 202–203; ghetto expansion, 1970 through 1990, 44–46; housing, occupancy status, **93**; income distribution, **149**, 152–156, **155**; neighborhood poverty, 1970 through 1990, 32–33; new metropolitan areas, 32–33, 214; population figures, comparison, **215**; poverty rate, **10**, 20–21; public policy, altering metropolitan system, 206–208. *See also* specific topic
metropolitan mean household income, 168, 178
Mexicans: city size, racial composition by, 1990, 65; Hispanic barrios, 1990, 80–81; 1990, neighborhood poverty, 61–62, 64, 70
Miami: Hispanic barrios, 1990, 80
middle class blacks: inner city neighborhoods, flight from, 132–138, 144, 178, 183, 203, 263*n*16
Midwest: generation of income, 162; neighborhood sorting index, 195; 1990, neighborhood poverty, 70, 73, 77, 81–82; residential segregation, 171–172
migration: blacks, 13; middle class blacks, outmigration, 132–138, 144, 178, 183, 203, 262*n*9, 263*n*16; selective outmigration, 138; social problems, rise of, 107
Miller, Elizabeth I., 205
Mills, Edwin S., 124–125
Milwaukee: ghetto expansion, 1970 through 1990, 45, 49–57, 116, 138, 202; middle class blacks, 133; 1990, neighborhood poverty, 81; poverty and population change, 1970 through 1990, **53–54**
Mincy, Ronald B.: city size, racial composition by, 1990, 65; metropolitan areas, examination of, 33, 85; neighborhood poverty versus underclass, 18; non-metropolitan areas, high-